BusinessSpeak

Other Books by Suzette Haden Elgin, Ph.D.

The Gentle Art of Verbal Self-Defense

More on the Gentle Art of Verbal Self-Defense

The Last Word on the Gentle Art of Verbal Self-Defense

Success with the Gentle Art of Verbal Self-Defense

Staying Well with the Gentle Art of Verbal Self-Defense

The Gentle Art of Written Self-Defense Letters Book

Genderspeak: Men, Women, and the Gentle Art of
Verbal Self-Defense

"You Can't Say That to Me!": Stopping the Pain of
Verbal Abuse—An 8-Step Program

BusinessSpeak

Using the Gentle Art of Verbal Persuasion
to Get What You Want at Work

Suzette Haden Elgin, Ph.D.

McGraw-Hill, Inc.

New York   San Francisco   Washington, D.C.   Auckland   Bogotá
Caracas   Lisbon   London   Madrid   Mexico City   Milan
Montreal   New Delhi   San Juan   Singapore
Sydney   Tokyo   Toronto

Library of Congress Cataloging-in-Publication Data

Elgin, Suzette Haden.
    BusinessSpeak : using the gentle art of verbal persuasion to get
what you want at work / Suzette Haden Elgin.
        p.   cm.
    Includes bibliographical references and index.
    ISBN 0-07-019999-X (alk. paper). — ISBN 0-07-020000-9
(pbk. : alk. paper)
    1. Business communication.   2. Oral communication.   I. Title.
HF5718.E424 1995
650.1'3—dc20   94-43457
                                                                    CIP

Copyright © 1995 by McGraw-Hill, Inc. All rights reserved. Printed in the
United States of America. Except as permitted under the United States
Copyright Act of 1976, no part of this publication may be reproduced or
distributed in any form or by any means, or stored in a data base or
retrieval system, without the prior written permission of the publisher.

2 3 4 5 6 7 8 9 0   DOC/DOC   9 0 0 9 8 7 6 5 (HC)
1 2 3 4 5 6 7 8 9 0   DOC/DOC   9 0 0 9 8 7 6 5 (PBK)

ISBN 0-07-019999-X (HC)
ISBN 0-07-020000-9 (PBK)

*The sponsoring editor for this book was Betsy Brown, the editing supervisor was
Jane Palmieri, and the production supervisor was Suzanne W. B. Rapcavage. It
was set in Palatino by Estelita F. Green of McGraw-Hill's Professional Book
Group composition unit.*

Printed and bound by R. R. Donnelley & Sons Company.

McGraw-Hill books are available at special quantity discounts to use as
premiums and sales promotions, or for use in corporate training
programs. For more information, please write to the Director of Special
Sales, McGraw-Hill, Inc., 11 West 19th Street, New York, NY 10011. Or
contact your local bookstore.

This book is printed on recycled, acid-free paper containing a
minimum of 50% recycled de-inked fiber.

Contents

3. "How Did We Get into This Stupid Fight, Anyway?!"   49
Staying Out of Hostility Loops

4. "Over My Dead and Bleeding Body!"   67
Combining the Communication Techniques

5. "No Decent Person Would Do Such a Thing!"   81
Making Complaints and Criticism Effective

Preface

Does this sound familiar?

"How could you possibly have done that? I told you what our strategy was—TWICE! What happened, for crying out loud?"

"You've gotta be kidding! This is nothing like what we had in mind! Where did you get such a crazy idea?!"

"How on earth did your people get the impression that *this* was the plan? They're doing it backwards!"

"But you were in the strategy meeting! You heard the presentation! How in the world did everything get so mixed up?"

"What's the matter with you people?! You must not have heard a single word I said! NOW what are we going to do?!"

Have you ever worked hard to put together a strategy, worked hard to explain it to those around you—and then discovered, too late, that what they *heard* was very different from what you're sure you *said*?

This book will show you how to solve that problem. It will show you how to say what you mean, in a way that produces both understanding and commitment in your listeners, so that your strategy has a chance to succeed and all your hard work doesn't go to waste.

Acknowledgments

My grateful thanks go to so long a list of researchers, scholars, students, colleagues, clients, and readers that they cannot all be listed here. I am especially indebted for the work of Virginia Satir, Edward T. Hall, Leonard Newmark, Peter J. Blanck, George Miller, and John

Grinder. I want to express my appreciation for the invaluable support and assistance I have received from my editor, Betsy Brown, and from my agent, Jeff McCartney. Thanks are due as always to the members of my household, with special thanks to my daughter and colleague, Rebecca Haden.

If you have questions about this book, or about the Gentle Art of Verbal Self-Defense system, please feel free to write directly to me at the address below.

Suzette Haden Elgin, Ph.D.
Ozark Center for Language Studies
P.O. Box 1137
Huntsville, Arkansas 72740-1137

BusinessSpeak

Introduction

Strategy. It's a word we all use far too carelessly. We talk about our strategy for improving our tennis game. For getting our children into good schools. For winning our next election. For convincing our spouses to buy a minivan. We talk about our strategy for taking off five pounds, for getting a promotion, for taking over a third of the market share for our product. Anything we propose to do, from switching to a new brand of toothpaste at home to creating stable democracies planetwide, seems eligible to be called a strategy. And dictionaries define it only as "a means for achieving some end."

The word comes from the Greek *strategia*, originally used for the planning of wars. We follow that tradition when we refer to our workplace planning rooms as "war rooms" and discuss our plans in military metaphors. We are not alone; in *The Mind of the Strategist,* Kinichi Ohmae tells us that "the central notion of Japanese business strategy is to change the battleground." The use of military terminology builds in the idea that every outcome must clearly and unambiguously establish a winner and a loser, and this concept has in the past been accepted as the only rational way to look at the business world. In recent years there has been a move toward new visions of business strategy, with greater emphasis on achieving goals and less on destroying enemies, but this shift in thinking has not produced greater precision and rigor. As the editors of *The Economist* put it in their March 20, 1993 issue: "Though top managers of big firms devote the bulk of their efforts to formulating strategy, there is remarkably little agreement about what it is."

The term began appearing in the literature of business and management in the 1960s, as a succession of theories and models were introduced. Today it is divided into subterms; we read of *business strategy, corporate strategy,* and *institutional strategy,* of *strategic planning* and *strategic thinking.* According to Richard G. Hamermesh (in *The Portable MBA*), "The term *strategy,* or *corporate strategy,* is one of the most widely used and abused expressions in business today." Hamermesh goes on to observe that the more popular the use of the term becomes, the more we distort its meaning.

This book is not about *business* strategy, however well or badly defined; the question of precisely what such strategy is will be left for the leaders in those fields to struggle with. It is about an area of strategy that logically should always be attended to first, before any other step is taken toward a goal, but which is unfortunately handled primarily by the ancient method known as "winging it." I refer to the neglected field of *communication* strategy, where the combat model still reigns supreme, but in an astonishingly primitive form. If business communication were war, we would still be meeting to discuss the deployment of our slingshots, our battering rams, and our vats of boiling oil. We've got to get past this stage, and we can do that only by narrowing the focus of our attention to the language we use.

In this book, therefore, we will assume that everyone who is shown presenting a business strategy has chosen it on the basis of the most complete and current information, using the most powerful and effective decision procedures. Our concern will not be with the strategy chosen, or the reasons for the choice, but with *how that strategy is communicated to others.*

Why Communication Strategy?

Why communication strategy, on top of all the other kinds of strategy you must cope with? In the July/August 1993 issue of *Business Strategy,* Bristol Voss tells us that "some business strategies make sense only to the strategist. This is not because the concept is flawed, but that the idea is just not conveyed in the words the strategist has chosen." We can't afford that. It's inexcusable waste. The idea *must* be conveyed in the language of the strategist.

Michel Robert, in his excellent book, *Strategy Pure & Simple,* writes that "almost any strategy will work, unless it is completely invalidated by negative environmental factors." But, he goes on, we know from sad experience that no matter how good a strategy is, if we can't communicate it to others we're wasting our time and energy; it will succeed only by chance. People who are asked to implement a plan they don't understand and to which they aren't committed will comply if they must—but they will do it as badly as they dare, and the sum of the mistakes they make through ignorance, plus those they make deliberately, will almost guarantee failure.

A strategy must be communicated *clearly* enough so that others will understand it and *persuasively* enough so that others will commit themselves to it. Otherwise, its chances are slim to nonexistent. When millions, sometimes billions, of dollars depend on achieving those two goals, there is no excuse for just winging it when the time comes to communicate what is to be done and why. Nor is there any reason to proceed in that manner. Today, because of contemporary linguistic science, we can proceed as systematically when we use language as when we use any other tool or process. The purpose of this book is to show you how you can do that and do it well.

This introduction will set the stage and present basic definitions of terms needed for the balance of the book. In the 13 chapters that follow, you will find:

- A scenario in which one individual (or team) proposes a strategy to an audience in a business context, and the presentation is neither as clear nor as persuasive as it could and should be

- An analysis of the scenario, carefully explaining the often very different perceptions of the individuals who were present and identifying a major cause of the communication shortfall

- A thorough description of a communication technique that can be used to avoid the problem identified, based on contemporary linguistic science and communication theory; a practical and immediately usable technique for that purpose

- A careful revision of the scenario that opened the chapter, demonstrating how the communication technique just described could have made the outcome far more positive

- A Workout Section that offers opportunities to practice the technique introduced in the chapter (and those from previous chapters, where appropriate), together with additional dialogues, resources, and examples

The concluding chapter will draw together the theory and practice set out in the 13 scenarios and provide you with a thorough and coherent summary.

We will need a shared set of basic semantic concepts, so that as you read you will know what *I* mean by them. The basic concepts include the book's definitions for these six words: *goal, plan, strategy, technique, heuristic,* and *algorithm.*

Goal	Something you want or need that you don't have (including *freedom from* something you *do* have).
Plan	A broad outline of the steps you will take to achieve your goal.
Strategy	A specific and systematic method for carrying out one or more of the steps in your plan.
Technique	A specific formal process used as part of the implementation of a strategy. Elsewhere, the word *technique* is often used as if it were interchangeable with the word *tactic.* In this book, because a tactic tends to be less explicit and more a matter of trial and error, we will ordinarily rely on the term *technique.*
Algorithm	A procedure which—provided you start with accurate data and follow the steps exactly according to instructions and in the order specified—will always provide the right answer eventually.
Heuristic	A method which, if you happen to be correct in choosing it, may be much *faster* than an algorithm, but which lacks the algorithm's rigor and guaranteed success. A heuristic is much like an informed and educated guess, but with stronger foundations.

These definitions will serve us adequately as we discuss *plans* for achieving *goals,* through the use of *strategies* that include *techniques,* identifying *algorithms* and *heuristics* as needed.

We are not trained to think about communication goals. We do decide why we are going into a given language interaction, but we rarely consider what *our language itself* is intended to accomplish there, except in vague terms, such as "getting the other person to do what we want." We have to learn to select our communication goals in advance of the interaction with great care, because language that is likely to achieve one goal is often useless for achieving another and mixing up the goals makes their achievement extremely unlikely. The four primary communication goals are:

1. To express your own feelings. (When this is your goal, you are concerned with the listener only *as* listener.)

2. To carry out some formal action that is accomplished by language, such as marrying your listener to another listener, sentencing your listener to prison, etc.

3. To educate and inform your listener, in order to change the listener's state from ignorance to knowledge with regard to a particular subject; sometimes to "raise your listener's consciousness."

4. To persuade your listener to change one or more behaviors or attitudes—from sorrow to joy, from fear to serenity, from disbelief to belief, from prejudice to tolerance, from inaction to action, and so on. (In each case, of course, your goal could be to produce change in the opposite direction.)

For the first goal, it makes little difference what you say as long as you feel after speaking that you've satisfied your need to get whatever it was "off your chest." For the second, you often have little choice about what you say, since the language you use is ordinarily established by law or ritual or tradition. For the third and fourth, however, the two that are our concern in this book, you have to answer the following question: *What is the best linguistic form for the thoughts you want your listener(s) to hear and understand—and later act upon—as you express them in language?*

Let's suppose that I, with the wise counsel of my editors, have chosen the surface shape of my language correctly in writing this book; let's suppose that you have read the book with care. We can then be certain that when you choose a strategy to present to others you will know how to guarantee the two crucial outcomes:

1. So long as *you* understand what you're saying, the people you're talking to will understand it too.

2. Everything you say will reach its maximum potential for persuading those you're talking to to feel the same commitment and passion for your strategy that *you* feel.

Achieving understanding in others is done in only one way: by gathering enough accurate information and making it so much a part of your own knowledge base that you are able to tailor it to the needs of your audience and express it for them clearly and effectively. Evoking commitment in others, on the other hand, can be done in three ways: by force (negative or positive), by charisma, or by skill.

1. *Evoking commitment by using force.* This method (saying "Do it and you'll get a raise," or "Do it or you'll get fired," for example) achieves only temporary, and largely phony, commitment. It lasts only as long as the threat or reward is not outweighed by other factors, and is shallow at best. The only understanding it requires is at the level of which

button to push with which finger; there's no need to understand the theory or the process behind the button, the motives for pushing it, or the consequences of doing so. In even the most minor crisis, this sort of limited commitment breaks down.

2. *Evoking commitment by using charisma (irresistible charm).* This method works *very* well and requires no more understanding from the listener than that needed when force is used. I once sat through a lengthy talk by an associate who had been paid a handsome fee to present it and who had literally done no preparation at all. He said nothing—at great length—and I thought the audience was going to be truly (and justifiably) furious when he stopped. But there was thunderous applause at the end, and the woman sitting in front of me turned around and made it vividly clear that I was wrong. Still clapping wildly, she said, "I didn't understand a single thing he said, but I just know it had to be important!" If you have the ability to achieve that result, you don't need this book—but you do need immortality and the ability to be in a dozen places at once.

The problem is that the effects of charisma wear off even faster than the effects of coercion unless constantly renewed, and *charisma cannot be delegated.* Unless you're going to be able to step in at frequent intervals and renew the commitment personally, it won't last long; it is tied to you and to your presence. If you can't be there as inspirational focus at all times—if you have to be busy elsewhere, if the people who are to carry out the strategy are widely scattered and hard to assemble as a group, if you get transferred or suffer the standard human illnesses and accidents, if *anything* takes you out of the picture for more than a very brief period, reliance on mere charisma will fail.

3. *Evoking commitment by using skill.* This is the best method and the one this book will teach you how to use. When people are persuaded by skill in communicating, they understand what they are to do, when and how they are to do it, and why. They share your conviction that your strategy is the best possible choice. As long as they are given even minimal feedback, they will know how to determine at any point whether the strategy is succeeding. And this effect *can* be delegated: your listeners can manage without your direct encouragement and explain the strategy to others if necessary. This is an effect that lasts, that has a solid foundation, and that won't disappear just because you're not immediately available to reinforce it at all times.

Fortunately, you are superbly equipped to communicate strategies by skill, rather than by force or charisma—or, as is too often the case, by blind luck. You don't have to have been "born with a silver tongue in your mouth." You don't have to hire expensive experts or spend years taking courses *from* experts. All you need is your own reliable competence in your language, this book, and a sincere desire to get the job done.

Let's get started.

How to Use This Book

If you are someone with abundant time and energy, I suggest that you proceed as follows:

1. Read the book quickly and casually, skipping the Workout Sections and making no effort to get deeply into the content.
2. Go back to the beginning and read each chapter with care, completing as many items in each Workout Section as you feel you need to before going on to the next chapter.

But your particular time and energy may be limited; you may feel you don't have the resources to carry out that program. You may want to simply read the book as quickly as possible, perhaps skimming the Workout Sections for a rough idea of their content. In that case, I offer just one warning. Suppose you run into trouble when you try one of the techniques; suppose your first reaction is that it doesn't work for you. In that case—before deciding that your negative judgment is accurate—it would be wise to go back and reread the chapter in which that technique is explained and complete its Workout Section.

Much of this book is devoted to presenting you with dialogue—spoken language in written form. Because the English punctuation system is very inadequate for that purpose, I modify it slightly when I write. The result is still inadequate, but it's better than no modification at all. Take a look at the following examples:

1. Why are you reading a book?
2. <u>Why</u> are you reading a book?
3. <u>Why</u> are you <u>read</u>ing a <u>book</u>?
4. WHY are you reading a book?
5. WHY are you READing a BOOK?

Example #1 is a neutral request for information; the speaker is just interested in knowing the answer. Example #2 is still a request for information, but it's not neutral; the speaker shows some emotional involvement, either positive or negative. Example #3 is no longer a request for information; rather, it is hostile language and may be a direct verbal attack. The part of language responsible for making these distinctions is *acoustic stress*, which speakers of English perceive as higher pitch and longer duration on words and parts of words. If you were reading the three examples aloud, you would give no particular emphasis to "why" in the first example, emphasize it slightly in the second and third examples, and give it strong emphasis in the fourth and fifth examples. (The use of all capital letters always indicates very strong emphasis.)

One more thing. Obviously the punctuation mark that English uses to indicate a question isn't adequate when the sentence is really an attack *disguised* as a question. In such cases, I often use a question mark and an exclamation point side by side, like this:

"WHY can't you EVer do anything RIGHT?!"

A question mark alone isn't enough for an utterance like this one; we need the combination to convey the true meaning.

WORKOUT SECTION: INTRODUCTION

1. *Your communication skills profile as of* _____ *(date).* Before you begin using the techniques presented in the book, answer the questions below to establish a baseline profile of your communication skills. In each case, rate your present level of ability by grading yourself on a scale from 0 (for totally untrue) to 10 (for absolutely true).

a. I am a good speaker in business situations. _____

b. I am a good speaker in social situations. _____

c. I find it easy to give talks and speeches, and I do it well. _____

d. I am a good listener in business situations. _____

e. I am a good listener in social situations. _____

f. I am a good listener when someone else is giving a talk or speech. _____

g. I know English grammar well and use it with skill when I talk. _____

h. I know and understand the basic facts about how languages are learned and used. _____

i. I am good at persuading people to do what I want. _____

j. I am good at convincing people to believe what I say. _____

k. People usually understand and remember what I say to them. _____

l. I have a pleasant and effective voice. _____

m. I have no annoying language habits that distract from what I say. _____

n. I'm an <u>interesting</u> speaker; people enjoy listening to me and talking with me. _____

o. I find it easy to take control of a language interaction. _____

p. I find it easy to stay on the subject when I talk; I never wander off into digressions or forget what I was saying. _____

q. People find it difficult to make me lose my temper in language interactions. _____

r. People are usually enthusiastic after hearing me present a plan or strategy. _____

s. I don't have to worry about preparing for a presentation; I can rely on my personal charm and charisma to get me through. _____

t. I find it easy to put my plans and strategies into spoken words. _____

u. I am good at observing and interpreting body language. _____

v. I am in control of my own body language and I know how it is perceived by others. _____

w. I am confident about my communication skills and feel that they need only minor polishing. _____

x. I am a courteous speaker—I don't interrupt people and I don't monopolize the floor so that others get no chance to talk. _____

y. I always know what my communication goal is before I begin talking. _____

z. I am skilled at communicating with people from other cultures and repairing misunderstandings that have their source in language or dialect differences. _____

Additional comments. _____

_____

_____

_____

2. *Communication Strategy Notebook.* Set up a Communication Strategy Notebook in a sturdy three-ring binder or on a computer disk and file your Communication Skills Profile there. You will be using your notebook as you work through this book, to create a database of information about your communication strategy skills. If you strongly dislike writing, you can put all your records on cassette tape instead; just remember that reviewing material and finding information that you need quickly is more difficult in that format.

1

"What's the Matter with You, Anyway?!"

Using the Power of Active Listening

Scenario One

Nick Barstow leaned back in his chair, clasped his hands behind his head, and nodded at his partner.

"Okay!" he said. "I cancelled a golf date to come in here and hear this pitch from you, Larry; it better be good. Let's hear it!"

Across from Nick, Larry Noll set his file of facts and figures down on the other man's desk carefully. He'd been working on that information every night for the last two weeks; he wasn't about to treat it casually.

"Well, Larry?" Nick said impatiently. "Come on! What's your great idea?"

Larry took a deep breath and leaned forward. "What we're going to do, Nick," he began earnestly, "is just this: we're going to provide every single one of our customers with a free monthly newsletter, starting August 1st. And we—"

Bolt upright now, both hands flat on the desktop, eyebrows halfway up his forehead, Nick cut Larry off.

"A free newsletter? A free monthly newsletter? You're out of your mind, Noll! You dragged me in here on a Sunday afternoon, I cancelled a golf date I'd been looking forward to all week, and all you've got to offer me is a stupid idea like that? What's the matter with you, anyway?"

"Now, Nick, wait a minute! You—"

"Listen, buddy, this is not a publishing company here! We're not a newspaper! This is a travel agency, and it's a travel agency going down

the tubes! You've got a lot of NERVE, wasting my time this way, when
I could be out with potential CUStomers! I could—"
"All right, Nick!" Larry interrupted. "All RIGHT! Just forGET it!
Just go right on, doing all the same things we've always done—not one of
which has worked, remember, but don't let that stand in your way!
You wouldn't want to risk letting a new idea into that closed mind of
yours, would you? You might get pneumonia of the brain, for crying out
loud!" He shoved back his chair and stood up, clutching the file folder
that represented so much wasted work and so many hours of lost sleep.
"Go on! Go play golf! I should have KNOWN better than to try to talk to
you—YOU haven't listened to anybody in YEARS!"
    On his way out the door—with Nick now on his feet sputtering with
rage—Larry took time for one parting shot. "Don't come complaining to
ME again, fella!" he shouted back over his shoulder. "You just take
your business problems to your GOLF buddies from now on!"

What's Going on Here?

This language interaction between Larry and Nick is an example of the
most basic opportunity for persuasion and negotiation. Just two people, one-on-one, meeting to talk something over. They both have good
intentions. They both care about the issue—in this case an attempt to
stop the downward slide of their small travel business. Larry, whose
role is to present and persuade, has worked hard to prepare himself
for the meeting; Nick has given up a plan of his own for the period of
time set aside for talking. It doesn't get any more basic than this.

    And it doesn't go much more badly than this, either. Short of going
after each other with baseball bats, Larry and Nick could hardly have
created a more striking example of total communication breakdown—
in spite of the best intentions on both sides.

Larry's Point of View

Larry really put his back into the process of getting his plan ready for
Nick to consider; he was excited about his idea and looking forward to
seeing his partner equally involved. He had everything ready. He had
all the figures, all the sources, everything. He'd found three different
companies that prepare and mail out brief newsletters, providing a
finished product with boilerplate stories and just dropping in bits and
pieces to make it look as though it was done entirely in-house. There'd
have been almost no work for either Larry or Nick or their staff of one.
He had figures proving that just two new deals closed as a result of
every 100 newsletters mailed out would pay for the whole thing—any-

thing else would be gravy! He had figures on the word-of-mouth pay-off from newsletters; he had figures on increased goodwill; he had case studies. He had a stack of short clippings he'd put together from papers all over the area, things they could drop into the newsletter to make it seem like their own product. He'd talked to all three of the suppliers to get comparative costs on a six-month trial. He had absolutely everything he needed; he was prepared to answer every question.

And Nick didn't even give him a chance to finish his opening *pitch*! As usual! As Larry sees it, Nick is an uninspired, plodding man with a closed mind who gets a rash just from *hearing* anything new, and this encounter was just another piece of evidence for that opinion. Larry is beginning to wonder if he shouldn't cut his losses and get out of the partnership as quickly as possible.

Nick's Point of View

The way Nick perceives matters, he is saddled with a business partner long on imagination and short on common sense. Like Larry, he knows that what they've been doing hasn't been producing good results; even with the economy recovering, their business has been going steadily downhill. But Nick believes that if he and Larry just hang in there and work hard—without wasting time and resources on crackpot ideas—they'll be able to turn things around. He just wishes he knew some way to get through to Larry on the matter, maybe get *him* out on the golf course where he can make useful contacts and take some of the burden of stroking potential customers off Nick's back.

Nick feels that he went into the inconvenient Sunday meeting ready to listen, ready to hear a case presented that would justify the inconvenience, only to learn that Larry had nothing in mind but a flaky fantasy. And at the worst possible time, when what they need to do is *cut* costs! Who, he wonders, would *write* this monthly newsletter? Who'd *type* it and *mail* it? How could Larry possibly be so ignorant of the company's financial position as to think they could afford a frill like a customer *news*letter?

Nick is insulted. As he sees it, Larry didn't do his homework, didn't bother to get his facts together, didn't care enough about their problems to do anything *solid*. Nick had been ready; he'd taken the time to go over the books, to review every projection on the spreadsheets, to check out every potential problem, so that he would be prepared to discuss Larry's idea without having to stop to look up dates or do a lot of calculations. He's beginning to wonder if maybe he and Larry ought to cut their losses and shut the business down before they get in any deeper.

What Went Wrong?

What went wrong is simple and obvious: neither of the two men allowed the other to present a case. Not because they were unprepared. Both had done everything necessary to get ready for the meeting. Not because they were actively working against each other; they had the common goal of turning their business around and were both willing to put plenty of effort into doing so. But neither man was willing to take the first and most important step in any successful language interaction, which is to *listen*—with full attention and a relatively open mind—to what the other person has to say.

This kind of communication breakdown happens all the time. Whether two individuals or dozens of people are involved, whether the interaction lasts ten minutes or ten days, whether the topic is choosing a new brand of envelopes or a multimillion-dollar advertising campaign, the same principle holds: *Unless people listen to one another, no useful communication can take place.*

Communication interactions don't have to be like the one in Scenario One, even when people are determined to disagree. But the usual recommendations on how to improve your communication tend to be too vague to be helpful. They tell you to listen; they may tell you to listen carefully, or with respect. They tell you to be polite and be patient and "make an effort to show interest." That's not specific enough to help. It doesn't tell you what changes should be made in your communication behavior. Let's take a look at a technique that goes beyond the platitudes and provides you with more specific information.

Communication Technique: Using Miller's Law

We are forever being told that we have to listen, but that's about as far as it goes. Nobody tells us how true listening (sometimes called *attending*) is done, or what to listen for in an ongoing language interaction. That's not because we don't *know*; we do.

In 1980, psychologist George Miller said something so critically important for listening, and for all human communication, that I call it *Miller's Law*. He said:

In order to understand what another person is saying, you have to assume that it is true and try to imagine what it could be true of. *("Giving Away Psychology in the '80s: George Miller Interviewed by Elizabeth Hall,"* Psychology Today, *January 1980, p. 46)*

Notice that Miller doesn't say you have to *accept* what the other person says as true. He says only that you need to *assume* that it is, temporarily; and then you need to try to imagine what it could be true *of*. You need to ask yourself these three questions:

1. In what sort of world would it be true?

2. Under what sort of circumstances would it be true?

3. What *else* would have to be true if the other person's words are not—as you are tempted to conclude—false and outrageous and ridiculous?

Much of the time, in business and elsewhere, we don't apply Miller's Law. Instead, we apply what can best be referred to as *Miller's Law In Reverse.* Let's compare the two:

Miller's Law

1. You hear someone say something and you have an immediate negative reaction to their words.

2. You assume that what they said is true.

3. You try to imagine what it could be true of.

4. *Listening* happens, and communication has a chance to succeed.

Miller's Law In Reverse

1. You hear someone say something and you have an immediate negative reaction to their words.

2. You assume that what they said is false.

3. You try to imagine what could be wrong with the *speak*er that would account for their saying something so unacceptable to you.

4. Listening *stops,* and communication is guaranteed to fail.

As will now be obvious to you, in Scenario One both Nick and Larry immediately applied Miller's Law In Reverse. As predicted by Step 4, the result was a communication breakdown.

When we fail to apply Miller's Law, we react to *language* with a judgment about the person speaking. We leap to conclusions like these:

- "He's only saying that because he's determined to stand in our way."
- "She's only saying that because she didn't do her homework and doesn't know what she's talking about."
- "He's only saying that because he's scared."
- "She's only saying that because she dislikes me and she'll do anything she can to hold me back."
- "He's only saying that because he's a bigot."
- "She's only saying that because she's a snob."
- "He's only saying that because I'm not able to drive a fancy car and wear expensive suits like he does."
- "She's only saying that because I don't have a fancy degree from some big university."
- "They're only saying that because they're stupid."

In every case, these hasty conclusions introduce serious confusion. *The important element in the interaction is the language being used, and that gets lost when you decide that what's important is some aspect of the speaker's character or personality or motivation.* And all listening stops, because you have rejected the language in advance and concluded—*without listening to it*—that it isn't worth hearing. When this happens, communication is doomed.

What Is Listening? How Does It Work?

Listening is a familiar activity, something we all do from birth, and common sense tells us that surely we must understand how we do it. The commonsense answer to the question above goes something like this:

Step 1: You hear the words being said.

Step 2: You figure out what each word means.

Step 3: You put it all together to find out what the whole utterance means.

This sort of obvious pronouncement is often labeled "self-evident"; however, like the equally obvious "The earth is flat," it's false. This is easily demonstrated, because it also happens to be impossible.

When we take what we know about the speed at which language is heard and processed and we do the basic math needed, we discover that nobody could follow those three steps. It is physiologically impossible, just as running 80 miles an hour is physiologically impossible, and no amount of practice or study or intense effort can change that.

Suppose you tried to apply the commonsense answer to a ten-word sentence, and the person talking to you did not stop talking at that point. Before you could attach a meaning to each of the ten words, long before you could combine the ten meanings to get the meaning of the full sentence, the speaker would be several words into the next sentence. And with each successive sequence of language, you would find yourself farther and farther behind. Steps 2 and 3 make Step 1 impossible; the time it takes to process the first 10 words makes it impossible for you to *hear* words 11, 12, and 13.

What really happens when you listen to someone talk is that, with the first few words you hear, you begin *generating hypotheses*—language sequences of your own—about what the final utterance is going to be. Your hypotheses are based on information you already have: information about the situation you and the speaker are in, which constitutes much of the *context* for the utterance; information about the speaker, about yourself, and about your relationship to one another; information about what you would say in the same situation if *you* were talking; information about what you would *not* say; information about the grammar of your language. All these different kinds of information enable you to use a linguistic strategy for listening that is *heuristic* rather than algorithmic. That is, you can be wrong, but you're not just making wild guesses; most of the time, you will be right. The only time you bother to make any serious effort at checking word meanings one by one is when you suddenly realize that what you're generating is way off the mark. When that happens, you will often ask for extra time, saying, "Wait a minute! I don't understand. What was that again?"

This process doesn't require much conscious knowledge on the part of the listener. It's on automatic pilot—on one condition. It will operate without your having to give it much conscious thought, *as long as you don't do anything to interfere with it.* When you apply Miller's Law In Reverse and start thinking about what's wrong with the speaker, that's interference. You can't do that and listen to the language at the same time; the human brain doesn't work that way. Reading while someone talks to you is interference, as is wondering whether your parking meter has expired or rehearsing what you're going to say when it's your turn to talk. Interference cancels the natural listening process, and effective communication becomes impossible.

There's one more thing you should know about listening before we move on. We now have abundant evidence that true listening—listening with your full attention—is actually good for you. It lowers blood pressure and heart rate and moves the whole body toward a more relaxed and balanced physiological state. (This is relatively recent information, discovered only since it has become possible to follow people with 24-hour computer monitoring.) If you've always listened to people "with half an ear," you're missing out on this bonus, but you may find it difficult to deliberately listen more attentively. Using Miller's Law will help, because you can't get the data you need to answer "What could it be true of?" unless you are really listening. If you're not willing to listen because it's courteous, or to improve your communication, please consider doing it for your health's sake.

Now let's go back and look at Scenario One again in the context of the information presented so far in this chapter, giving both Larry and Nick a chance to apply Miller's Law. We want to see how matters might, in that case, go differently. Let's see how Larry, who is in the active role of persuader, could structure his communication in such a way that Nick might be more willing to listen and less likely to leap to negative conclusions. Let's see how Nick could structure his objections in such a way that Larry might stay to discuss them instead of losing his temper and leaving. And finally, let's find out how each of these men could make it easier for the *other* to use Miller's Law.

Another Look at Scenario One

If Nick Uses Miller's Law

This alternative is easily described. Nick hears Larry's words: "We're going to provide every single one of our customers with a free monthly newsletter." He ignores his initial tendency to reject that out of hand and assumes that it is true. Then he asks himself, "What could it be true of? What else would have to be true if that's true?" He realizes that the answer to his question is, "I don't have enough information to decide," and that the only way he can *get* the information is by listening to the rest of what Larry has to say. If Nick wants to say anything at all, the appropriate line from him is simply, "Go on."

If Larry Uses Miller's Law

Larry's role in an improved scenario is more complicated. That's to be expected, because he is the one whose goal is to persuade someone else to agree to his proposal; the burden of proof is on him. Suppose the scenario begins as in the original, and Nick responds with his lengthy and hostile objections. We could summarize those objections as, "You're out of your mind suggesting a free monthly newsletter. That's a ridiculous idea. You're wasting my time."

But this time Larry applies Miller's Law. He ignores his initial negative reaction to Nick's words. He assumes that they are true, and he asks himself, "What could they be true <u>of</u>?" The answer is that they would be true of a situation in which the newsletter would be so expensive and burdensome for the company that it would make no business sense at all. This tells Larry what the problem is: Nick doesn't have the information he needs to perceive the proposal differently. Instead of saying "Now, Nick, <u>wait</u> a minute!" Larry says:

> "I'll bet you're thinking that the newsletter would cost a lot of money and add tremendously to our workload. That's <u>my</u> fault—I should have given you the information that <u>I</u> have, so you'd have known that it's not like that. Let's start this conversation over again, and I'll try to do it <u>right</u> this time."

And then Larry begins repairing the damage.

Both revisions of the scenario are an improvement over the original. However, Larry and Nick could do even better...

If Nick Makes It Easier for Larry to Use Miller's Law

Tension and stress make it harder for people to process language efficiently. Consider Nick's opening utterance:

> "Okay! I cancelled a golf date to come in here and hear this pitch from you, Larry; it better be <u>good</u>. Let's hear it!"

That is, *Larry, I'm here under protest, I'd rather be someplace else, and you're going to have to convince me that I made the right choice.* Anyone who has a presentation to make has to be prepared for that message, because it's very common—but it's no way to help the other person communicate. It's confrontational; it says "<u>Prove</u> it!" before Larry can even get started. And Nick tops it off by intensifying the pressure with an impatient, "Well, Larry? Come on! What's your great idea?" It must also be mentioned that the posture Nick originally chose—leaning back in his chair with his hands clasped behind his head—is in many cases a posture of challenge and a poor choice for putting someone at ease.

Nick could have improved the chances of a successful exchange of information by sitting in a more neutral posture, relaxed and attentive, and saying something like this:

"Okay, Larry, I'm ready to listen to your idea. Tell me about it."

Sometimes it's good strategy to make the person you're talking with nervous; sometimes that's your goal. But it's a very *bad* idea when you need to get quick and complete and accurate information from someone, as was true in this case. Suppose Nick is convinced in advance that Larry's idea won't be any good, and is just going through the motions, humoring him for friendship's sake. Even so, quick and complete information will get him off to the golf course faster. It's in Nick's own best interests to open the meeting by saying something that will put Larry at ease and help him do his best.

If Larry Makes It Easier for Nick to Use Miller's Law

There are a number of techniques Larry could use as part of a strategy to make it easier for Nick to apply Miller's Law and increase his chances of being properly understood. We're going to look at just two of these here; more will be presented as you read the rest of the book.

George Miller has been the source of more than one piece of crucially important information. He was the first to explain that the human *short-term memory*—the part of processing that holds information until something is *done* with it—is limited to roughly seven items at a time. He called this quantity "the magic number seven plus or minus two." Think of your short-term memory as a moving belt with five to nine hooks attached that moves along over a vat of information and can dip into it to pick up items from the whole. Each hook can pick up only one item, but there's some choice about what the item is, based on the person's efficiency at packaging the information into *chunks*. That is, if the vat contains two paragraphs of instructions for running a machine, each hook could pick up one letter of a word, or one word, or one phrase, or one of some larger unit. *The more information packed into a single chunk, the more information will be transmitted and processed.*

One way to help listeners do this chunking efficiently is to cue them to establish some mental pigeonholes in advance, because a major task of information processing is sorting items into sets and indexing them for possible storage in *long-term memory*. Suppose you hear someone say, "In the first quarter, we will identify a narrow marketing niche. In the second, we'll move on to select a product." Because of information you already have—that there are always four quarters arranged in a particular order—you will automatically set up four pigeonholes to drop information into as soon as you hear, "In the first quarter..." And you will expect to hear at least three more objectives stated. That takes some of the processing burden off your short-term memory and makes it easier for you to package what you hear into larger chunks.

Larry can take advantage of this information about listening by using structures like these as he begins his presentation:

"Nick, the idea I'm going to tell you about in just a minute is going to mean four separate and important positive changes for this company."

"Nick, I want to begin by making four important points. First..."

"Nick, I'd like you to reserve judgment while I take you through four important pieces of information. First..."

Such openings relieve the listener of some of the processing burden and increase the efficiency of the short-term memory by giving the message: *"Open four pigeonholes for the information that's coming."* Making it specific by labeling the pigeonholes in advance—as four questions, or four sales figures summaries, or four contract provisions—helps even more. If Larry is prepared to use specific terms rather than "four pieces of information," he would be well advised to do so.

And then he must be sure he lives up to what he's promised! You can probably remember a time in a classroom when an instructor told you to expect three important items and then proceeded to give you only two. Once you had come to what appeared to be the end of item two, everything from that point on was made harder to understand by your short-term memory's constant interruptions: "Hey! Where's item three? I set up that pigeonhole and I don't have anything to put in there! Where is it?" That message is static, and it interferes with comprehension. The same sort of problem is created by the person who says to expect three items and provides half a dozen.

If Larry says he's going to present four items of information, he needs to be sure he presents four and only four, in the order he's prescribed, and that he doesn't wander off inside items into digressions that don't belong in that pigeonhole.

It's important *never* to say that you are getting ready to present ten (or more) chunks of any kind. Nine is the upper limit; seven or fewer is much better than nine. This is not for stylistic reasons but for scientific reasons based on the capacity of the short-term memory. These same reasons have caused bureaucracies and businesses to divide the seven-digit numbers they want people to remember into three digits, a hyphen, and four digits. If you absolutely *cannot* avoid putting ten separate items into a single presentation (as the Social Security Administration was unable to avoid putting nine digits into a single number), always subdivide them in advance. Let's use *point* as a cover term here for whatever specific type of chunk you might be providing ten of. Then you would say something like this:

"I'm going to discuss two major points, each of which has five important subpoints."

or

"I'm going to cover three major points, together with their subpoints."

Usually it's best to present information your audience will need for judging your proposal *before* telling them what the proposal is if that can be done without causing confusion. Larry would be far wiser to first tell Nick the benefits that his idea would provide for the company if accepted and *then* tell him that the idea is a free monthly newsletter for their customers. Dropping the idea into an informational void is far more likely to provoke "You're out of your mind!" than dropping it into a short-term memory already prepared to receive it. The military version of this strategy is "Tell them what you're going to tell them, then tell them, then tell them what you've told them." When this is overdone, listeners feel that the presentation is being "dumbed down" for them and find it insulting, but when it's used carefully, it's good strategy.

"I Know You Know This"

One more thing Larry could do is use the "As You Know" opening. A dermatologist once told me that one of his worst problems was the colleague from another specialty who would call and say something like, "I've got a patient in my office with psoriasis. What should I prescribe for him?" How, the dermatologist wanted to know, could he handle this and protect both physician and patient without making his colleague angry, given the fact that many diseases look like psoriasis if you're not an expert? "Easy," I told him. "You just say, 'As you know, many diseases look like psoriasis and can easily be confused with psoriasis...' and then go on and tell him or her all the rest—up to and including, 'And as you know, you're less likely to find yourself in a malpractice suit if you refer the patient to a dermatologist.'" I am told that this single strategy dramatically improved the doctor's professional life.

"As you know..." followed by whatever you want to be sure your listener knows, diminishes tension and stress. It *presupposes*—that is, it establishes as something that can be taken for granted in advance—that the listener does know whatever it is and is only being told about it by you because the repetition is in some way part of your presentation. It says "I respect you; you and I are equally well informed. I know I can count on you to be familiar with this item of information already." Larry could put this to use in his presentation to Nick by saying things like these:

"As you know, Nick, research shows that keeping an old customer is much cheaper than acquiring a new one and will generate far more income in the long run."

"As you are aware, newsletters that are brief and interesting to read have proved to be one of the most reliable ways to keep customers happy and make them remember your company and its products or services."

"As we both know, methods exist today to produce and deliver newsletters so easily and cheaply that only one additional order for each one hundred mailed will cover the costs."

You can overdo this, too, of course. You don't want to start every sentence this way. You don't want to use it when it would sound patronizing, as when there's no plausible reason whatever to assume that the listener would know the information. You don't want to use it when it would make someone who *doesn't* already know feel embarrassed to ask a question about the item. But a judicious sprinkling of "As you know's" and "As you are aware's" and "As you will remember's" between individuals of roughly equal rank can be extremely helpful. Such individuals always have the option of stopping the speaker and saying, "Wait a minute—I *don't* know that!" if that becomes necessary. To summarize: You increase your chances of being understood when you make it easier for your listener to apply Miller's Law to what you're saying. One way to do this is to improve the performance of your listener's short-term memory by:

- Taking on part of the processing load whenever possible (as by setting up mental pigeonholes to help with the task of sorting and labeling).

- Decreasing distractions that interfere with processing by helping your listener feel less tense and less ill at ease.

WORKOUT SECTION: CHAPTER 1

1. For your Communication Strategy Notebook (on paper, computer disk, or tape), set up a Miller's Law file and begin keeping track of relevant information. For example, to serve as a database for planning strategies, record incidents in which you used Miller's Law. For each case, record the following:

What was the situation?

Who was there?

What was said (and by whom) that struck you as false, outrageous, or unacceptable?

What did you say back as a way of using Miller's Law?

What was the response?

What happened next?

How did things turn out?

What was surprising?

Did anything go wrong, and if so, can you determine why?

2. Complaints that sentences are "awkward" are common, but the term is never explained. Let's make it clear: *A sentence will be perceived as awkward when it places an undue burden on the short-term memory of the person at whom the message is aimed.* For example, in language processing, the listener first finds the verb and then assigns the various other chunks their roles relative to the verb. The sentence below makes that process difficult, and is therefore awkward:

"That the man who insisted on seeing the manager in charge of product development waited only ten minutes annoyed the secretary."

The problem is that the whole subject (from "that" through "minutes") has to be held in the short-term memory until the verb "annoyed" is located. It's 18 words long—twice the upper limit. If you talk like this, your chances of producing understanding and commitment are very slim. One simple way to fix the sentence is to move the verb to the beginning, like this:

It annoyed the secretary that the man who insisted on seeing the manager in charge of product development waited only ten minutes."

Notice that it's not true that sentences are awkward just because they are *long;* the revised example is one word longer than the awkward original. What matters is not the length but the ease with which the material can be processed.

Using the principles outlined above, find the constituent that makes the examples below awkward, and make the necessary revisions to reduce the short-term memory burden for the listener.

a. "That a moral crisis of monumental proportions exists in this country and is growing worse with every passing day is obvious."

b. "What's needed in order to turn this economic stagnation around and establish a vigorous recovery is a program of bold reforms."

c. "If action—firm and innovative action that can be relied upon to produce results instead of just rumors of results—isn't taken immediately, the company will fail."

d. "For Congress to have passed so many significant pieces of legislation that year in spite of the pressure from special interests all around the country surprised the voters."

e. "Whether the stocks purchased in a moment of enthusiasm after a spirited presentation by a charismatic speaker turned out to be profitable is something we have to find out."

Sentences like examples a–e pose a challenge even in written language, where the reader can go back over them if necessary. In spoken language, where they have to be processed as new language continues to come in, they distract the listener from what the speaker says next, making understanding—and applying Miller's Law—almost impossible.

3. The example below is one of the worst examples of awkwardness I've ever seen. If it had been used in a spoken attempt at persuading others, it would have failed miserably. Rewrite it so that the reader's short-term memory isn't put into an agonizing cramp.

"Although Nader advocates minute regulatory enforcement for others, preferably with criminal penalties, his own organizations display a remarkable 'pattern' of filing delinquencies—to borrow the jargon of RICO, the Racketeer Influenced Corrupt Organizations Act, extending which to just such technical white-collar crime is a pet Nader cause." (*Peter Brimelow and Leslie Spencer, "Ralph Nader, Inc.,"* Forbes *magazine, September 17, 1990, p. 122.*)

4. If you find it difficult to listen to others with full attention, train yourself by working with your television set; you can't hurt *its* feelings. Find a program where someone is actually talking—giving a speech, presenting a sermon, something of that kind. It doesn't matter if it's boring; listening to a boring speaker is a greater challenge—and a better workout—than listening to an interesting one. Sit down and give the speaker your full attention. Don't take notes; just listen. Every time you realize that you've let your mind wander, grab it and bring it firmly back. Keep practicing until you are able to listen to the televised speaker attentively for ten full minutes—and then start trying the same workout with people who are present in the flesh.

5. Jot down or record the language you hear in half a dozen prime time television commercials. Then try applying Miller's Law to each of them. What could they be true of? What else would have to be true if they were true?

2

"I Don't Feel Like You See What I'm Saying"

Speaking the Other Person's Language

Scenario Two

Mark Engstrom was in the small conference room Friday morning
at five minutes after eight, giving himself time to check every detail and
still get away well before anyone else arrived. He would show up again
at precisely 9 a.m., relaxed and comfortable, with no sign that he'd
been there earlier but knowing that all was well. That mattered to him,
as *everything* about the presentation mattered; Mark left nothing to
chance, ever. He and his staff had spent the last two months making sure
that today's presentation urging Hadleigh, Inc., to move aggressively
into the Hispanic market with a product line tailored *for* that
market would be perfect down to the last comma. He was very pleased
with the results.

The red notebooks at each place, holding the information packets,
were *exactly* the color of chili peppers; Mark had gone through dozens
of color samples to find the precise red he wanted. Inside the binders
were printouts of the best of his slides, plus many pages of
supplementary materials. He'd spared no expense. Handsome borders,
top-quality white paper toned down just enough to set off the charts and
graphs—everything done in red and white and green, the colors of
the Mexican flag—with all the little extra graphics frills that make the

difference. Every page layout had been done professionally, with lots of white space, no crowding anywhere, crisp black type in Mark's favorite font, and all the blocks of text arranged to lead the eye easily from one crucial point to another. Everything on the table, everything in the binders, looked the way it was *supposed* to look. Sophisticated. Current. Exciting. *Beautiful.* Not a flaw to be seen. And he'd had his best people check to be sure that every fact, every smallest item of data, was current and correct; that mattered to him too.

The presentation itself went well. Mark had seen other people ruining their chances with slides that were upside down or in the wrong order or just plain ugly. He'd seen people forced to ask for delays while somebody found them an extension cord or fixed a glitch in the equipment. He'd sat many times, bored out of his mind, while people droned on and on explaining what was already *on* their slides as plain as day, as if everyone in the room were either blind or illiterate. Mark made none of those mistakes.

He began with the most basic fact—that the Hispanic market is worth $189.5 billion—on a spectacular slide all its own. The graphics were top of the line; he could have looked at that slide all day. He said only "See that?" and moved on to the next one, the one showing them that by the year 2010 Hispanics would be the largest ethnic group in the United States: 30 million people with money to spend! He was careful not to overdo it; he had 35 slides and he kept them moving right along, taking his audience step by step through the plan that he was proposing. And he let the slides speak for themselves. None of that annoying patter that spoiled the effect. Just the occasional word or two when it was really appropriate and necessary.

When the lights came back on he stood there relaxed and smiling, sure he'd made his case, certain that all the weeks of hard work and scrupulous attention to detail were going to pay off for him now.

"All right!" he said. "I'm sure you can all see that we need to move on this and move fast, and my people are ready. Now, are there any questions before we leave? Anything I need to clarify for you?"

The response he got floored him. He could hardly believe it! *They'd get back to him. There was plenty of time; no reason to push things along too fast and make mistakes. They'd have to think it over. They'd let him know. He'd be hearing from them.* He had to struggle just to get an appointment to discuss it some more, and they put him off for more than a week when they gave in on that. Mark knew what the message was. It was "thanks, but no thanks."

Why? he thought, stunned and bewildered. *What more could they possibly want? What had gone wrong?*

What's Going on Here?

Mark's Point of View

The way Mark sees it, the three people in his audience should have had nothing to say at the end of his presentation but "Where do we sign?" He had done *everything* right. All the research to establish that the new Hispanic line would fit right into the business; all the research to gather the facts and statistics and figures that proved what a bonanza the line would be for the company. All the hours put into laying out the information so that the picture would be crystal clear. All the preparation, all the time and money and energy. Sure, he'd known there might be some requests for changes—maybe a little haggling—and he could understand that they might not have wanted to look eager. But he had expected the resistance to be only symbolic; he had been positive that the answer would be a swift and vigorous *yes!*

It wasn't as if Hadleigh, Inc., hadn't been looking for a new line; the company was actively looking and anxious to get on with it. It wasn't as if he'd done a sloppy job on the presentation; he had given it 100 percent. It wasn't as if he hadn't made sure he knew his subject inside and out. He'd been ready to answer every question, no matter how detailed, no matter how obscure, but they hadn't given him the chance. His presentation had been a sure thing; it should have worked.

It seems to Mark that the only possible explanation is that his listeners had made up their minds in advance to say no—maybe because he's younger than they are, and they can't stand seeing him out in front on anything big, anything new—and so they just let him go through the motions. What a terrible waste!

The Managers' Points of View

Suppose we asked the three managers who attended Mark's presentation to explain why they responded so negatively. We would get these three summary comments in reply:

> JIM HANSEN: I just didn't hear anything that convinced me. Lots of pretty pictures, sure—but it all sounded superficial. It didn't sound to me like Mark really knew what he was talking about. Under the circumstances, I couldn't say anything positive.

ELIZABETH BAKER: Well, I listened carefully, because I had been sort of halfway convinced before Mark started talking. But he didn't really say anything. Lots of flash, but nothing that told me loud and clear, *This is what we ought to do.* Before I say yes to a plan that's going to cost us a fortune, I have to hear something that really rings a bell with me. That didn't happen today.

LEE CARTWRIGHT: I have to hand it to Mark; he does good work. He puts a lot of energy into everything he does. But he only scratched the surface this morning, know what I mean? All those slides and stuff come in handy when you're rushed. But I didn't get the feeling that Mark had a firm grasp of what he was trying to lay on us here. I didn't feel like he had come to grips with the material the way he should have if he wanted us to feel safe trusting his division with that much money and that much responsibility. I couldn't go along with it.

The managers felt they had given Mark a chance to convince them, and he'd blown it. And they would agree with him—it was a terrible waste, for everybody involved.

What Went Wrong?

The problem that caused Mark Engstrom to fail in spite of all his careful hard work can be simply stated: *He'd offered a completely visual presentation of a case to an audience composed of two people who rely on their ears for information processing and one whose dominant sensory system is touch. None of the three people he was trying to convince cares at all about how things* look.

If Mark had been talking to three total strangers on the spur of the moment, this total sensory mismatch could be considered a stroke of bad luck, the way a sudden snowstorm that makes you arrive 20 minutes late is bad luck. But this was no off-the-cuff performance; we know Mark had two whole months to prepare for it. And one of the things he needed to know, right up there with how many potential profit dollars there are in the Hispanic market, was *which sensory system each member of his audience relied on most heavily.* He had more than enough time to find this out; he just didn't realize that it made any difference. Like most sight dominant people, it never crossed his mind that there is any other way to look at the world than the way *he* looks at it. In Mark's world, what matters if you're going to understand and remember information is color and pattern and arrangement for the eye. He would be amazed to know that this isn't true for every competent and intelligent adult he works with, because it seems to him to be so obviously the only possible way to perceive the world.

Mark is mistaken. Different people have different sensory preferences, and any strategy that fails to take those preferences into account risks failing, no matter how good it may otherwise be. Let's turn to this issue and discuss it thoroughly, to find out how Mark might have avoided getting into such deep and unprofitable water.

Communication Technique: Using the Sensory Modes

It's estimated that human beings are bombarded with at least 10,000 sensory stimuli *per second* from their external and internal environments. If attention were to be paid to every one of those 10,000 sensations, the result would be information overload; we would collapse under the impossible weight of such a processing burden. To avoid that, we have to reduce the incoming information to a manageable quantity, noticing some stimuli and discarding others, remembering some only with our short-term (working) memory, indexing others for transfer to long-term memory storage. Our brains carry out this formidable task by working with our sensory systems: sight, hearing, touch, taste, smell, and perhaps a dozen less familiar systems, such as the sense of *proprioception*, which tells us about our position in space and our balance. In this book we will restrict our discussion to the senses of sight, hearing, and touch for reasons of space, but we have no reason to believe that what is said here doesn't apply to all the others as well.

We need *all* our sensory systems, and in the best possible working order. When one system is drastically limited, as when the sense of sight is limited by darkness, we rely more heavily on the others, but we ordinarily use them all together. However, no later than the age of five every child has discovered that *one* of the sensory systems works best for him or her and is more useful for information processing than the others. That system becomes the preferred or dominant one for that child. We don't know whether this preference is inborn or learned, or (most probably) both; we do know that it is extremely difficult to change—much as left- or right-handedness is. We also know that ignoring it can interfere significantly with understanding and learning. Talk to any teacher of young children, and you'll hear statements like these:

"Just talking to Johnny is a waste of time. If you want him to understand what he's supposed to do, you have to give him something to look at."

"You can show Helena pictures all day long—it's no use. You have to <u>tell</u> her; she has to hear the information or she's lost."

"The only way you can get Brett to understand anything is by letting him tackle it hands-on. He can take a clock apart and put it back together blindfolded, but he has a terrible time learning with his eyes or his ears."

By the time we're adults this preference is usually less obvious. We learn over the years to make good use of our other sensory systems, and we become far less likely to blurt out in public that we can't do something. However, the task of determining sensory preferences is simplified by the fact that they are reliably reflected in *speech*.

Suppose you've made a brief presentation to three people that you outrank, presenting your idea for a new product or service and then asking them to tell you their opinions. Suppose each of these persons has a different sensory preference, and they all dislike your idea. In such a situation you can expect answers like these:

"I'm sorry; I don't really see it as very promising. I hate to be negative, but I just can't picture our division doing that."

"I'm sorry; it really doesn't sound very promising. I hate to be negative, but it just doesn't ring any bells with me."

"I'm sorry; I don't feel as if it would be a good idea. I hate to be negative, but it just falls flat with me somehow."

Notice that you immediately recognize which sensory system each utterance comes from; you don't have to go look anything up to make that determination. This is because one of the features of everyone's *mental* grammar is an internal dictionary where the words of your language are indexed and cross-indexed in many different ways; one way is by their association with one or the other of your sensory systems. The task of recognizing a sensory vocabulary—called a sensory *mode*—is not something you will have to learn; it's a skill you already have available and ready for use.

It was important for me to specify in the example that the person presenting the idea outranked the three listeners and that they all reacted negatively. When people are relaxed and at ease, they use *all* the sensory modes as they talk, shifting from one to another without difficulty. Often they mix the modes, as in this chapter's title: "I don't feel like you see what I'm saying." In casual discourse the sensory modes aren't particularly important. But when people are tense—as when they must respond negatively to a presentation by someone who outranks them—they tend to become *locked in* to the sensory mode that corresponds to their preferred sensory system. The more tense they are, the stronger that lock will be.

If you were attending one of my seminars and I suddenly began talking in Navajo rather than in English, you would have an immediate—and justifiable—negative reaction. You would feel distrust and suspicion. You would think, "This woman isn't interested in communicating with me; she isn't concerned about me at all; she has some secret agenda of her own that she's pushing here." My seminar would be a failure and I would have to give you your money back. (Unless, of course, you were a native speaker of Navajo, in which case your reaction would be exactly the opposite.)

The sensory modes are not languages, but they function like languages during communication under stress—which is an accurate description of most business communication. This makes the technique of systematic use of the sensory modes a powerful tool in that language environment for building rapport, for increasing understanding, and for persuading others to agree with what you say. It has two parts: recognition and response. Recognition, as you have already noticed, is automatic; it's just a matter of paying attention. And the basis for choosing your response will be obvious to you from the Navajo/ English situation I described in the previous paragraph. Rule 1 is: *Match the sensory mode coming at you.* That is, speak your listener's language, so that the reaction will be, "I may find out that I don't agree with this person; but I can tell that I'm listening to someone who perceives the world the same way I do. This is someone I can work with."

And if you can't follow Rule 1? Sometimes you can't. Sometimes English *has* no word or phrase for what you want to say that is in the sensory mode you're trying to match. For example, I can refer to the sight dominant as "eye people" and the hearing dominant as "ear people." But English offers no corresponding term for individuals who are touch dominant. "Skin people" would be understood in a very different way and is totally unsuitable. Sometimes the matching word or phrase is one you can't remember or don't feel comfortable saying; often eye or ear dominant people perceive touch mode language as crude or in other ways undesirable. (We'll be coming back to the prejudice against touch mode later in this chapter and elsewhere in the book.) If we were talking about languages, a fallback rule would exist only in the rare situation in which speakers of two different languages have a third *shared* language they can use. For the sensory modes, however, we're more fortunate. Rule 2 is: *If you can't use Rule 1, try to use no sensory language at all.* That is, when you can't match your listener's language, stay neutral to avoid clashing with it. Here are three brief examples to illustrate how this works.

Using Rule 1

> FRED: "I don't see why you're reacting so negatively to my proposal. It's clear, it's sharp, and from my point of view it is <u>exactly</u> what this company needs to do."
>
> ELENA: "I understand that that's the way you see it; I wish I could agree with you."

Fred addresses Elena in sight mode; she answers in sight mode. This is sensory mode matching.

Using Rule 2

> FRED: "I don't see why you're reacting so negatively to my proposal. It's clear, it's sharp, and from my point of view it is <u>exactly</u> what this company needs to do."
>
> ELENA: "I understand that that's your opinion; I wish I could agree with you."

Fred addresses Elena in sight mode. Because she is for some reason unable or unwilling to match that mode, she answers neutrally, using an utterance that contains no vocabulary from any of the sensory modes.

Breaking Both Rules

> FRED: "I don't see why you're reacting so negatively to my proposal. It's clear, it's sharp, and from my point of view it is <u>exactly</u> what this company needs to do."
>
> ELENA: "I understand that that's how you feel about it; I wish I could agree with you."

Fred addresses Elena in sight mode; she answers in touch mode. This is sensory mode mismatch.

Match the other person's sensory mode if you can; otherwise, avoid using sensory language, so that you can stay neutral. Matching sensory modes sets up a feedback loop of trust and good feeling; that's the best move. Mismatching has the opposite effect; that's the *worst* move. Avoiding sensory language allows you to remain neutral, and that's a great deal better than mismatch.

This technique will strike you as incredibly easy to do, and you are right in your assessment. It's a piece of cake. That's not a flaw, that's an advantage; be glad there is something easy you can do that is both valuable and powerful. And notice that it is not only easy, it's *free*. This is a gift that should not be rejected because of "no pain, no gain." You took care of all the pain you are responsible for when you went through the process of acquiring your language in infancy; you can relax now and reap the gain.

To the extent that algorithms are possible for language—which has far more "give" to it than mathematics does—the sensory mode technique is an algorithm. That is, if you match the mode you hear, good feeling between you and the other speaker will always increase to the degree allowed by the context. If you use sensory-neutral language when you can't match the other's mode, bad feeling along the lines of "This person isn't even trying to speak my language!" will be avoided—again, to the extent that this outcome is allowed by the context. Numbers don't *have* contexts in this way; if you add 2 and 2, no matter what the situation is and no matter who does the adding the sum will always be 4. Language can't quite achieve that rigor, and it's a good thing; the flexibility of language is something human beings need. But the sensory mode technique is as close to being a language algorithm—a lalgorithm, maybe?—as you can get. It's *very* reliable.

The Special Problem of Touch Dominance

We need to turn our attention just for a moment to the problem of touch dominance, which is at the heart of many communication breakdowns and all too often goes unrecognized.

The American Mainstream English culture is biased first in favor of sight and then in favor of hearing; it is biased *against* touch. We are a "Don't touch!" and "Keep your hands to yourself!" society. Those who ignore the "No touching" rules find themselves constantly in trouble; in today's environment of intense concern over issues like child abuse and sexual harrassment, it can be very serious trouble.

We would never send our kids to school with the commands "Don't look!" and "Don't listen!" We would consider it absurd to expect children to learn while wearing blindfolds or earplugs. We don't hesitate, however, to send touch dominant children off to school ordered not to touch, which is like sending them to a typing class wearing heavy mittens. People whose preference for touch is strong have few callings open to them that combine high earning potential with high status. Many positions in which people "work with their hands" mean low pay or low status or both; there are relatively few openings in our society for sculptors, weavers, and ceramists, for example. The ideal profession for a touch dominant person—surgery—is out of reach for a large proportion of the population.

The bias against touch is so pervasive that it permeates everything we encounter in our lives. In Tom Peters and Nancy Austin's book, *A Passion For Excellence*, for example, we read that "The values of any organization live most humanly through stories, pictures." Stories are for the ear if heard and for the eye if read; pictures are for the eye alone. What about the people in that organization whose dominant sensory system is touch? There's no provision here for giving such people equally good access to the organization's values—and, you'll notice that there's no comparable way to *say* so. I can say that something has been designed to appeal to the eye and the ear. But if I say that something has been designed to appeal to the skin, I will very probably get a negative reaction. Even the vocabulary for touch is impoverished.

All this combines to make touch dominance a genuine handicap. Touch dominant people face constant rejection and reprimand in our society, and by the time they reach adulthood they have come to *expect* rejection. Usually they have also acquired a label. If it comes from experts, it may be "slow learner" or "hostile and withdrawn" or "underachiever"; if it comes from others, it can be summed up as "pain in the neck." A great deal of the time, touch dominant people have had to work twice as hard to get ahead and have managed it only by a dogged stubbornness that is easy to misinterpret.

Because the majority of successful people in our society are eye or ear dominant individuals with no understanding of touch dominance, they tend to leap to negative conclusions about a touch dominant individual, blaming misunderstandings and interpersonal difficulties on flaws in his or her personality and character. This creates tension, of course, which will lock the touch dominant individual into touch mode, which makes the tension worse—and so on, round and round the loop. The result is constant negative interactions, most of which could be avoided by following the rules for using the sensory modes.

Remember, the person you view as a pain in the neck may only appear that way to you because he or she is touch dominant. If that's the source of the communication problem, speaking in touch mode yourself will improve matters dramatically. If it's not, no harm will have been done. It can be difficult at first if you are eye or ear dominant, but it becomes easy with practice and it's always worth a try.

Now let's go back to the scenario that opened this chapter and examine it again, to find out how proper use of the sensory modes could make it possible for Mark Engstrom to achieve the maximum positive effect for the presentation he worked so hard to prepare.

Another Look at Scenario Two

Let's assume that Mark Engstrom has taken time to find out—*before* he starts preparing his presentation—that he has to communicate effectively with a man and a woman (Jim Hansen and Elizabeth Baker) who are hearing dominant, and one man (Lee Cartwright) who is touch dominant. This is important information. For one thing, it lets him avoid spending a lot of money unnecessarily. He knows in advance that the three people he wants to persuade will not be impressed by color choices or typeface selections or anything of that kind. He can save money by putting together information packets and slides that are simply neat and informative and easy to deal with. No need to search for binders the exact color of chili peppers for this audience!

If Mark is the sort of speaker who can keep a roomful of people on the edge of their seats just by talking, he could do without the slides altogether. But let's assume that—like most of us—he is a competent speaker but not star quality. In that case, if he likes to use slides he should feel free to do so. He should still be careful that they're in the right order and not upside down, and he should still be sure his equipment will work without glitches. He still needs to come in ahead of time and check the details to be sure all is well. An overall impression of competence remains important. However, his slides need not be fancy, he doesn't need so many of them, and, above all, he can't *rely* on them. He will have to present the information by talking. Let's rewrite the scenario to reflect this changed context; we can leave the opening paragraph just as it was and begin at paragraph two.

Scenario Two, Revised

As the managers came into the small conference room and took their places around the table, Latin music was playing softly in the background. At each place was a notebook holding an information packet carefully put together. Because the two hearing dominant people present wouldn't care what kind of paper the notebooks held, Mark had chosen a good-quality stock with a rough linenlike texture that he knew would appeal to Lee Cartwright. For the same reason, he had passed up the standard slick vinyl binders for three of the old-fashioned blue fabric kind; they had texture, too.

"Nice music," Jim Hansen said, and Elizabeth Baker agreed.

"You like it?"

"Very much," Elizabeth said.

"That," Mark said, "is Caballero—Caballero Spanish Media. They have ninety Spanish-language radio stations in this country." As he expected, all three wrote that down. Jim and Elizabeth made a note because radio was important to them; Lee did so because the act of writing—holding the pen, moving the arm and hand, and pressing on the paper—helps touch dominant people establish a mental index for information they want to remember.

Turning the radio down low, Mark began showing his slides, beginning with the one that established the size of the market.

"This may surprise you," he said as it came up on the screen. "It certainly surprised <u>me.</u> Notice that the Hispanic market in 1993 was $189.5 billion—that's <u>billion</u>—dollars. That's no lightweight market, my friends. In my opinion, that's substantial. How does it sound to you?"

"Substantial," said Jim. "Very substantial."

"It's news to me," Elizabeth said. "I knew it was large, but I hadn't heard that figure before."

"And," Mark went on as he brought up the next slide, "here are some of the basic facts I'd like you to hold onto as we go along." He read the data off the slide, changing a word here and a word there so that he wouldn't appear to think they were incapable of reading it for themselves. He was aware that Jim and Elizabeth would rather hear the facts than look at them, and he knew that in the absence of any tactile information it would help Lee to have the data presented in both sight and sound. "The U.S. Census Bureau," he told them, "says that we'll have a Hispanic population in the U.S. by 1997 of <u>28 million people</u>. The word from the bureau is that by 2010, Hispanics will be our largest ethnic group. We're talking 30 million people with money to spend…"

The presentation went well. Mark talked his audience through all 20 slides, adding small bits of extra information whenever it was appropriate, answering Jim and Elizabeth's questions as he went and carefully salting what he said with enough touch mode vocabulary to stay in good contact with Lee Cartwright.

When the lights came back on, he stood there relaxed and smiling, sure he'd made his case, certain that all the weeks of hard work and scrupulous attention to detail were going to pay off for him.

"All right!" he said. "I'm sure you hear the potential loud and clear, just as I do. I feel like we ought to move on this <u>fast,</u> and my people are ready to dig in. Just say the word."

The response he got satisfied him. All three had minor items to argue with him about; he had expected that. Naturally they didn't want to give him the impression that they were eager; they were handing over a lot of company time and money and they wanted him to understand that they didn't feel casual about it. They had asked for another meeting before setting a firm starting date; Mark had been expecting that also. But they were *convinced.*

I don't want to give the impression that the sensory modes technique will always work like this. When a presentation is otherwise poorly done, this technique won't save it. When there are compelling business reasons for the audience to refuse to go along, it won't cancel those reasons. But in the situation set out in Scenario Two, where the presentation is excellent, the homework has all been done, and the course proposed is a good fit, it can work wonders. And even in a bad situation, even when the presentation *doesn't* succeed, proper use of sensory modes can help ensure that everyone leaves the room still feeling good about the others present. That's capital that can be used another time, and it's well worth having.

The Workout Section for this chapter will give you an opportunity to explore the technique further and practice your skills; in the meantime, you can begin using it immediately. For this and all the subsequent techniques in the book, *begin by using it when the outcome isn't critical.* Use it at the grocery store and the public library and the gas station. Use it with good friends who, if they ask you why you're "talking funny," won't be offended to hear that you're practicing a new communication technique. You want to get over being awkward with sensory modes; you want to get past the fumbling stage. You want the technique to become so familiar and so easy that you can do it almost without thinking about it. Then, when you need it suddenly in a crisis, you'll be ready.

Notes

1. It's not possible to give a first source for the information about sensory preferences and sensory modes. The earliest reference I've found in print is a passing mention in the work of Carl Jung. Edward T. Hall has written about it extensively; it comes up in the work of Virginia Satir; and it is prominent in the system created by John Grinder and Richard Bandler called Neurolinguistic Programming, under the heading of "representational systems."

2. In literature on the subject of sensory preferences you will find a variety of different terms used; in order to search the literature you'll need to be familiar with them. The most frequent are "visual" for the sense of sight, "auditory" for the sense of hearing, and "tactile," "tactual," and "kinesthetic" for the sense of touch.

WORKOUT SECTION: CHAPTER 2

1. In the same way that you need to know the addresses and phone numbers of people you interact with frequently, you need to know their preferred sensory modes. Begin with the people closest to you, and observe their language carefully, *especially when you know that they are under stress*. You're watching for a *consistent* vocabulary pattern from a single sensory mode. As you work, remember these four points:

a. People ordinarily lock in to their dominant mode only when they are under stress; such behavior is in fact a reliable indication that they are under stress, which can be a useful thing to know. Their vocabulary choices when they're relaxed may or may not come from that mode and should not serve as your data source.

b. An item that is part of someone's professional or group jargon is not a reliable clue to their preferred mode. For example, the fact that a therapist frequently uses the sentence, "And how did that make you feel?" doesn't mean that he or she is touch dominant; a teacher's frequent use of "I see" doesn't indicate sight dominance. Teenagers' use of the expression "I smell ya" for "I understand what you're saying" certainly doesn't indicate that they are smell dominant.

c. An item from a particular sensory mode doesn't count as evidence when the speaker has no other choice. If English has alternatives only from the vocabularies of hearing and touch, for example, the fact that someone uses those rather than an item from sight mode says nothing about his or her reliance on visual information.

d. Finally, it's best not to rely on someone's written language as evidence. People often use very different vocabularies when they write than when they speak, and the touch mode alternatives in particular may seem to them to be too informal or "colloquial" to use in writing.

When you've been working with this process a while, you'll be able to do it almost automatically. At first, however, I recommend the following steps:

a. Select the person you want to observe.

b. On a small piece of paper, draw lines setting up three columns, headed S for sight, H for hearing, and T for touch.

c. Each time you hear the person use an item from one of the sensory modes while talking in a nonrelaxed situation, make a small mark in the proper column. (Obviously you will do this only when you can do it unobtrusively.)

d. When you have a large sample, total up the marks in each column to determine the person's preference.

e. Make a note of any additional evidence. For example, suppose you ask someone to tell you about a business dinner and you're given lots of detailed information about what people said there and how people sounded but no information about how anyone looked or what people were wearing. That's typical of the hearing dominant person; record it as supporting evidence of that preference.

Once you're sure of someone's preferred mode, enter it on a Sensory Mode Directory page in your Communication Strategy Notebook. Also add it to your regular address and phone number list for that person, so that it will always be readily available when you need it.

2. Identifying your *own* preferred sensory mode may provide you with the answers to questions that have always baffled you in the past, such as why you have so much trouble learning something that everyone else finds easy (or vice versa), why you seem unable to get along with someone whom you feel you have no reason to dislike, or why—as in Scenario 2—you were unable to persuade people to go along with a proposal that you *knew* was well presented and desirable. It's harder to observe your own language than that of others; you may want to ask your family and close associates for their input. Here are a few questions to get you started.

a. When you understand and approve of what someone says to you, which are you more likely to say: "I see what you mean; it looks great"; "I hear you; it sounds great"; or "I get it; that feels right to me"?

b. Do you understand and remember best when you get information from watching a video, listening to a cassette, or from hands-on experience? Which method of obtaining information do you enjoy most? My husband finds it impossible to listen to recorded language unless he has his glasses on. Do you have any quirks of that kind?

c. Are there particular kinds of vocabulary items that you feel you would almost never use? Are there any particular methods for processing information that you would find difficult or boring and would use only under duress?

Take your time doing this workout. Often your first judgment will turn out to be incorrect; the task of getting it right may take weeks. For example, because I kept hearing myself say, "I see," and because I am a voracious reader, I assumed that I was a sight dominant person. My children, who were very familiar with my speech when I was angry or frustrated with them, were able to help me make the more accurate determination that I'm hearing dominant. My experience is not unusual.

3. For your Communication Strategy Notebook, set up a Sensory Mode file and begin keeping track of relevant information. For example:

a. Record incidents in which you used the sensory mode technique to serve as a database for planning strategies. What was the situation? What was said? What happened? What was surprising? Did you find a particular mode difficult to deal with? Did anything go wrong, and if so, can you determine why?

b. Make a list of words and phrases that you use frequently and that are important to you. Identify them by sensory mode, and then translate them into the other two major sensory vocabularies if you can. As with "eye people, ear people, and [skin?] people," you'll find that it's not always possible. In such cases, find an equivalent that is sensory neutral, like "I understand" for "I see/I hear you/I get it."

c. Set up a file of lexical items from each of the sensory modes and keep adding to it; the larger it is, the more useful it will be to you. The lists below will get you started.

    Sight: vision; focus; peer into; insight; see the light; pretty as a picture; sight unseen; shine some light on the problem; see my way clear to; point of view; apple of his eye.

    Hearing: doesn't ring true; full of static; out of tune; off pitch; music to my ears; sound off; now hear this; the way I hear it; hear on the grapevine; an earful; hear me out.

    Touch: think straight; get through the week; break off with; grasp at straws; rub someone the wrong way; get a grip on yourself; roll with the punches; heap praise on; heavy-handed.

    Mixed: keep an eye on something; take a look at something; hit a sour note; I see what you're saying.

4. Jack Kahl of Manco, Inc. (following Walt Disney's lead), insists on trying for active involvement of all of the customer's sensory systems when designing a product. Kahl "even gave special attention to the sound of duct tape, the scrunch that it makes as consumers unroll it," according to Joshua Hyatt in "Steal This Strategy" (*Inc.* magazine,

February 1991). Does your company follow this practice in the language used to describe its products and/or services? If not, how could you add it to your standard procedures? Choose one product or service and think carefully: When you talk or write about it, what steps are you taking to appeal to the customer's sight, hearing, and touch? (And taste and smell, if those are appropriate.) What could you do, linguistically, to cover all the sensory bases more effectively?

5. Because touch is at the bottom of the sensory totem pole in our culture, most successful people are eye or ear dominant—which means they have trouble using touch mode easily. Similarly, touch dominant people often find themselves "at a loss for words" because they can't readily put their hands on a sight or hearing equivalent for something they want to say. All of the examples below are in touch mode; translate them into a sight and a hearing version that will convey essentially the same meaning. Your translations don't have to be a perfect match or in elegant language, and it doesn't matter whether or not they are utterances you would be comfortable saying yourself. If you're sure English has no translation for some item that's in the sensory mode you need, use an equivalent that contains no sensory language. The first example has been done for you.

a. "But for the grace of God we would have got in some quicksand that would have sunk Sonic." *(J. Vernon Stewart, quoted by Seth Lubove in "People Talk Thin but Eat Fat," Forbes magazine, April 2, 1990, p. 57)*

   Sight mode: "But for the grace of God we would have been looking at some kind of disaster that would have meant seeing the end of Sonic."

   Hearing mode: "But for the grace of God we would have been hearing the kind of static that would have made people say goodbye to Sonic for good."

   Sensory-neutral mode: "But for the grace of God we would have been involved in problems that would have meant failure for Sonic."

b. "We didn't want to gum up Quicken with a lot of extra features that our home users didn't need." *(Scott Cook, quoted by Julia Pitta in "The Crisco Factor," Forbes magazine, July 10, 1992, p. 307)*

c. "Goldsbury knew he had a hot number in the salsa. He convinced Pace to drop the peppers, relishes and spicy cheese dip to concentrate on building the sauce line." *(Claire Poole, "Please Pass the Hot Stuff," Forbes magazine, April 27, 1992, p. 155)*

d. "If you own shares of a hot little concept company and you're counting on press releases and crowd psychology to push the stock higher (or keep it from drifting lower), my advice is to think very seriously about getting out while you still can." *(Frederick E. Rowe, Jr., "Weasel Words," Forbes magazine, December 23, 1991, p. 184)*

e. "In a crash, my Brooklyn neighbors were inclined to believe, such trading would give a plunging human investor little in the way of an outcropping to grab onto, or a level terrace on which to rest, recuperate, and, above all, think." *(L. J. Davis, "The Next Panic," Harper's magazine, May 1991, p. 39)*

f. [Asked to identify his greatest career achievement:] "Steering the company with a sense of direction, and maintaining its momentum during my tenure as CEO." *(Roberto Goizueta, quoted in a "Top 50" profile, Forbes magazine, May 30, 1988, p. 130)*

g. "We've never seen a reason to compress authority into a single person. Whenever there's a question, we get together and massage it around. And it works." *(Albert Elia III, quoted in a "Top 500" profile, Inc. magazine, December 1985, p. 80)*

h. "Critics suggest that the creation of category managers will further clog an already slow-moving system." *(Zachary Schiller, "The Marketing Revolution at Procter & Gamble," Business Week, July 25, 1988, p. 73)*

i. "You'll have to sharpen your pencil." *(Identified in a book review as Steve Jobs's "favorite phrase to suppliers," Success magazine, September 1989, p. 54)*

j. "The goal of contingency planning is to remove from a tough situation the panic element of 'What the hell are we going to do now?'....When you're under pressure, the mind can play tricks on you." *(Bill Walsh, "When Things Go Bad," Forbes magazine, March 29, 1993, p. 13)*

k. "If the poor believe that most wealthy people are exploiters and thieves who squash other people into poverty for personal gain, they will not be likely to climb the ladder of economic success." *(Michael Bauman, "The Dangerous Samaritans: How We Unintentionally Injure the Poor," Imprimis magazine, January 1994, p. 4)*

You may find this workout hard to do. That's fine; that means you get the point. Someone who is locked into a particular sensory mode by stress has exactly that sort of difficulty dealing with communication in other sensory modes. This workout will give you a feeling for how frustrating that can be and how much it can increase a person's tension.

6. A Touch Dominance Network was founded in May 1994 to serve as a clearinghouse for information about touch dominance and to provide a networking forum both for touch dominant individuals and those who interact with them. For information, write TDN, Ozark Center for Language Studies, P.O. Box 1137, Huntsville, Arkansas 72740–1137.

7. The quotations below are typical examples of the bias toward sight as "the best of all senses" in our culture.

a. "The ordinary creativity of ordinary human beings, which is the ability to look, not to conceptualize, can be trained. But not in the behavioral way." *(Peter Drucker, quoted by Elizabeth Hall in ",",* Psychology Today, *December 1982, p. 62)*

   Why just "the ability to look"? Why aren't hearing and touching also part of ordinary creativity?

b. ...I(t) would seem to provide additional evidence that there might be a 'deep structure' of visual form underlying human art that is wired into the human brain." *(Betty Edwards,* Drawing on the Artist Within, *New York: Simon & Schuster, 1986.)*

   Why just visual *form? What does this mean for sculpture and other tactile media? Are they excluded from art? Edwards's book is one of the most useful volumes I own, but it is written as though vision were the only valuable human sensory system.*

c. "As you begin the imagery, picture a place where you feel safe...." Make yourself a participant in the vision, not just an observer.... Picture the setting you are trying to change...." *(Sally Squires, "The Power of Positive Imagery: Visions to Boost Immunity,"* American Health, *July 1987, pp. 56–61)*

   Like the majority of the material available on the process of creative visualization (and like its various names), almost no attention is given to any sense except sight. To the sight dominant person this seems entirely natural; how else would you do it? Squires certainly isn't alone. But this approach shuts out those who prefer hearing and touch. Is that necessary? Is there any reason why the instructions couldn't refer to sounds and textures? Try to find eye and ear translations for the three quoted instructions. What happens?

d. *The Mind's Eye* (This is the name of one of the leading catalogues of
    informational audiotapes, books on tape, and the like)

> *The name is certainly clever. However, are its implications accurate? Does*
> *everyone who listens to a tape of a novel begin to see it, rather than hear it?*
> *If your answer to that question would be an unhesitating yes, ask some of*
> *your friends and associates. Ask an auto mechanic; ask a plumber; ask a*
> *surgeon. You may be surprised at their answers.*

3

"How Did We Get into This Stupid Fight, Anyway?!"

Staying Out of Hostility Loops

Scenario Three

Rebecca Linwood had done her best to prepare for her meeting with Elaine Clark, gathering every item of information she could possibly need. She knew, absolutely, that she was right; the company *had* to increase its spending for research if it was going to have any hope of remaining competitive. Nevertheless, she was dreading the session, because Elaine was hard to get along with; Rebecca was very sorry there was no way to avoid running this issue by the woman. She took her place at the conference table, already tense, and opened her file to the first set of statistics. *I will not let her get to me this time,* she promised herself as she began talking.

"As you know, Elaine," she said, "we're here this morning to discuss this company's pathetic investment in research, and our crying need to do something about that. I'll begin with a presentation of the basic facts and figures. I'll be as brief as possible."

"Oh, take your time, Rebecca!" Elaine answered, laughing. She waved one careless hand. "You know me—I'd never ask you to rush! Just do your best, dear." She paused, smiling sweetly, and added, "I've cancelled all my appointments for this morning."

"You didn't have to do that!" Rebecca said. "If you'll just give me your full attention for once, I'm sure I can get through this material in an hour. I KNOW I told you that when I asked for this meeting!"

"Oh, goodness," said Elaine, "I've up<u>set</u> you again, <u>haven't</u> I? I'm <u>so</u> sorry, dear. Please just ignore me. You go <u>right</u> ahead with your presentation. I <u>prom</u>ise you—I'm <u>all</u> ears!"

Rebecca stared grimly at the sheet of paper in front of her, and when she spoke again it was through clenched teeth. "In the past nine years," she began, "TC-Plex has spent only <u>three</u> <u>percent</u> of its budget on basic research. This is in <u>marked</u> <u>con</u>trast to the practice in our industry, where six percent or more is the <u>stan</u>dard. It's clear that—" She jumped as she felt Elaine's fingertips touch her wrist, and she stopped and looked at the other woman. "What?"

"I'm <u>sorry</u> to have to <u>stop</u> you, Rebecca," said Elaine; she certainly *looked* sorry. "You <u>know</u> how I hate to interrupt."

"Then why <u>did</u> you interrupt?" Rebecca snapped. "We've been here ten minutes, and I've hardly gotten <u>started</u>!" She smacked the thick folder of papers down on the table hard. "<u>Why</u> do you go out of your way to make things difficult, Elaine?" she demanded. "How do you expect us to ever get <u>through</u> with this discussion? It's imPORtant!"

Elaine sighed and made a soft "tsk" sound with her tongue. "As I told you, Rebecca," she said patiently, "I cancelled <u>every</u>thing this morning. I <u>do</u> wish you would just re<u>lax</u> and stop <u>worrying</u> about the <u>time</u>! I am <u>at</u> your dis<u>pos</u>al! There's just one thing: Your figures, dear. Heaven knows, I make <u>many</u>, many mistakes, but it does seem to me that <u>six</u> percent is just a tiny bit <u>high</u>. I know for a fact that W.D.X. only puts <u>five</u> percent into research, and—"

"Elaine, the <u>six</u> percent figure is an <u>average</u>! Of <u>course</u> some firms spend less, and some spend <u>more</u>! That's how you <u>arrive</u> at an average, for heaven's sakes! I'm <u>sure</u> you learned that at <u>some</u> point in your education! Now will you <u>please</u> stop playing games and let me get ON WITH THIS???"

What's Going on Here?

Communication is going on, certainly, but it's not communication about whether TC-Plex should increase its research budget or not. And it's not *going* to be. Rebecca is quite right; Elaine is playing games. However, this game requires two players, and Rebecca is providing Elaine with the partner she has to have if the game is to continue. We know that no action can be taken on the budget change until Rebecca finds a way to get the other woman's approval. If Scenario Three is a typical example of the way the two women communicate, many more meetings will take place and much more time will pass before even the first stage of that process—the simple presentation of the basic facts—can be completed.

Rebecca's Point of View

Rebecca's perception of the situation is that Elaine Clark is a silly, manipulative woman who has somehow managed to lodge herself at a critical point in the chain of command at TC-Plex and whose only goal in life is to use that position to block any idea that isn't her own. Rebecca goes into every interaction with Elaine tense, expecting the worst, prepared to be infuriated, knowing that she will come out of it sick to her stomach and with a pounding headache. As far as Rebecca is concerned, Elaine is an *impossible* person to deal with; she cannot imagine how Elaine rose so high or how she can hold *on* to her authority, behaving as she does. "If it were up to me_," she has told her husband many times, "I wouldn't let her be a receptionist for this company!"

However, whether she's correct about Elaine or not, Rebecca is stuck with her. That's terrifying, because in her opinion Elaine cares nothing about the company nor her colleagues; it's impossible to carry on a civil discussion with her; and she takes some kind of twisted pleasure in wrecking everybody else's plans. This makes everyone else's work twice as hard as it should be, and Rebecca is determined to find *some* way to either bring Elaine down or get past her.

Elaine's Point of View

Elaine considers Rebecca to be a mildly annoying, overwrought woman with no manners and limited talent who has a driving need to take charge of anything she encounters and dominate everyone around her. Elaine is rather sorry for Rebecca, and she always goes into any interaction with her determined to be pleasant no matter *how* the other woman behaves. She certainly is not going to stoop to Rebecca's level and engage in aggressive confrontations with her; she handles her much as she would handle a child. She is well aware of the negative opinions Rebecca has of her and is entirely indifferent to them.

What matters to Elaine is the welfare of the company. Rebecca is valuable to TC-Plex for her skill with computers and spreadsheets; Elaine is prepared to put up with any number of grandiose project proposals and absurd accusations in order to hold on to those skills for the company; she's careful to set things up in such a way that she is the only person who has to put up with either one very often. It's important to Elaine to keep Rebecca's nervousness and irritability as isolated as possible; she knows how contagious such emotions can be in a group and has no intention of letting them spread in *her* division. "I've dealt with worse," she tells her husband. "<u>Far</u> worse! You know me; I'll manage."

What Went Wrong?

Nothing at all has gone wrong for Elaine Clark. Her goal is to prevent any of Rebecca's plans for change from going anywhere, while at the same time offering her no cause for complaint (an outright refusal to meet with her, for example) that would justify an attempt to go over her head. The technique of endless delay serves her well; she is highly skilled at it; and she has no reason to be concerned. If Rebecca were ever to show signs of substantial improvement, or if she were to come up with a proposal that showed promise, Elaine would be the first to give her support. Until that happens, however, she is satisfied with matters as they stand.

For Rebecca, however, things are going from bad to worse. <u>Her</u> goal is to convince Elaine Clark, just once, to accept a proposal for increased research and carry it to a higher level in the company so that it will have some chance of being implemented. She knows that each time she loses her temper with Elaine she moves farther away from that goal, but the woman is so maddening that she just can't *help* it.

And for the company? There are two problems. In the first place, perhaps Rebecca is *right*; perhaps TC-Plex *should* be doing more research. No one will ever know as long as Rebecca continues to let herself be tied up in silly delaying games. And in the second place, an ongoing power struggle of this kind inside a company cannot be kept a secret, even when both parties make an effort to be discreet. It fuels gossip; people tend to take sides; and it's a constant distraction that can interfere with productivity and morale. It also wastes a lot of time. It could be set right by firing Elaine or Rebecca, but that would have obvious negative consequences. For someone they both report to to order them to behave differently would only create resentment and make things worse. What the company needs is for one or both of the women to find a way to end the communication deadlock that has been established, using language, without causing some *new* difficulty for the firm as a side effect.

That's possible. It can be done. I will step in with author's license here and say that we are going to *assume* that Elaine and Rebecca can be motivated to look for such a solution. In the real world that might not always be the case. The task of persuasion might fall to someone else and might shift to *finding a way to change their attitudes*. If we start from the assumption that the motivation already exists, however, there is a reliable technique that either woman—or both—can use to improve matters.

Communication Technique: Using the Satir Modes

Like the sensory mode technique you learned in Chapter 2, the five *Satir Modes* are examples of *language behavior modes*, patterns of language that can be identified by specific predictable characteristics and put to strategic purposes in communication. They are based on the work of therapist Virginia Satir, who discovered over the course of a lifetime of professional practice that the language of English speakers communicating under stress tended to fall into one of these five patterns. They include *Blaming, Placating, Computing, Distracting,* and *Leveling.* As you read their descriptions below, you will recognize them immediately—because they are part of your internal grammar— even if Satir's labels are unfamiliar to you.

Recognizing the Satir Modes

Blaming. The characteristics of *Blaming* include: a surface impression of open anger and hostility; extensive use of very personal language ("I, me, you, your, us, this," etc.); frequent use of extra acoustic stresses— emphasis—on words and parts of words; frequent use of words like "everything, everybody, never, always," etc.; angry and hostile body language. For example:

"What's the <u>matter</u> with you, an<u>y</u>way, have you <u>lost</u> your MIND?"

"<u>You</u> can't follow even the <u>sim</u>plest in<u>struc</u>tions, <u>can</u> you?"

"You could at <u>least</u> try to carry your share of the LOAD around here once in a while!"

"<u>Why</u> don't you <u>ever</u> consider what everybody <u>else</u> might want to do? <u>You</u> never think of <u>any</u>body but yourSELF!"

"<u>Every</u>body in the de<u>part</u>ment says you ALways act like this!"

The utterances above would be accompanied by frowns, jabbing fingers, clenched fists, gritted teeth, tense shoulders, a harsh tone of voice, and so on. Blaming body language is threatening body language.

Placating. The characteristics of *Placating* include: a surface impression of apology and deprecation and eagerness to please; heavy use of very personal language; frequent use of extra stresses on words and parts of words; body language to match. For example:

"You know how I am—anything you want is okay with me!"

"Shoot, what do I know? I don't care. You decide!"

"I hope you won't think that I'm trying to criticize you, dear! Goodness, I'd never do that; now would I?"

"I'm so sorry! I didn't mean to cause so much trouble, you know I didn't! I was only trying to HELP!"

"You know I'd never tell you what to do, dear...goodness, I'm no expert! But if you don't try to get along with your colleagues, how do you expect to get ahead?"

These examples would be accompanied by head bobbing, eye blinking, leaning, fidgeting, clinging, exaggerated smiling or pouting, and the like; Satir said that Placating reminded her of the behavior of cocker spaniel puppies.

Computing. The characteristics of *Computing* include: a surface impression of neutrality and control; personal language used only when it cannot easily be avoided; frequent use of abstractions and generalities and hypothetical expressions; stresses on words and parts of words only when they are absolutely necessary; very restrained body language at all times. For example:

"There is undoubtedly a good reason for this delay; no rational person would be alarmed."

"People tend to object when they are kept waiting for scheduled appointments."

"If executives forget to look after their pension funds, grave consequences are not unusual."

"Files are located on the hard disk whenever possible."

The body language that would go with these examples would be sparse and unemotional: a neutral facial expression and posture, a flat tone and intonation of the voice, and very few gestures.

Distracting. You don't need to learn new characteristics for identifying the *Distracting* mode. Distracters cycle through the other modes, using a sentence or two of one and then of another, with body language switching right along with the words. The surface impression is one of panic and disarray.

For example, suppose a person who relies on Distracting is sitting in a waiting room and it's now an hour past time for the scheduled appointment. A typical utterance would sound like this:

> "Why is it that every time I come here I have to sit around waiting for hours! MY time is important TOO, you know! *(Blaming)* But heck...I shouldn't complain! I mean, what do I know? And I don't have anything to do at home anyway, you know what I mean? *(Placating)* Nevertheless, patients are entitled to some minimum degree of courtesy. *(Computing)* And if they think they can push me around, they'd just better think aGAIN!" *(Blaming)*

Leveling. This brings us to *Leveling,* and to an aspect of language that is often hard for people to accept at first. Leveling is what is called in medicine "a diagnosis of exclusion"; that is, if the communication pattern of someone under stress does not have the characteristics of the other Satir Modes, it is Leveling. Our culture places so much emphasis on the use of "exactly the right word" and the need for a "powerful vocabulary" that we tend to have a distorted impression of the importance of words. In Chapter 8 we will take up this issue specifically, in detail. For now, it's important to realize that *you cannot tell the Satir Modes apart by the words that are used.* There are certain tendencies within the modes and they have been outlined above. But *any* word or phrase may be used in an utterance in *any* Satir Mode. What distinguishes one mode from another is not the words but the tunes the words are set to, and the rest of the accompanying body language. Look at these two examples:

1. "Why are you taking the file home with you?"
2. "WHY are you taking the file HOME with you?"

These two sentences contain exactly the same words, but they mean different things. Example #1 is a neutral request for information. It may be rude, it may be none of the questioner's business why you're taking the file, but so far as we can tell from its written form, it's Leveling. It's not hostile or confrontational or accusatory. Example #2, on the other hand, is Blaming; it is deliberately confrontational and provocative. The difference between the two is signalled only by the intonation, not by the words.

Someone who is in Leveling mode, then, may use very personal language or abstractions and generalities, may frequently use words like "everything" and "never" or use them rarely, may apologize or threaten. Only the accompanying body language—only the way it's said—distinguishes it as Leveling. This isn't trivial, obviously. A threat from someone who is Leveling is a serious matter; a threat from someone in Blaming mode is probably nothing but hot air.

WARNING: You will find people talking and writing of "Blamers" and "Placaters" and "Levelers." I've tried to avoid that up to this point, but I can't go on that way; always writing "someone who is using Blaming" is cumbersome and becomes annoying. It's important to understand, however, that to call someone "a Blamer" is only shorthand for "someone who is at this time using the language pattern called Blaming." Nobody *is* a Blamer in the way that a person *is* a Spaniard or a brunette. *Blaming is not a part of the character or personality or genetic identity. It is a behavior—specifically, a language behavior that is linked to the context of communication under stress.*

As is true for the sensory modes, people tend to have strong preferences for one particular Satir Mode over all the others. However, the sensory mode preference is an across-the-board phenomenon. The Satir Mode preference, on the other hand, is ordinarily linked to a specific role or setting. For example, many people rely on Placating or Computing for stressful communication at work but prefer to use Blaming for stressful interactions at home—or vice versa. It's very common for people to Placate with a doctor and switch to Blaming with the doctor's nurse—or vice versa.

Responding to the Satir Modes

Now that the information about these patterns has been made specific for you, you will realize that I was right: you do recognize the patterns without any difficulty. The question is then, how do you *respond* to them? For most people, the choice among the Satir Modes is either based on habit—"That's how I always talk to my salespeople!"—or is unconscious and reactive. Successful communication requires that it be systematic and deliberate instead. The choice is based on the same metaprinciples that underlie the choice of the sensory modes:

1. All language encounters are interactive feedback loops.
2. Anything you feed will grow.

However, while the sensory mode technique is an algorithm, using the Satir Modes properly requires a heuristic process. It's not guessing; it's based on substantial evidence and reliable principles. But so many different variables are involved, depending on the context and the individuals who are interacting, that the word *algorithm* cannot be stretched to fit. This makes it no less systematic, but it can't be done mindlessly; thought and care are required.

With the sensory modes, when someone speaks to you in his or her preferred mode you recognize this input and adjust your output to respond in a matching mode if possible, whereupon the other person responds to *you* in that mode—and so on round the interactive feedback loop. Because speaking to someone in their own sensory mode creates trust and rapport and good will, the more you feed that loop, the stronger the positive feelings grow. This is a simple paradigmatic system, and it's fail-safe; there is no plausible human situation in which good feeling is not helpful.

When you apply the same metaprinciples to the Satir Modes, things are more complex, but they are consistent. Just as feeding a goodwill loop creates more goodwill, feeding a hostility loop creates more hostility. After you recognize a Satir Mode, you have to stop and ask yourself: "Do I want this to grow?" Rule 1 is: *When matching the Satir Mode coming at you would result in something you approve of, match that mode.*

The second rule, as with the sensory modes, is a fallback rule to use when you can't follow Rule 1. It is intended to let you take a *neutral* position. Rule 2, therefore, is: *When you don't know what to do, go to Computer mode and maintain it until you have a good reason to change.*

For example, let's go back to the question about why someone is taking a file home, and see how following these two rules would work out.

Using Rule 1

FRANK: "WHY are you taking the file HOME with you?"

TRACY: "Whadda you MEAN, why am I taking it?! It's none of your BUSINESS why I'm taking it!"

FRANK: "Oh, YEAH? LISTEN, it's not YOUR file!"

TRACY: "Well, it's sure not YOURS!"

(And so on.)

Tracy responds to Frank's Blaming with more Blaming, setting up a hostility loop that Frank feeds with *more* Blaming, and so on, around and around.

Using Rule 2

FRANK: "WHY are you taking the file HOME with you?"

TRACY: "Taking a file home over the weekend is easier than going back and forth between home and the office."

FRANK: "That's true. You need to work on it all weekend?"

TRACY: "I won't get it done in time if I don't."

Frank opens with Blaming; Tracy responds with Computing. This defuses Frank's hostility and he switches to Leveling. Tracy perceives this as a good reason to change, and he switches too, matching Frank's Leveling with his own. (This sequence—Blaming/Computing; Leveling/Leveling—is one of the most common patterns.)

Here are the feedback loops that reliably result from matching each of the Satir Modes:

1. Blaming at a Blamer guarantees a fight.

2. Placating at a Placater yields undignified delay. ("You decide."/ "No, YOU decide!"; "I don't care; YOU pick."/ "No, I wouldn't think of it! YOU pick.")

3. Computing at a Computer yields *dignified* delay, which is the most neutral stance in verbal self-defense.

4. Distracting at a Distracter is panic feeding panic and guarantees communication disaster.

5. Leveling at a Leveler is the simple truth going both ways.

Blaming and Placating loops are hostility loops. Like Distracting loops, they should be avoided except in those very rare cases when you have a specific strategic reason for *wanting* a fight or an undignified delay. Both interfere with communication by increasing tension; both decrease the chances of transmitting messages other than hostility because they are static on the line. Last, but far from least, both are bad for your health and well-being. The two most serious risk factors for all diseases and disorders across the board are chronic exposure to hostility and loneliness, and few methods for achieving loneliness are more reliable than being hostile toward others; the two factors work together to put you in danger. Your usual choice, therefore, will be between Leveling and Computing. Leveling is theoretically the most perfect communication of all, but in the real world it may be inappropriate or dangerous. When that's the situation—or when you aren't sure which mode to choose—your best response is a Computing utterance, ideally one stating something innocuous that would be hard for any rational person to disagree with. Compare these two dialogues:

A Leveling Loop

MANAGER: "You don't like me, do you?"

EMPLOYEE: "No, I don't. I never have liked you."

MANAGER: "That's what I thought. I suggest seeing if you can't find a job somewhere else where you'd be happier."

Leveling, Then Computing

MANAGER: "You don't like me, do you?"

EMPLOYEE: "Employees are rarely equipped to make accurate judgments about managers."

MANAGER: "That's true. I couldn't agree with you more."

In deciding between Leveling and Computing you have to take into account the knowledge you have about the situation, about the person you're interacting with, and about any special circumstances that may apply. This choice is not automatic, and it has to be made each time, in the context of the particular situation in which the communication is taking place. However, reducing the five modes to these two will result in a substantial improvement in your language environment.

When Satir Mode Choices Are Not Deliberate

As noted earlier, for most people the choice among the Satir Modes is the result of habit or is reactive. We need to explore this a bit further.

You have three communication channels available to you for speech. One is the words you say; another is the body language that accompanies the words. The third channel is something for which we have no good English label, but which is sometimes referred to as your *vibes*—the expression of your inner feelings as perceived by others. When a stranger walks into a room and—before a word is said or a move is made—you feel somehow threatened, you are reacting to that stranger's vibes.

The only time all three of these channels can be counted on to *match* during communication under stress is when Leveling is taking place. Otherwise, the situation is as follows:

Blaming

Words and body language:	"I have ALL the power!"
Inner feelings/vibes:	"I don't have any power."

People use Blaming when they're convinced that nobody would do anything they wanted or needed if they don't throw their weight around.

Placating

Words and body language: "I don't care!"
Inner feelings/vibes: "I care; I care desperately."

People use Placating when they're afraid that people will get angry and are afraid of the possible results of that anger.

Computing

Words and body language: "I have no emotions."
Inner feelings/vibes: "I have one (or more) emotions that I pre-fer not to share."

Distracting

Words and body language: "I'll say anything! I'll say everything!"
Inner feelings/vibes: "HELP—I don't know what to SAY!"

(In Chapter 8 we will take up the question of what happens when there is not only conflict between the speech and the inner feelings but also conflict between the words and the body language.)

Now let's go back to the scenario that opened this chapter and see how a systematic and deliberate use of the Satir Modes could make things go more smoothly.

Another Look at Scenario Three

Rebecca Linwood opens like this:

"As you know, Elaine, we're here this morning to discuss this company's pathetic investment in research, and our crying need to do something about that. I'll begin with a presentation of the basic facts and figures; I'll be as brief as possible."

Every English sentence has to have an acoustic stress *peak*—a syllable that is more strongly stressed than any other. This stress has no particular semantic significance. Then there are two situations where other stresses are needed. The first is *contrastive* stress, as in, "The contract wasn't for three years, it was for <u>four</u> years." The second is *emphatic stress*, used when you want to be absolutely certain that some item is understood, as in defining words or specifying dates and times, and in making "announcements," as in, "That was the <u>President</u> of the United <u>States</u> who just called me!" Any other use of acoustic stress (perceived as higher pitch and longer duration) is a warning sign. When more than one acoustic stress not needed for any of these purposes appears in a single sentence, it will almost always signal hostility; if highly personal language is also present, the odds that it's not hostile are vanishingly small.

Rebecca's opening utterance is mild Blaming, her usual choice when she is uneasy. It contains four acoustic stresses (marked in the quoted dialogue by underlining) and not one of them is a stress that is needed for any of the nonhostile purposes outlined above. They therefore *signal* hostility. When Elaine hears them, she recognizes the hostility, even if she's not consciously aware of doing so. *And that predisposes her to resist persuasion from Rebecca.* The *first* thing Rebecca could do to improve her chances of getting Elaine's approval for her proposal is to get rid of those extra stresses. We know from the analysis of the scenario that it is Rebecca's usual practice to talk this way when she's tense. That's unfortunate, but it can be fixed. She needs to give up this habit for the simple reason that it provokes automatic resistance in everyone who hears it.

Elaine's response is equally undesirable:

> "Oh, take your <u>time</u>, Rebecca! <u>You</u> know me—<u>I'd</u> never ask you to rush! Just <u>do</u> <u>your</u> best, dear. I've <u>can</u>celled all my appointments for this morning."

Those lines, together with the laughing and waving, are classic Placating, filled with acoustic stresses needed for no positive purpose. Elaine is afraid of two things: that Rebecca will get angry enough to quit her job, depriving the company of skills she values; and that she will take her complaints to someone else. In such a situation, Elaine's preferred Satir Mode—because it ordinarily works well for her—is Placating. The fact that Rebecca opened with Blaming (plus the effects of past negative experience with her) makes Elaine tense and ill at ease, which means that she will automatically use her preferred Satir Mode for her response. That's a mistake. Since she feels unsafe Leveling with Rebecca, she should rely on Computing, like this:

> REBECCA: "As you <u>know</u>, Elaine, we're here this morning to discuss the company's pathetic investment in <u>research</u>, and our crying need to <u>do</u> something about that. I'll begin with a presentation of the basic facts and figures; I'll be as brief as <u>possible</u>."

ELAINE: "The question of how much money should go into research is a major issue in business today."

Throughout their discussions, Elaine and Rebecca could move from feuding to negotiating by a proper use of the Satir Modes. Neither one can maintain a hostility loop alone; no matter which of the women sets up the loop, it has to be fed by the other or it will collapse. It's just a matter of being willing to give up a linguistic habit that nourishes conflict and delay for one that nourishes successful and effective communication.

Notes

1. For a detailed examination of the link between language and your health, see *Staying Well With the Gentle Art of Verbal Self-Defense*, by Suzette Haden Elgin, Ph.D. (Englewood Cliffs, N.J.: Prentice Hall, 1990.)

WORKOUT SECTION: CHAPTER 3

1. Just as you did for the sensory modes, begin identifying your own and others' preferred Satir Modes to add to your informational database. Knowing that particular individuals typically lock into Blaming (or one of the other modes) when communicating under stress at work allows you to make predictions about their behavior in advance of interactions and then tailor your communication strategies to the occasion. Knowing your *own* Satir Mode habits lets you predict what *you* are most likely to do in stressful communication situations, so that you can be wary of potential errors and can plan changes where they might be needed.

Remember that (unlike the sensory modes) the Satir Modes are linked to roles and situations, so that people almost never have only one preferred Satir Mode choice. Set up your Satir Mode Directory in your notebook with at least three columns for each person, to record the preferred Satir Mode in business situations, in social situations, and in some other situation of your choice. For example, if you know that Jack Jones ordinarily communicates with Blaming in both tense business situations and uncomfortable social ones, but always switches to Placating if Bill Smith is present, that's valuable information. It should go into the Other column for Jones.

The more detailed the information you have about your *personal* Satir Mode choices, the better; you'll spend a lot less time asking yourself questions such as "Now why in the world did I say that?" Carry with you a small piece of paper with a blank column for each of the Satir Modes. When you notice that you're using one of them, put a check mark in that column; if you can do so unobtrusively and without losing track of what's going on around you, make a note that will let you identify the circumstances later. Total the check marks as they accumulate, watching for patterns. You want to know *what situations and which individuals you reliably react to with which Satir Modes.*

2. For your Communication Strategy Notebook: Set up a Satir Mode file and begin keeping track of relevant information. Record incidents in which you used the Satir Mode technique, to serve you as a database for planning strategies. What was the situation? Who was present? What was said, in which Satir Mode? What was your response, in which Satir Mode? What happened? What was surprising? Did anything go wrong, and if so, can you determine why? If you had it to do over again, would you make different Satir Mode choices?

3. For the following examples, identify the speaker's Satir Mode and then translate the utterance into one of the others. The first one has been done for you.

a. "We're not running a CHARity here, don't you KNOW THAT?"

   Blaming. Translated to Computer mode: "People who mistake a business for a charity often run into unexpected difficulties."

b. "Inactivity almost inevitably leads to physical decline."

c. "You have to stop pounding on the desk when you don't like what I'm saying. It slows us down."

d. "YOU know how I am—I'd NEVer put my personal FEELings ahead of the company's well-BEing unless I just absolutely HAD to!"

e. "I'm angry. I mean....of course, I NEVer get angry, I don't know why I SAID that! I mean, anger only makes people SCARED, right? Nothing significant is ever accomplished with anger."

f. "When you LOOK at me like that I FEEL like SOME kind of CREEP!"

g. "When you look at me like that I feel like some kind of creep."

h. "When you look at me like that I feel like some kind of creep."

The final three examples above will make it clear to you why I can't use quotations from real speech as I did for the sensory mode workout section. Without information about the speaker's intonation or some indication like "he thundered, pounding the desk," there's no way to identify the Satir Mode being used. Look at this example:

"If getting labor costs down requires our taking a strike, we will, and we will publish through it." (*Nicolas Pennimay, quoted by John Herns in "Why Ingersoll picked St. Louis,"* Forbes *magazine, July 24, 1989, p. 55.*)

Is that Leveling, Placating, or Blaming? Could you base a strategic decision on it? Rewrite it in each of these three modes, so that a reader could be sure of the emotional message attached to it.

4. If we make the assumption that the intonation for all of the examples below is neutral, they are all Computing sentences. In each case find out what it *accomplishes* for the speaker, by deciding what would have to be done to translate it into Leveling Mode. The first has been done for you.

a. "What's done in medicine is done for the convenience of medical professionals."

   To translate this into Leveling, you would have to identify the person or persons who have been left unlexicalized, as in "Doctors and nurses and technicians [*or some more narrowly identified set of medpros*] choose their medical acts for the convenience of medical professionals." By leaving this information unspecified, the speaker avoids having to name any names.

b. Of swizzle sticks, first developed during the Depression, Joshua Levine explains that they were invented to replace the expensive demitasse spoons used by restaurants and hotels, which "had an annoying habit of disappearing with patrons." *(Joshua Levine, "Stirring Story,"* Forbes *magazine, November 12, 1990, p. 310)*

c. "'There is a limit to what can be done,' huffed the bureaucrat." *(Richard C. Morais, "Tale of Two Tombs,"* Forbes *magazine, November 12, 1990, p. 76)*

d. "Over the past 20 years book prices have risen at double the rate of inflation." *(Fleming Meeks, "Mom-and-Pop Publishing,"* Forbes *magazine, September 17, 1990, p. 170)*

e. "When rates rise, the value of fixed-rate portfolios goes down and mortgage yields can wind up no longer sufficient to cover the cost of money." *(Jack Willoughby, "Teasing the Teasers,"* Forbes *magazine, April 3, 1989, p. 68)*

f. "Attaining a negative energy balance is central to the successful management of obesity." *(John F. Wilber, "Neuropeptides, Appetite Regulation, and Human Obesity,"* JAMA, *July 10, 1991, p. 258)*

g. "The patient was treated with moderate restriction of energy intake...without anorexigenic medications." *(John F. Wilber, "Neuropeptides, Appetite Regulation, and Human Obesity,"* JAMA, *July 10, 1991, p. 259)*

   5. For examples 4f and 4g, what else can you say about the communication strategy being used? Why "anorexigenic medications" rather than "diet pills"? Why "attaining a negative energy balance" instead of "eating less and exercising more"? *Remember that the effect of Computing is to establish neutrality and remove as much emotional information from the language as possible.* Does the patient whose doctor says "Pat, you're hyperphagic" get a different emotional message than the patient who hears "Pat, you eat too much"?

6. You're probably careful about your cholesterol level, about your exposure to smoking and alcohol, and about getting enough exercise; you probably do your best to avoid contaminated food and polluted water. You do these things in an effort to reduce your health risks. But what about your exposure to chronic hostility, with all its proven health dangers? Answer the questions below, on a scale from 1 (totally untrue) to 10 (absolutely true), to find out; the test identifies Type A hostility.

Date:_____

a. I always do everything exactly on time, and I expect others to do the same. _____

b. Whatever I do, I do as quickly as possible; I don't have any time to waste. _____

c. Trusting other people is stupid; you have to get them before they get you. _____

d. There's no such thing as making too much money; money is how you keep score. _____

e. Whenever possible, I do two or more things at once, like reading while I watch television. _____

f. I'm shocked by how little work other people get done. _____

g. It's hard for me to pay close attention to what other people say, because I have a lot of more important things on my mind. _____

h. My time is too valuable to spend waiting in line; I just refuse to do it. _____

i. My computer is way too slow. _____

j. I lose my temper pretty often, but I always have a good reason. _____

k. Half the people I know take so long to get to the point that I have to finish their sentences for them. _____

l. If you don't interrupt people you never get anything done. _____

4

"Over My Dead and Bleeding Body!"

Combining the Communication Techniques

Scenario Four

Stan Petry knew he had an uphill battle ahead of him, and he was as nervous as a sack of cats. The three men he was up against this afternoon were known companywide as the Three Immovable Objects—except when the project for discussion was *their* idea, in which case they were known as the Three Irresistible Forces. Stan was very much aware that the reason he'd been told he had to get his plan past them was because the chief was positive they'd stop him. On the other hand, despite the unpleasantness he was facing, he felt a certain amount of excitement and anticipation. The *plan* might not survive this encounter, but he himself was in a perfect position. If he got past any one of these three silverbacks, if he even scored a few points on one of them, people would see him as somebody to watch out for. But it was safe to *lose* against these three men, too; everyone else had. There was no shame attached. It was an opportunity.

He looked at the three of them, a solid lineup at the other end of the table. Paul Hansen; Joe Fisk; Tony Martinez. Arms folded over their chests; eyebrows knotted into frowns; jaws tight and lips narrowed. *Get ready*, he thought, *here we go!* And he leaned on the table with both hands, gave them his most confident smile, and began explaining why it was time for AJW Polymers to start putting women on its outside sales force, with their own territories. He was driving his points home, punctuating each one with a solid smack of his fist into the palm of his other hand, moving fast; he managed to get almost three minutes into his pitch before they stopped him.

"Cut!" bellowed Fisk. He crossed his hands in the air in front of his face and then uncrossed them with a fierce chopping motion that left nothing to the imagination. "CUT!"

Stan raised his eyebrows. "I'm sorry?"

"You damn well better be sorry!" Joe told him. "Who do you think you are, wasting our time with that garbage? We've got work to do, Petry, and you're in the way!"

"It's not garbage, Joe, it's common sense," Stan said calmly, riding the adrenalin rush. "You've got to join the real world someday, you know—I'm just trying to show you where you apply!"

Zing! One point for him! In his mind Stan touched the tip of his index finger to his tongue and posted the point in the air high above his head. Way to go, he told himself. Way to go!

"In the real world," Tony Martinez put in over Joe's snort of outrage, "you don't put girls on the field to do a man's job."

"Women!" Paul Hansen drawled. "You can't say 'girls' any more, Tony; it makes them cry."

Zing! They all chuckled as Hansen added that he hoped they'd all noticed that Stan was politically correct.

Stan seized his chance and charged through the next three sentences he'd memorized for this occasion.

"Over my dead and bleeding body!" That was Tony, drowning him out. "You can cut that in stone, in great big letters!"

"Tony," Stan objected, "you're out of touch!"

"Oh, yeah? You're the one running down the field in the wrong direction, Petry! I've got nothing against women; I love women, one and all! But they cannot go into a waste treatment plant and sell polymers, and nobody with his brain hooked up straight would suggest that they can!"

"It scares you, doesn't it?"

Stan leaned toward them, his heart pounding; there was a certain amount of risk in that line.

"What's THAT supposed to mean?!"

"That's supposed to mean, Joe, that you can't face the idea that a woman might be just as smart, and just as savvy, as you are! You need a lot of women bowing and scraping around you to prop yourself up with!"

That hadn't been in his script; he was surprised to hear it come out of his mouth. The silence told him he'd gone a bit farther than he should have.

"Hey," he said carefully, keeping his voice casual, "that's a joke, Joe! But you've got to realize: If we go on being the only company in the business that hasn't got a single female rep, we're the joke!"

Joe turned to the man beside him. "What do you think, Paul?" he asked. His voice was level and quiet and smooth. "You think this meeting's over?"

"You <u>got</u> it!" Paul answered.

"Second the motion," said Tony.

"Everybody in favor say aye? The ayes <u>have</u> it!" Joe stood up, shoving his chair back out of his way, and the other two followed his example.

"Now <u>wait</u> a minute, you guys!" Stan protested. "YOU can't just—"

They could, of course, and they did. And as they walked out the door, Tony Martinez looked back at Stan and said amiably, "<u>This</u> is the real <u>world</u>, Petry—and <u>we</u> <u>run</u> it!"

Standing in the empty room, Stan sighed, a wry grin on his face, and shrugged his shoulders. *Oh, well,* he thought as he gathered up his notes. *You win some; you lose some.*

What's Going on Here?

We have all seen scenarios like this played out. They're a staple of business communication, and the one above is a typical example. But they're not business, of course; they're sport. Sometimes, as in this case, they're ritual sport; sometimes they're a strategy for establishing a pecking order. The problem is that they're not a *healthy* sport. This game is bad for the heart and the stomach and the spirit. When people are present who don't know how to play the game, they can get badly hurt. Golf or tennis or baseball would be a far wiser investment of this company's resources.

Everybody's Point of View—What Went Wrong?

The culture at AJW Polymer is driven by the metaphor of The Football Game; it is hypermasculine and very traditional. (You'll find a detailed discussion of this metaphor and its place in contemporary AME communication in Chapter 9.) The top executive knows in advance that no women are going to be hired as sales reps by AJW. But he needs to be able to look at others in his field when the subject comes up and say gravely, "We've been discussing it; we had a meeting about it just the other day." Stan Petry is one of his best younger people; the chief is happy to give him a chance to spar with Fisk and Hansen and Martinez. Nothing will come of it, of course, but it gives Stan a chance to practice his skills, maybe even pick up a move or two. It's training for the day, some years down the road, when Stan will be on the other side of the table and somebody *else* will be trying to break through the line. And if Stan *can't* handle it, of course, a session like this—where nothing important is hanging in the balance—is the best way to find that out, so he can be replaced by somebody who can.

I have occasionally mentioned to the managers of companies like this that I disapprove of this process, that it's a waste of time and energy, that a lot of useful work could be done in its place. But even when those I'm speaking to readily acknowledge, in private, that I'm right, they usually say one of the following three things:

"Yeah, but it's part of the way we run things around here. We've always done it this way. People <u>expect</u> it; they'd think we'd all turned into <u>wimps</u> if we tried to stop it."

"Yeah, but dropping that kind of sparring takes all the <u>fun</u> out of life! Lighten <u>up</u>!"

"Listen...I get a kick out of getting people going, you know? It's a <u>high</u>."

There are people who will tell you that the macho culture I've described above no longer exists. They're wrong. As a consultant, a seminar leader, and a troubleshooter, I see it a dozen times a year. And I see it in every field, including scientific and academic fields and professions at the highest level. The issue of whether communication of this kind is good clean fun essential to morale, a hallowed tradition that must be protected, or a foolish and hazardous waste of resources is not one it would be appropriate to examine here—but you might give it some thought.

Let us suppose, however, that the situation in Scenario Four is different in two significant ways. First, Stan Petry, as the person sent to propose that women should be sales representatives, takes the matter seriously and is determined to get the change under way. And second, he has the support of the man in charge, at least in philosophical terms. When those are the circumstances, it *is* appropriate to investigate the question of whether Stan would still be doomed to failure. Let's assume that Stan is familiar with the information you now have about Miller's Law, the sensory modes, and the Satir Modes, and explore that question.

Combining the Communication Techniques (Review): Another Look at Scenario Four

Sensory Modes in Scenario Four

One of the reasons that Stan Petry and the three managers get along so well and have such a good time playing their game is that all four rely most heavily on the sense of touch. Although Stan actually believes that women *should* be hired as reps at AJW Polymer and the others are adamantly opposed to any such idea, their shared sensory preference and its expression in their language make it possible for them to communicate with considerable ease. Here is a list of lexical items from the scenario that are unambiguously touch mode:

1. "<u>Cut</u>! CUT!"
2. "We've got <u>work</u> to do, Petry, and you're in the <u>way</u>!"
3. "You've got to join the twentieth century...."
4. "...you don't put <u>girls</u> on the field to do a <u>man's job</u>!"
5. "Over my dead and bleeding body! You can cut that in <u>stone</u>, in great big letters."
6. "Tony, you're out of <u>touch</u>!"
7. "<u>You're</u> the one running down the field in the wrong di<u>rec</u>tion, Petry!"
8. "<u>I've</u> got nothing against women...."
9. "...nobody with his brain hooked up straight would suggest...."
10. "You <u>need</u> a lot of women bowing and scraping around you to prop yourself <u>up</u> with!"
11. "...you've got to realize...."
12. "...the only company in the business that hasn't got a single female <u>rep</u>...."
13. "You <u>got</u> it!"
14. "...and <u>we run</u> it!"

Two or three of those items could come up in the course of any language interaction on the same subject. But their consistent use in such numbers, as shown here, is likely only when speakers are touch dominant. To demonstrate that, let's "translate" the list so that none of the items is taken from touch mode.

1a. "All <u>right</u>, that's ENOUGH!"

2a. "We're <u>busy</u>, Petry, and you're being a <u>nuis</u>ance!"

3a. "You have to be part of the twentieth century...."

4a. "...I can't see <u>girls</u> in a <u>man's</u> <u>role</u>!"

5a. "Not if <u>I</u> have anything to say about it! And I am <u>serious</u> about that!"

6a. "Tony, you just don't see what's <u>happ</u>ening!"

7a. "<u>You're</u> the one who sees everything <u>cock</u>eyed, Petry!"

8a. "<u>I'm</u> not sexist...."

9a. "...nobody who has a clear perception of the world would suggest...."

10a. "You <u>need</u> a lot of women singing your praises all the time, so you can maintain your self-image!"

11a. "...you have to realize...."

12a. "...the only company in the business that doesn't have a single female <u>rep</u>...."

13a. "You're absolutely right!"

14a. "...and <u>we're</u> in <u>charge</u>!"

You will have noticed that six of the fourteen sensory mode changes involve replacing "got" with "have." And you may have thought that people who consistently use sequences like "I've got time" instead of "I have time" are demonstrating inelegant (or even "incorrect") grammar. That's possible, certainly. But unless the rest of their usage is nonstandard—unless, for example, they also consistently say "I ain't got time"—it's unlikely. It would be wiser to assume that the many "got's" are there because they are touch mode vocabulary.

When I wrote Scenario Four, I was assuming that all four of the male characters used touch mode because it was their personal preference. However, any one of them *could* have been "talking touch" because he knew about the use of the sensory modes and was using the technique deliberately. The resulting dialogue would be the same in both cases.

Satir Modes in Scenario Four

All four men in the scenario appear to rely most heavily on Blaming when they are under stress. (In this case, where they're playing games, the stress is caused by the pressure of competing with one another.) All four use personal language almost exclusively; all add extra acoustic stresses to words and parts of words; and all use threatening body language throughout their interaction. What if Stan Petry were skilled in the Satir Modes technique? Is there anything he could do to use that technique to help him make his case for the change in hiring practice?

It won't be easy. Stan is facing a solid *team* of Blamers. All are male, all outrank him, and all are opposed to his position. He will need to plan carefully. His final goal is to have all three men saying sincerely, even if reluctantly, "You're right. We <u>do</u> need to start hiring women reps." *But he has another goal, a communication goal, without which the final goal hasn't a prayer: the goal of being allowed to present his facts and arguments while the other men listen.* His best move is to work toward *that* goal first. We know that proper use of the Satir Mode technique means that his best choice in response to Blaming will always be either Computing or Leveling. Let's take a look at these two possibilities.

If Stan Chooses Computer Mode

> JOE: "Who do you think you <u>are</u>, wasting our time with that garbage? We've got <u>work</u> to do, Petry, and you're in the WAY!"
>
> STAN: "It's hard for people to keep their minds on a complicated subject when there's a lot of work piled up on their desks." (Computing)
>
> JOE: "It sure <u>is</u>!"
>
> STAN: "Tell you what...you give me fifteen minutes without any interruptions—just let me tell you what the facts are, and what I think they mean—and I promise you that you'll be able to get back to your work in a hurry. Can you go along with that?" (Leveling)
>
> JOE: "I guess so. Sure. Fair enough."

This is a major improvement. Joe (or one of the others) may not keep the bargain about listening without interrupting, but at least the stage has been set for it and an agreement has been arrived at. In addition, the first sequence of verbal attack and counterattack has been avoided altogether. With this revision, Stan has no motivation for the confrontational, "You've got to join the real world <u>some</u>day, you know— I'm just trying to show you where you ap<u>ply</u>!" In the original scenario that utterance, with its clever metaphor, gave him a lot of satisfaction and the feeling that he'd scored a point, but it did nothing whatsoever to help him present his case or persuade the others to support him. And it was that zinger that launched him into the competitive loop where he eventually went too far and provided his audience with an excuse to walk out on him.

Notice that in the revision we see the sequence that I have told you is so common: Joe opens with Blaming, Stan responds with Computing, whereupon Joe switches to Leveling, and Stan matches him by Leveling back. That might not happen this quickly; it might take several repetitions of Blaming-met-with-Computing to make Joe switch. In that case, the challenge for Stan is keeping his temper and not allowing Joe to provoke him into Blaming or Placating. For reasons of economy of space, I've shown the switch out of Blaming happening immediately—and I want to assure you, it often <u>does</u>. It depends on such factors as how dedicated to picking a fight the Blamer is, how skilled the other speaker is with Computing, and so on.

NOTE: Instead of "It's hard for people to keep their minds on a complicated subject, Stan could say, "It's <u>hard</u> to keep your mind on a complicated subject"; in that case, "your" would not be personal language. If Stan spoke British English or extremely formal American English, he could say, "It's hard to keep one's mind on a complicated subject." The nonpersonal "you" is the AME equivalent of that lofty "one," which sounds pedantic to the average American ear and is an unlikely choice for American men in a situation like that shown in the scenario. Even if Stan goes further and says, "It's hard to keep your mind on a complicated subject when you have a lot of work piled up on your desk," he would still be using Computer mode. None of those "you's" refers to anyone present as he speaks; they refer to some entirely hypothetical person and would be understood that way by any native speaker of American English.

If Stan Chooses Leveling

Stan had another choice, he could have decided to meet Joe's Blaming with Leveling. Let's consider what might have happened if he'd gone that route.

> JOE: "Who do you think you <u>are</u>, wasting our time with that garbage? We've got <u>work</u> to do, Petry, and you're in the WAY!"

> STAN: "Joe, you don't want to listen to what I have to say; I know that. I also know that you and Paul and Tony can interrupt me every couple of sentences to tell me how opposed you are to what I'm saying. However, you'll be able to get back to your work faster if you just hear me out."

JOE: "And why, exactly, should we want to do that, Petry?"

STAN: "It's called getting it over with, Joe."

JOE: "Okay. You've got a point. Let's get on with it."

This is also an improvement over the original scenario, although it creates a more unfriendly atmosphere than the Computing alternative does. Stan is the only one who can make the choice between the two, and he has to base it on his personal knowledge of the circumstances. Leveling is more risky; it's also more impressive. When you can be sure it's both appropriate and safe, it's always the better choice. When you can't be sure, Computing is better.

What About Miller's Law?

In both proposed revisions of the scenario we see Stan Petry applying Miller's Law in three ways.

1. *When he matches the other men's touch mode utterances.* It's a way of saying, "I notice that you're telling me touch is the best sensory system for processing information in this situation. I'll assume that that's true; and I'll use touch mode myself to find out what it could be true of."

2. *When he responds to Joe's, "we've got work to do" by agreeing that it's hard to get your mind off a desk piled with work and give your attention to a complicated subject.* He doesn't assume, as Joe does, that his case is garbage and that it wastes time, but he accepts the proposition that someone buried in work might perceive things that way and lets the criticism pass unchallenged.

3. *When he responds to Joe's opening blast of Blaming by saying, "I know you don't want to listen" and pointing out that the men will get back to their work faster if they don't struggle with him.*

In the original scenario, by contrast, what Stan does is apply Miller's Law In Reverse. He instantly challenges the truth of Joe's opening words with, "It's not garbage, it's common sense!" And he underlines his disrespect for Joe's perceptions by topping off the challenge with an open attack that claims Joe not only isn't part of the twentieth century yet, he doesn't even know where you go to *apply* to be part of it. This is a way of saying, "What you say is false and the reason you say it is because you're so far behind everybody else."

Don't misunderstand me: None of these revisions is magic. The men may still turn Stan down. He may still have to go through a half dozen more meetings to get their agreement. He may have to have help from his boss. It may take a long time. But he will at least have succeeded in getting the Three Immovable Objects to let him state his facts and his arguments, and that is the first step. He will have persuaded them to change from inattention to attention, which prepares the way for persuading them to consider the case he's trying to make. Until that has been accomplished, he *is* wasting time.

We've now taken a look at how the first three communication techniques could be used together in a single scenario. From now on we'll assume that each time a new technique is added to the set it will be used in combination with all the others, as would be the case in real life.

WORKOUT SECTION: CHAPTER 4

1. For your Communication Strategy Notebook, set up a page for keeping track of language interactions in which your strategy is to use a variety of techniques in combination. Here's a suggested layout:

Strategy Log

Date: _____

Description of the situation (where, when, who, why, etc.):

My communication goal(s):

My final goal(s):

Techniques I planned to use:

Techniques I did use:

    Technique 1:
    What was said:
    Result:
    Technique 2:
    What was said:
    Result:
    Technique 3:, etc.

Final results, measured against my goals:

Things I would change if I had this to do over again:

Comments:

2. Obviously you won't be able to remember every word that is said in your language interactions, and you can't participate while taking notes. However, as you continue to make an effort to remember and record as much of the dialogue as you can, you'll find that training your memory is just like any other kind of training: the more you practice, the easier it gets and the better you're able to do it. You'll want to record the body language as well as the words; that, too, will get easier with practice. At first it's best just to record everything you can remember except completely irrelevant items. But you will quickly learn what's important and what can be ignored, especially as you begin to observe patterns that occur over and over again.

3. Take advantage of opportunities to observe the communication strategies and behavior of *others* as well as your own. When you have a chance to observe people whose communication strategies are extremely good (or extremely bad), it's like an opportunity to attend a really valuable seminar. Ask yourself questions like these. Why is he or she saying that? What communication goal is he or she trying to achieve? What final goal? Why did he or she respond to that remark in that way? What were some of the things that could have been said, but weren't? What is the effect of the body language used? And of course, how did the person DO that?! When you're participating in an interaction primarily as an observer you can often take notes on the spot; take advantage of that. *Don't forget to watch as well as listen.*

4. One of the best ways to become skilled at techniques like those you've been learning in this book is to practice in groups of three: Speaker A (who gets first turn to speak), Speaker B (who responds to Speaker A), and a Coach. Suppose you're practicing the sensory mode technique. Speaker A says something in one of the sensory modes; Speaker B either matches the mode or, if that's impossible, responds with sensory-neutral language; the Coach observes what happens, taking notes if necessary. After a few rounds, practice stops while the Coach tells the speakers how they did, what was observed, etc. Then everyone switches roles, until each person has had a chance to practice all three. Start with a single utterance and response; then work up to more extended dialogues.

When working with one technique starts getting easy, go on to work with more than one at a time. For example: Speaker A opens with a touch mode utterance that is also in Blaming mode and that is designed to strike the listener as clearly false. Speaker B then tailors a response using the rules for Miller's Law, the sensory modes, and the Satir Modes. The Coach observes carefully, takes notes, and provides the necessary feedback.

5. Try some role-playing sessions that deliberately *violate* the rules for the techniques you've learned. (This is called The Game of Verbal Pollution.) Work in teams of threes, but do everything *wrong*. Violate Miller's Law; mismatch the sensory modes; make Satir Mode choices that create hostility loops and undignified delays. *Pay close attention to emotional reactions. If people start feeling angry or frustrated or overstressed, call the session off.*

6. Leveling is of course the most efficient way to transmit information, theoretically. Computing is the most *neutral* way to do so. About 99 percent of the time, your choice in business communication will be between these two modes. Getting to Leveler mode is simple: just speak the whole truth as you know and feel it. Getting to *Computer* mode, when you feel that Leveling is either dangerous or inappropriate, is more complicated. However, English offers you a variety of resources for this purpose.

Suppose the basic message, if Leveling were your choice, would be this sentence, spoken with body language that unambiguously expresses your disgust and distress: "Your company has spilled thousands of gallons of oil in the Gulf." What could you say instead, using Computer mode? You want to remove as many "I/you" items and items that carry emotional messages as is possible without totally destroying the meaning. Here are five of the patterns available to you:

a. Thousands of gallons of oil have been spilled in the Gulf.

You can't take the subject "you" out of the basic sentence, because English doesn't allow "Has spilled thousands of gallons of oil in the Gulf." But if you use the passive form of the sentence, English then lets you delete the subject, as above. (All languages are not alike in this respect. Some— Spanish and Navajo, for example—allow sentences without full subjects. Some—Arabic, for example—allow the passive but don't allow deletion of the subject, so that the final sentence would still have to be "Thousands of gallons of oil have been spilled in the Gulf by your company.")

b. What has been spilled in the Gulf is thousands of gallons of oil.

c. The spilling of thousands of gallons of oil in the Gulf was unfortunate.

d. Some oil companies have spilled thousands of gallons of oil in the Gulf.

e. There are oil companies that have spilled thousands of gallons of oil in the Gulf.

7. Many of the patterns that can be used in this way have as their function what linguists call the "promoting or demoting" of nominals (chunks that fill roles that nouns can fill, like the role of subject or object). All else being equal, the position that is assumed to be most important to the English speaker is at the beginning of the sentence. To draw attention away from the person or entity that actually carried out some act, you can promote another constituent to the beginning of the sentence, thereby demoting all the others.

Now rewrite the examples that follow in Computer mode, using as many of the five patterns as are possible for each one.

a. "You lose three files a day."

b. "You are inexcusably careless."

c. "Your secretary has left the phone off the hook again."

d. "This plan of yours is full of flaws and errors."

e. "Take this prototype down to the third floor and fix it."

5

"No Decent Person Would <u>Do</u> Such a Thing!"

Making Complaints and Criticism Effective

Scenario Five

Andrew Carter was absolutely sure he was right in what he was proposing: The company had to pull their barbecue sauce off the shelves, coast to coast, right *now*. But he was stunned by the reaction he was getting from Jeff Smither, without whose agreement he couldn't order that action taken. Andy had only had time to say his opening line—"Jeff, you have to stop stalling and give me your okay for a recall—you can't put it off any longer!"—and before he could say another word, Jeff had told him flatly that they weren't going to pull a single bottle.

"You can't be serious, Jeff!" Andy said. "You can't possibly <u>mean</u> that!"

"Well, I <u>do</u> mean it. We'll stonewall on this, Andy."

"And what if somebody gets <u>sick</u>?" Andy asked hotly. "What if, god forbid, somebody <u>dies</u>?"

"Oh, come <u>on</u>, Andy! <u>One</u> bottle was tampered with. <u>One</u>. If we let that panic us and we start pulling product, the bottom will fall out of our market share. You know as well as <u>I</u> do that—"

Andy cut him off, slamming one fist on the desktop hard. "That's disgusting!" he said. "No decent person would even <u>consider</u> that in a situation like this one!"

"Now <u>wait</u> a minute, Andy!" Jeff protested, the outrage on his face unmistakable, his hands clenching the desk in front of him. "You're <u>way</u> out of line!"

Andy ignored him. "When you put <u>mar</u>ket share ahead of people's <u>lives</u>," he went on, "it makes me <u>sick</u>! I'm telling you, and I'm telling you straight, we have to pull that stuff, and that's all there is TO it! You <u>know</u> I'm right; you're just too pigheaded to <u>admit</u> it!"

Jeff stared at Andy, his eyes narrowed and his lips tight; there was a long silence while the two men glared at each other.

And then Jeff stood up abruptly, folded his arms across his chest, and leaned forward. "<u>All</u> right!" he snapped. "<u>That's</u> it!"

"What do you mean, 'that's it'?"

"Just what I said. Get out of my office, Andrew. So I can get somebody in here to help me put together a press release that will let people know we stand solidly behind what we make."

"Jeff, you can't just run me out of here like that! You have to calm down and <u>listen</u> to what I have to <u>say</u>. You haven't even let me tell you <u>why</u> I'm so sure that—"

"Right! I haven't. And I'm not <u>going</u> to, either!"

"When YOU ACT this way, Jeff, like you RAN the whole damn WORLD, like nobody ELSE'S opinions are even worth HEARing, you make me so mad I could—"

"OUT!" Jeff bellowed, slicing the air with one I'm-cutting-your-throat-buddy slash of his right hand. "OUT, Carter! NOW!"

What's Going on Here?

If these two men were arguing about what colors to use for the label on their barbecue sauce, we could let the scenario go with a judgment that it represents an unfortunate waste of time and energy for the company and for both speakers. However, the issue is far too serious to make that possible. Both men are in the wrong here, and there's a grave danger that a decision with potentially life-threatening (and company-destroying) consequences is going to be made on the basis of emotion and ego rather than facts and logic.

Andy's Point of View

Because the one bottle that was found tampered with had been laced with a pesticide that could cause paralysis or death even in small quantities, Andy is deeply concerned. The way he sees it, the only factor to be considered in this situation is the possible hazard to human beings. Sure, just the process of recalling the stock and destroying it would cost a lot of money. And then there'd be the loss of time while a new batch was produced and moved into the stores, plus the problem of people being scared away from it for a while. Andy understands Jeff's concern and knows full well that anyone holding his job must always keep in mind the shareholders and the bottom line. But it seems to Andy that this is one time when all that has to be set aside. Morally, he knows he is right: Human lives come first. And he is furious that Jeff feels free to ignore that fundamental principle and move to protect the company without so much as a discussion. Andy perceives Jeff's behavior as arrogant and callous and just plain *wrong*. No matter what happens in the long run, even if no additional tampering ever takes place, Andy will find it hard to have any respect for Jeff in the future.

Jeff's Point of View

Because only one tampered bottle of barbecue sauce was found, and tests in that store and 50 others have turned up no additional adulterated product, Jeff's initial feeling is that perhaps drastic measures can be avoided. Like Andy, he would be heartsick if people were injured or killed by the barbecue sauce; Jeff is a decent and caring man. But it seems to him that an immediate and total withdrawal of the product on the basis of just one incident would be an overreaction. His original intention was to discuss the possible company actions carefully with Andy, going over the consequences of each one in detail in both human and financial terms. He had intended to keep sales on hold for 24 hours longer while he consulted a few other people and gave the matter long and careful thought.

But when Andy marched into the office and started giving him orders as though he were speaking to a mail clerk—not to mention laying on a tirade of insults to top off his commands—it was just too much. Nobody who acts the way Andy did has any right to be considered as a source of facts and rational argument, in Jeff's opinion, and he isn't about to change his original judgment on the basis of an emotional hothead's ravings. And the next time he wants to discuss anything of importance, Andrew Carter will not be on the list of people he consults if he has any choice in the matter.

It may be that Andy has compelling arguments for the product recall, and that after hearing them Jeff would have agreed with him and given the necessary orders. It may be that Jeff would have been able to counter those arguments with compelling arguments of his own, and that in the end *Andy* would have been the one who said, "You know, you're right. I've changed my mind." As matters stand, it makes no difference who has the stronger case. The men might as well not have bothered even to think the issue over, much less to prepare arguments.

All of the information exchanged in the scenario was *emotional* information, which is a very weak foundation for making decisions.

You will have noticed a number of problems with the language in the scenario. In particular, the heavy use of Blaming by both men makes hostility inevitable and puts massive barriers in the way of meaningful communication. But suppose we could wave a magic wand and change the intonation, removing most of the extra stresses from the speech used by Andy and Jeff. Suppose we could reduce the amount of personal language a little bit. The result might be less dramatic and less confrontational, but the outcome would probably be unchanged.

Andy's goal was neither to prove his moral superiority to Jeff nor to demonstrate his horror at the crime of product tampering. *His goal was to change Jeff's behavior from careful waiting to the bold action of pulling the barbecue sauce off the shelves.* To achieve that goal, no matter how right he may be in moral terms, his linguistic choices—the choices that make up his communication strategy—were all wrong.

What Went Wrong?

Adults in our society have an automatic negative reaction to being told what to do, especially when the telling is done face to face. That reaction is the primary source of the communication failure in Scenario Five.

The English speech patterns (called *speech acts*) that are used to convey a desire for behavioral change in others include *direct commands, indirect commands, complaints,* and *requests.*

> *Direct command:* "Stop yelling at the staff." Or "Stop yelling at the staff!"
>
> *Indirect command:* "I'd appreciate it if you'd stop yelling at the staff."
>
> *Complaint:* "The way you're always yelling at the staff is just not acceptable."
>
> *Request:* "Would you please stop yelling at the staff?"

People ordinarily react more strongly to commands than to complaints and requests, but *all* these patterns tend to produce a negative feeling in those who hear them. Whether the reaction is mild annoyance or a fierce, "WHO do you think you ARE, telling me what to do like that?" the results are predictable. The person experiencing it stops listening and communication breaks down. When listening stops, communication is impossible. The negative reaction is not to the *content* of the utterance—the person might not even have any objection to making the change requested—but to the speech *act* itself, to having been spoken to in a way that carries this metamessage: *There's something about your behavior that should be changed, and I have the right to tell you so.*

What is needed is a technique for constructing messages about desired behavioral change that will bypass, or significantly reduce, this knee-jerk negative reaction.

Communication Technique: Using the Three-Part Message

You're probably familiar with a language pattern called *the I-message;* it's a staple of talks and seminars on such subjects as conflict resolution, mediation, and negotiation. The I-message reformulates "You talk too much!" or "Stop talking so I can say something once in a while!"—both likely to provoke hostility—as the two-part message "I feel distressed when you don't give me a chance to talk." This is an improvement, and has been helpful to many people over the years. However, Dr. Thomas Gordon (an expert in effectiveness training) took the I-message and improved it greatly by adding a third section. The resulting pattern looks like this:

$$\text{"When you } [X], \quad \text{I feel } [Y], \quad \text{because } [Z]."$$
$$1 \qquad\qquad 2 \qquad\qquad 3$$

This pattern has three variables: X, Y, and Z. They are filled as follows:

- Part 1 states the single item of behavior that the speaker wants changed [X.]

- Part 2 states the emotion [Y] that the speaker feels with regard to the item of behavior.

- Part 3 states the real-world consequences of the behavior [Z] that justify the whole utterance.

Each of the three variables must be filled with something that is concrete and verifiable in the real world, and that no rational person would be likely to argue about. This means they must not contain moral judgments, polemics, personal opinions, or any other content that encourages contradiction and verbal struggle. Here's a paradigmatic example to use as a model:

"When you don't water the tomatoes, I feel angry, because plants die if they're not watered."

The verifiability of Parts 1 and 3 of a three-part message will be obvious and objective and based on real-world facts. That is, it will be obvious and verifiable that the person being addressed did or did not water the tomato plants and that plants left unwatered die. Part 2 can never be quite that concrete, because it refers to an inner state. A speaker's claim to feeling angry has no objective proof in the outside world. However, it is verifiable in that the emotion named is one that makes sense in the situation and is backed up by the speaker's body language. In cases where the message is being made on behalf of someone else—"When you don't return the files after you're through with them, people feel frustrated, because they can't do their work without those files"—the emotion is verifiable in that it is appropriate to the situation and backed up by body language *observed and reported by* the speaker.

Let's compare the three-part message pattern with the way Andy Carter structured *his* messages about a desired behavioral change in Scenario Five. Here are the relevant lines:

"You have to stop stalling and give me your okay for a recall—you can't put it off any longer!"
A direct command, and insultingly worded; Jeff is accused of stalling and procrastinating.

"That's disgusting! No decent person would even consider that in a situation like this one!"
An open and insulting moral judgment; verbal abuse.

"When you put market share ahead of people's lives, it makes me sick!"
More verbal abuse.

"I'm telling you, and I'm telling you straight: We have to pull that stuff, and that's all there is TO it!"
A direct command, with the "I have the right to tell you what to do" message made explicit and intense.

(The rest of Andy's lines, below, are just more of the same; they don't require additional comment.)

"You can't just run me out of here like that!"

"You have to calm down and <u>listen</u> to what I have to <u>say</u>."

"You haven't even let me tell you <u>why</u> I'm so sure that—"

"When you ACT this way, Jeff, like you RAN the whole damn WORLD, like nobody ELSE'S opinions are even worth HEARing, you make me so mad I could—"

You see the problem. Instead of a neutral statement of the change desired, the emotion felt, and the justifying consequences, Andy's utterances are filled with accusations and moral judgments and verbal abuse. When he states commands, they are not only direct but insultingly so. These are typical examples of commands and complaints in our society, unfortunately; it's no wonder that we react to them as we do.

However, it's important to understand that *even if the intonation were changed so that the verbal abuse was eliminated,* Andy's utterances would still be confrontational; they would still guarantee a negative reaction. Their metamessage, over and over again, is this one: "I'm the one who has the power and I can tell you what to do, and you have to do what I say because you're totally in the wrong." There's no way Andy can expect Jeff to tolerate that and be willing to listen to the case he'd like to make. Even if Andy is absolutely right, this manner of expressing himself guarantees that he will fail to achieve even his preliminary goal of persuading Jeff to listen to what he has to say. The end goal— persuading Jeff to recall the product for safety reasons—hasn't a prayer.

For Andy to achieve his goals, he would have to do two things. First, he must eliminate all the direct commands. The only time a direct command between civilian adults is justified is in emergencies, as in "Look out for that TRUCK!" In all other cases, there are better ways to say what must be said. Second, he would have to substitute three-part messages for his various complaints about Jeff's behavior and language.

We'll come back to the question of avoiding direct commands. Right now, let's look at how three-part messages are put together.

Constructing Three-Part Messages

It's best to construct your three-part message in advance, in writing or with a tape recorder, whenever you have enough lead time to make that possible. You're more likely to get it right that way, and the practice will make it easier for you to get it right when you have to do it *without* any advance preparation. In addition, if the message is one you'd be sorry to have transmitted, you won't be in the unpleasant position of hearing it for the first time only as you're *saying* it, when it's too late.

To construct Part 1, you must identify the *exact* item of behavior— just one such item—that you want changed. It should be stated without extra frills. It should be concrete and verifiable in the real world. And it should be something difficult for a rational person to argue about; you should not proceed if there's any uncertainty about whether your listener actually has carried out the action you're objecting to. Here are some Part 1 examples:

A–1. "When you take files home for the weekend and don't bring them back on Monday,"

B–1. "When you yell at the staff,"

C–1. "When you use the last blank disk and don't tell anybody that we're all out of them,"

D–1. "When you tie up the copier for long periods copying personal items,"

E–1. "When you bring the company car back with an empty gas tank,"

Part 2 states your emotion, or the emotion of the person(s) on whose behalf you're making the complaint. *Be careful not to change the wording of Part 2.* That is, stick with "I feel angry." Don't say, "It makes me angry," or "You make me angry." (If someone else has the power to determine your emotions, keep that information to yourself.) Examples:

A–2. "...everyone in the department feels frustrated,"

B–2. "...I feel distressed,"

C–2. "...I feel angry,"

D–2. "...we all feel angry,"

E–2. "...I feel outraged,"

The English vocabulary for stating emotions has many flaws; it's not precise enough and it doesn't offer enough choices. That's why people are so likely to say things like "I feel as if you're taking advantage of me" and "I feel like a second-class citizen"; they're trying to make the emotion more *clear*. Resist that temptation, because your intended clarifications will almost always add *unintended* extra messages that muddy the waters and introduce confusion.

Part 3 is the hardest section to construct. We don't *want* to have to specify real-world consequences. We want to be able to tell people that they must change because we say so, or because they're wrong, or because it's obvious that we're right. *But all of these claims are invitations to argue.* If there *is* no real-world consequence of the behavior you're asking your listener to change, there's one obvious question: what gives you the right to make the request? You can be sure that question will occur to your listener. When you are unambiguously the boss, you can say *that* gives you the right, and if you never need to complain to anyone except your subordinates, you're home free. However, you will still have to contend with the resentment adults feel when you exercise that right. Three-part messages are far more likely to accomplish your goals.

Now let's add Part 3 examples to complete the messages we've been working on in this section.

A–3.   "When you take files home for the weekend and don't bring them back on Monday, everyone in the department feels frustrated, because we can't begin <u>our</u> work without those files."

B–3.   "When you yell at the staff, I feel distressed, because people can't type accurately when they're crying."

C–3.   "When you use the last blank disk and don't tell anybody that we're out of them, I feel angry, because it costs almost twice as much to buy disks locally as it does to order them by mail."

D–3.   "When you tie up the copier for long periods copying personal items, we all feel angry, because everyone working here needs at least half an hour of copier time daily for <u>business</u> purposes."

E–3.   "When you bring the company car back with an empty gas tank, I feel outraged, because a car with an empty gas tank is useless."

Sometimes when you try to construct a three-part message, you'll find that you can't do it because you can't fill all the parts. In such cases, it's better not to transmit the message that you feel entitled to request a behavioral change. *If you don't know exactly what item of behavior you want changed, or how you feel about it, or what real-world consequences give you the right to ask for the change, it's irrational to expect your* listener *to know these things.* That means that utterances beginning with, "When you keep clicking your ballpoint pen...." probably can't be made into three-part messages.

It doesn't *mean you can't object.* You can certainly go ahead and state your feelings when that's appropriate and safe. You can say, "I really find it distracting and annoying when you keep clicking your ball-point pen," or "Constantly clicking a ballpoint pen is inconsiderate and annoying, in my opinion." That's your privilege, always. But the only way you can use the three-part message technique in such a situation is if you have been able to make and compile the records necessary to support a statement something like this one:

"When you keep clicking your ballpoint pen, I feel distressed, because I make three additional clerical errors for every sixty seconds you spend making that noise."

Three-Part Messages and Sexual Harassment

A moment's thought will make it clear that the difficulty we all have constructing Part 3 of three-part messages lies at the heart of the difficulty people have in constructing complaints and requests for behavioral change with regard to sexual harassment. For example, suppose a woman has begun a three-part message on her own behalf and on behalf of her female colleagues that goes something like this:

"When you walk in here and call us 'sweetie' and 'honey,' we feel angry," because....

What can she use as Part 3, to finish it? All the following sequences and many more of the same kind have been suggested to me at one time or another:

- "...because it means you don't respect us."
- "...because it's rude and boorish behavior."
- "...because no man has the right to talk to a woman that way without her permission."
- "...because it makes us so flustered that we can't work."
- "...because it's sexual harassment, and it's <u>wrong</u>."
- "...because it's humiliating and degrading."
- "...because that kind of language is illegal."

When the woman's goal is to express her anger, or to educate the offending male, or to state an opinion, those utterances will serve quite well. However, because all of them are subjective judgments, they are invitations to argument and further harassment. Even the last example—which could be factual if the harasser used explicitly forbidden words or phrases, such as obscenities or open sexual invitations—is subjective in this case. There's no objective definition of the phrase "that kind of language," and no law forbids "sweetie" and "honey" specifically. The same facts hold when the harasser is female and the object of the harassment is male; they also hold when the harassment involves ethnic origin, sexual preference, physical appearance, etc., rather than gender. Finding a real-world consequence in such situations can be extremely difficult.

The following example, constructed in a large health care facility at my suggestion and backed up by six weeks of meticulously graphed statistics, *did* stop one man's objectionable behavior:

> "When you come on the floor and call us 'sweetie' and 'honey,' we feel angry, because we have an eighteen-percent increase in errors on the days when you do that."

When this option is available, it's an excellent move. In a medical setting, where even minor errors can mean the difference between life and death, it's a compelling argument. However, in many cases it's not available because there is no easily tracked concrete task that can be measured in this way. In many other cases it's not *safe*, because the harasser in question is likely to use it as evidence for punishing or firing those who make the complaint.

I want to be quite sure that I make myself clear here, because this area of communication is so charged with emotion. *I am not defending those who harass others with offensive language of any kind.* I agree that such language is morally wrong, that it is unacceptable, and that it constitutes harassment. I am not claiming, in any way, that the person harassed is the one responsible for setting matters right.

However, our topic here is *communication strategy for achieving goals.* When the goal is to change someone's behavior, responses like those on page 90 are almost always useless. In an ideal world where everyone lived by the highest moral principles, they would always work. In the flawed world we live in, they work only in those rare cases when the person who uses the language is genuinely unaware that it causes offense and is immediately willing to apologize and agree not to use it again. However right the statements are philosophically and morally, they are *strategic errors* when the goal is behavioral change. The deliberate harasser either becomes angry and defensive upon hearing them, or is delighted with the opportunity they offer him or her to argue and continue the abusive interaction.

Three-Part Messages and Negotiation

Three-part messages are an almost magical tool for negotiation between groups, especially when the semantic field has been badly contaminated by anger and resentment. Suppose Group A and Group B are "at each other's throats" and attempts to improve matters have not been getting anywhere. The procedure is as follows:

1. Each group meets alone and prepares a list of its complaints about the other group.

2. *No complaint can be put on the list unless it is in the form of a three-part message.*

3. The two groups exchange their complaint lists.

4. Each group meets alone again and goes over the other group's complaints to decide what the members are willing and able to do in response.

5. Now the two groups meet together for joint negotiation.

Following this procedure means that both sides know exactly what the disagreement is *about* and both sides know what they can do to resolve it. No meeting time is wasted in wrangling over phony issues, defining vague terms, or any of the other unproductive matters that make most such meetings ineffective.

Avoiding Direct Commands

There are languages (Navajo, for example) where it is literally a violation of the grammar for an adult to use a direct command to another adult other than in emergencies. English is not one of these languages, and many English speakers feel perfectly free to order other adults around as long as they can plausibly be perceived as outranking them. This is a matter of personal choice; even if you are neither a military officer nor a law enforcement professional, you may not wish to give up the direct command option. I will say only that avoiding direct commands is one way to increase loyalty and improve morale, and that English offers a wide variety of resources for the purpose.

Suppose that you want someone to total the sales figures for the preceding six weeks and give you a printout of that information. You could say "Total the sales figures for the past six weeks, Jan, and bring me the printout." Or you can say any of the following to Jan instead:

"Would you total the sales figures for the past six weeks weeks and bring me the printout, please?"

"I need a printout of the totals for this past six weeks' sales figures."

"I wonder if you could get me a printout of the sales figures for the past six weeks."

"The sales figures for the past six weeks need to be totaled and printed out."

"A printout of the totals for our past six weeks' sales figures is badly needed."

It takes very little effort to use these constructions instead of the flat-out direct command, or, at absolute minimum, to add "please" to your commands. I recommend it.

Another Look at Scenario Five

Now, what about our friend Andy? How could he structure his communication so that he would have a chance to make his presentation, with a reasonable probability that it would be listened to and understood?

First, he should open the interaction with a neutral statement instead of the abusive direct command used in the original. For example:

"Jeff, I know you've made a tentative decision to issue a press statement saying that we consider the contaminated bottle of sauce an isolated incident and assuring people that it's safe to go ahead and buy the product. I also know that there are plenty of solid financial reasons for doing that. However, I'd like to offer a couple of reasons why that's <u>not</u> necessarily the best move."

He could follow this opening with a careful comparison of two famous tampering cases: Tylenol and Gerber Baby Food. After cyanide was found in some bottles of Tylenol (with serious consequences), Johnson & Johnson pulled every bottle off the market, issued instructions for people to return Tylenol already purchased (for a full refund), and replaced the product with a new package that made tampering difficult. Gerber responded to the finding of fragments of glass in its baby food the way Jeff wants to respond to his firm's problem with its barbecue sauce. The consequences of the two moves are quite clear. Tylenol not only maintained its market share, it *increased* it; the product became synonymous with safety and reliability. The outcome for Gerber, on the other hand, was far less rosy. Jeff might or might not find that comparison an adequate reason to change his mind, but Andy would at least have had the opportunity to present it.

And what if Jeff's reaction to the neutral opening above is a negative one? What if the opening goes this way:

> "Jeff, I know that you've made a tentative decision to issue a press statement saying we consider that contaminated bottle of sauce an isolated incident and assuring people that it's safe to go ahead and buy the product. I also know that there are plenty of solid financial reasons for doing that. However, I'd like to offer a couple of reasons why that's <u>not</u> necessarily the best move."

> "I hear you, Andy—but I think you'd be wasting your time. I've already considered all the options and my mind is made up."

In this case, Andy should immediately offer a three-part message as his response:

> "Jeff, when you tell me that your mind is made up before you hear the arguments I've prepared, I feel surprised, because I know you're aware that judgments based on incomplete information are dangerous."

Jeff may not go for this. He may insist that his information *is* complete and that he's not going to let Andy try to add to it. But the chances for success with this approach, though not guaranteed, are excellent. Since Andy's chances with his approach in the original scenario were essentially zero, "excellent" is a substantial improvement and well worth the effort.

WORKOUT SECTION: CHAPTER 5

1. Write a three-part message to go with each of these situations:

a. Your assistant has brought back the company car—the only one available at the moment—with the gas gauge right on "Empty." Now you'll have to stop for gas on your way to your next appointment, and you will be late.

b. One of the managers at your company consistently loses his temper and yells at the clerical staff when they make even the most trivial errors. This upsets them, so much so that their number of errors increases every time. Sometimes they cry. You want your colleague to stop this counterproductive behavior.

c. Every time you bring up a proposal for a new format for your company newsletter you are buried in lengthy objections and monologues about all the reasons the format can't be changed. As a result, the meeting always ends without your having a chance to explain how the change could be made.

d. Every time you try to explain something to a client at one of your company's business receptions, your boss steps in with, "What [your name] means is...." and takes over the explanation. This leaves you with nothing to say.

2. For your Communication Strategy Notebook, set up a Three-Part Message file and begin keeping track of relevant information. For example:

■ To serve as a database for planning strategies, record incidents in which you used the three-part message technique. What was the situation? Who was present, and why? What was said? What happened? What was surprising? Did anything go wrong, and if so, can you determine why?

■ Record incidents in which you wanted to use a three-part message but were unable to complete one of the parts. (Usually this is because you aren't sure exactly what item of someone's behavior you want changed or you are unable to find any concrete and verifiable real-world consequences of the behavior.) Record the details of the incident and the partial message, so that if the time comes when you see a way to complete it you can do so.

■ Record incidents when you complained to someone directly and openly; record the situation and the details. Then revise your complaint, turning it into a three-part message instead—for next time.

■ Identify situations that occur regularly in your business life—situations in which you typically find yourself wanting to request a change in someone's behavior. (For example, the weekly sales meeting in which it takes your supervisor half an hour just to get the meeting started.) Record the details of the situation and work out a three-part message that you could use there. Even if circumstances make it unwise for you actually to deliver the message, it's good practice to construct it. Circumstances can change.

3. The examples below are disguised direct commands. (In some cases, only body language and the context would make that clear; the words alone aren't sufficient.) For each one, what was the direct command? What did the speaker do to avoid using the direct command? What goals do the speakers accomplish in this way?

a. "Laundry is put in the hamper beside the stairway."

b. "Children are accompanied by their parents at all times."

c. "I wonder if that window behind you opens?"

d. "Do you suppose this letter could be mailed today?"

e. "Why don't you suggest adding a new parking lot?"

f. "Maybe you would be more comfortable sitting in that other chair."

g. "When you catch that plane for Detroit, do you want to leave your car here and take a cab, or would you rather drive yourself?"

h. "I'm sure you could do that hammering somewhere else."

i. "The copier should be turned off before employees leave."

j. "Would you rather type this information for use on folded brochures or format it as a letter?"

k. "If files are not returned by 10 a.m., the clerks find it impossible to get them put away before noon."

l. "I'm sure you would rather order minivans for the company fleet this year instead of station wagons."

m. "Your proposal is unacceptable as written."

6

"Don't You Even Care?!"

Avoiding and Defusing Verbal Attacks

Scenario Six

"I appreciate the opportunity to discuss this issue with you again," Anita Winters said as she hung her flipchart on the easel at the head of the table. "It's <u>very</u> important."

"And very ex<u>pen</u>sive," Richard Hart observed. The others at the table—a second man and one woman—nodded their agreement, and Mary Begay made a soft "tsk!" sound of disapproval.

"Not <u>that</u> expensive," Anita countered. "In fact, when you figure in what it costs the company in absenteeism—not to mention lost productivity because parents are worried and distracted—having an on-site child care program turns out to <u>save</u> money. Just take a look at the figures on this chart. They show quite clearly that—"

"Just a minute!" Walter Hedrick broke in. "Just hold on a minute. We don't need to sit here and watch you flip charts, Anita—we're as familiar with those facts as <u>you</u> are. You're not the <u>only</u> person around here who's concerned about <u>child</u> care, you know!"

"Then <u>why</u> don't you ever <u>listen</u> when we bring you a <u>plan</u>?" Anita asked him. "You could at <u>least</u> give us a fair <u>hear</u>ing!"

"Anita," Richard said, "You're only <u>saying</u> that to cause <u>trouble</u>—you <u>know</u> it's not true! We explained to you <u>last</u> time: You may be right, long term, but the problem is the start-up costs. We just plain don't have the capital."

"If you <u>really</u> cared about the welfare of your employees," Anita snapped, "you'd stop making ex<u>cus</u>es and BORrow the capital!" She turned to her next chart, jabbing the air with her index finger to direct their eyes to the one titled "Alternate Plans for Financing an On-Site Daycare Facility." She'd spent a lot of time getting the information for that chart together; she hadn't had it with her last time. "Please—look at these figures before you tell me it can't be done!" she pleaded.

"Borrow?" Walter asked incredulously. "You are seriously suggesting that we take on <u>more</u> <u>debt</u>?"

"<u>Yes</u>! This is the biggest poultry company in the United <u>States</u>! We're not exactly short on <u>credit</u> lines—but our <u>employees</u> are! <u>They</u> can't <u>afford</u> nannies and private schools! Don't you even <u>care</u> <u>about</u> <u>the</u> <u>problems</u> <u>of</u> <u>ordinary</u> <u>people</u>?"

There was a brief silence; when Walter broke it to answer her, his voice was icy, clipping each word short. "EVen a WOMan," he said grimly, "should be able to discuss expenditures without a lot of cheap MELodrama and emotional BLACKmail!"

Anita stared at him, furious. "It is NOT melodrama!" she said fiercely. "And it is not BLACKmail! It is the TRUTH! And my GENder has NOTHing to DO with it!"

"WHY do you always do this, Anita?" Richard said, with a long sigh. "<u>Please</u> try to calm down!"

And Mary Begay backed him up, saying, "Yes. Please. There is too much commotion, Anita. It serves no useful purpose."

"WHY do you always tell ME to calm down?" Anita demanded. "WHY don't you ever take MY side when he attacks me like that? WHY is it always ME that gets chewed out?"

"Nobody has attacked you, Anita," said Walter. "And nobody has chewed you out. If you <u>really</u> wanted to make the case for a child care facility, you'd learn to stick to the <u>facts</u> instead of making emotional <u>speeches</u>!"

Anita swallowed hard, miserably aware that she was shaking and that her flushed face betrayed her disarray, wondering how she was going to rescue her presentation and get the meeting back under control. <u>Why</u>, she thought, *did this always happen to her? How did she get <u>into</u> these awful public confrontations?*

What's Going on Here: What Went Wrong?

Scenario Six presents a typical undignified verbal wrestling match caused not by careless preparation or bad intentions but by a flawed communication strategy. Both sides in this confrontation appear to be in agreement about the real-world data on company child care, as well as on the financial soundness of such a project over the long term. We have no reason to believe they don't also agree about the moral principles and social issues involved. It's clear that the topic Anita should be tackling in her presentation is the one area where obvious conflict exists: the initial expense of setting up a child care program on site. She may have been prepared to do that, but she has no chance to demonstrate it; instead, she allows herself to be drawn into one extraneous argument after another.

We don't need a detailed examination of the personal points of view in this case. They're obvious:

- Everyone agrees that employees need good child care and have trouble finding it or affording it.

- Everyone agrees that if an on-site facility could be set up—and the three managers don't see how it *could* be—it would pay for itself in the long run.

- The managers perceive Anita as an emotional woman who lets her heart overrule her good sense.

- Anita perceives the managers as obstinate barriers to change who bully and belittle her instead of working with her to solve mutual problems.

With the exception of Mary Begay, whose native language is Navajo rather than English, all the speakers in Scenario Six have a shared bad habit of language: they all freely use the abusive structures known as *the English verbal attack patterns*. These patterns (called *VAPs* for short) are so common and so pervasive that I suspect they account for at least a third of all verbal abuse in our society. Let's take a look at how they are put together and how they are used, and then we'll come back to the scenario to see how eliminating them from the interaction would improve matters.

Communication Technique: Managing the English Verbal Attack Patterns

By the time you started elementary school, you had an internal mental grammar of your language already established and stored in your long-term memory. (We will assume here that that language was English; the statements about language acquisition are true for every human language.) In that grammar, although it's unlikely that you had ever had a single lesson on the subject, all the information you needed for carrying on an English conversation was stored. The difference between that grammar and the grammar of an English-speaking adult isn't in the *rules* they contain; all the basic and crucial rules are present in both. The difference is in vocabulary size and linguistic sophistication, which require time and practice. The adequacy of that internal grammar is entirely independent of such external judgments as the grades you got in "language arts" courses during the process of your education. It is flawless (unlike attempts to write it down, which are filled with gaps and distortions), and you can rely on it absolutely.

In your internal grammar, along with your vocabulary and the facts about the English sound system, are all the *speech act* patterns that you need for constructing sentences. The patterns for commands and questions, for threats and promises, for pleas and announcements, are all there. And so, unfortunately, are the patterns for verbal attacks.

Most people aren't aware of the internal grammar or of its contents; certainly we don't learn about it in school. As a result, it's like a library that has no card index or other organizing system. *We can't use the information it contains as effectively or efficiently as we should be able to, because we have no reliable way to find the particular items that we need.* We know "it's all in there somewhere"; you can easily prove that that's true.

Suppose I asked you to give me the rule for forming English yes/no questions, like "Did you enjoy studying grammar in school?" You probably wouldn't be able to do it, but you'd be able to prove that you *knew* the rule by providing me with any number of *examples* of such questions. In exactly the same way, you will immediately recognize the English verbal attack patterns and be able to construct examples of each one, even though you were probably unaware that you knew them and would be unable to recite any rules for them. The material below will let you *index* the information about the VAPs for future efficient retrieval.

Recognizing the English VAPs

Let's begin by looking at and analyzing examples of the two most basic VAPs: the "If you REALLY" pattern and the "WHY..." pattern. (We won't have to spend much time on the technical and formal details because all of that information is already in your head.)

1. "If you REALLY cared about your job, YOU wouldn't come in LATE every single day!"
2. "WHY can't you ever get to WORK on TIME?"

Each of these familiar patterns has two parts. The first is an open and obvious attack (called the *bait*); this is the part designed to get the intended verbal victim's attention. The second part is a less overt attack sheltered in a presupposition. That is, although it doesn't appear openly in the surface of the utterance, every native speaker of English understands the second attack as part of the meaning. Every one of the VAPs has these two parts, sometimes clearly separated, sometimes mingled together in a more complex fashion. We can break down examples #1 and #2 to make this clear:

1. "If you REALLY cared about your job, YOU wouldn't come in LATE every single day!"

   Bait: "You come to work late every single day."
   Presupposed Attack: "You don't really care about your job."

   "You don't really care" is presupposed by "If you REALLY cared" (or "If you really CARED").

2. "WHY can't you ever get to WORK on TIME?"

   Bait: "You never come to work on time."
   Presupposed Attack: "Whatever your answer to this question may be, it's not good enough."

   The inadequacy of the answer is presupposed by the heavily emphasized "WHY" in the question.

In the theoretical sense, *any* sentence of English is a pattern, because there are an infinite number of ways to vary the words it contains. In the same way, any hostile sentence is potentially a verbal attack. But for a sentence to qualify for the technical term *Verbal Attack Pattern of English*, it must meet the following conditions:

1. It contains an open attack (the bait) and at least one attack sheltered in a presupposition.

   Example: "If you REALLY wanted to get ahead, YOU'D stop being so LAzy!" The bait is "You're so lazy," and the presupposed attack is "You don't really want to get ahead."

2. It is marked as hostile by the presence of extra acoustic stresses on words and parts of words and because it contains (or presupposes) very personal language.

   Example: "If you really CARED about your health, YOU'D stay on your DIet!" contains both 'you' and 'your' and has extra stresses on "cared," "you'd," and the first syllable of "diet." "People who really CARE about their health STAY on their DIets!" has extra stresses on "care" and "stay" and the first syllable of "diet." It has no personal language; but when used as a VAP, it presupposes "you" and "your diet" from the *context*, with reference to the intended victim.

3. It is used in a situation where it's reasonable to assume that the speaker has little or no interest in the response that would be expected if the utterance were neutral.

   Example: Suppose an emergency department doctor says to a bleeding patient, "If you <u>want</u> me to <u>help</u> you, you'll <u>have</u> to tell me your <u>blood</u> type, FAST!" It's true that this utterance contains many stresses and resembles the "If you REALLY" pattern; it's also clear that the doctor's interest in the normal response to 'Tell me your blood type!' is intense. Therefore, although this isn't the best way to communicate with a patient in a crisis, the utterance is not an attack.

With this information, plus the backup information in your mental grammar, you will be able to *recognize* a VAP when you hear one coming at you. That part is automatic, just like your recognition of the sensory modes and Satir Modes.

Obviously, you don't want to use these patterns in a presentation yourself. I say this not because I'm demanding that you be kind or courteous (although I approve of both kindness and courtesy), but because the VAPs always and without exception lead to a waste of time and energy. VAPs are *action chains* containing the following steps:

Step 1: The attacker throws out a VAP.

> ATTACKER: "If you REALLY cared about your job, YOU wouldn't come in LATE every single day!"

Step 2: The intended victim takes the bait and runs with it.

> VICTIM: "What do you MEAN, I come in late every day?! I do NOT!"

Step 3: Attacker and victim engage in a verbal confrontation until one of them gives up.

> ATTACKER: "Oh, YEAH? How about TUESday? You didn't show up until ten o'CLOCK on TUESday!"
>
> VICTIM: "That's not FAIR! I was late because my CAR broke down! THAT can happen to ANYbody!"
>
> ATTACKER: "Uh-huh...And what's your excuse for FRIday?"
>
> VICTIM: "FRIday I had a DOCtor's appointment!"
>
> ATTACKER: "You can ALways find SOME reason to skip out on your share of the work, CAN'T you?"
>
> VICTIM: "Listen, I work just as hard as YOU do!"

ATTACKER: "Oh, sure! YESterday I got here at SIX, buddy, and I didn't LEAVE until nearly MIDnight! When's the last time YOU worked a day like that?"

(And so on...)

This can take a long time—all of it time that should be going into something more productive. Every intended victim who *takes* the bait guarantees a dialogue like this one; however, it takes two to do this verbal violence tango. *Without the cooperation of the victim, the attacker is helpless and the attack fails.* VAP interactions have a direct negative impact on the bottom line, putting all useful communication on hold until they're over; this alone is reason enough to avoid the practice.

Responding to the English VAPs

We can assume, then, that you will recognize VAPs when they are coming at you and that you will refrain from using them yourself to open an interaction. The question then is: How do you *respond* to VAPs used by others? Here are the rules:

Rule 1: Ignore the bait, no matter how outrageous it is.

Rule 2: Respond directly to a presupposition.

Rule 3: No matter what else you do, transmit this message: "You're wasting your time trying that with me; I won't play that game."

Let's apply the rules to the attack example, "If you REALLY cared about your job, YOU wouldn't come in LATE every single day! Here are two appropriate responses, both replying directly to the presupposition, "You don't really care about your job."

ATTACKER: "If you REALLY cared about your job, YOU wouldn't come in LATE every single day!"

INTENDED VICTIM: "Of course I care about my job."

or

"When did you start thinking I don't care about my job?"

Neither response is what the attacker is expecting; each has the advantage of surprise. And neither one provides the "I'm taking your bait" response that will allow the VAP action chain to continue. The attacker can certainly start over with a *new* attack, but *this* one is over, and it has failed.

There's a third way to respond to this (or any other) VAP, using the emergency all-purpose reply called "the Boring Baroque Response" (BBR). BBR's reply directly to the vacuous presupposition that the attacker wants a response to a statement or an answer to a question. Here are two examples:

> "Hearing you say that reminds me of something that happened to me when I was just a little kid. We were living in Detroit at the time...No, wait. It wasn't Detroit, it must have been Minneapolis, because that was the summer my Aunt Grace came to see us and brought her dog. Anyway..."

> "Hearing you say that reminds me of an article I read only the other day in *The New York Times*. No, wait...it couldn't have been the *Times*. It must have been *The Wall Street Journal*, because it was Thursday, and Thursday is the day Allan always gets the *Times* and forgets to put it back. Anyway...etc."

Boring Baroque Responses are mildly punitive, in that listening to them is a miserable experience. They should never go on for one word longer than is necessary to transmit the "I won't play that game with you" message. And they must be used with neutral body language. When spoken with sarcasm, a patronizing expression, etc., they become counterattacks, and you *are* playing the verbal violence game. *If you're not confident that you can do a BBR neutrally, don't use one.*

Your choice among the three possible responses discussed so far will depend on the communication situation in which you find yourself. If you're in a meeting, you won't want to use a Boring Baroque Response because it takes too long and attracts too much attention to itself. If you don't have time to answer a question, you won't want to use "When did you start thinking that..." because it would require you to listen to the answer and carry on a conversation about it. When neither of those responses is appropriate to your situation, you would choose "Of course I care about my job."

The rules for responding to VAPs are simple and easy. What's *hard* is applying them and resisting the temptation to play the VAPs game instead. This is especially true for people who enjoy the game as a sport and get a kick out of playing it. Such people—who are more likely to be male than female, although there are exceptions—need to remember some basic facts:

- VAP interactions waste your resources—your time, your money, and your energy—not only while they're going on, but afterward, when you have to deal with their consequences.

- For all diseases and disorders across the board, *the major risk factors are exposure to chronic hostility and loneliness.* You may feel like you're having fun when you carry out a VAP action chain, but you pay for your pleasure by risking your health and well-being.

A Few More VAPs

The two patterns we've been analyzing are the most common ones and are the ones children appear to learn first. They are easy to understand and use, and they clearly separate the open and hidden attacks. The patterns below are more complicated, with the bait and the presupposed attacks mingled together. In isolation on a page, it's often hard to decide which insult in these examples is intended as bait. In context, however, the bait is usually obvious because of what both the attacker and victim already know about the situation.

"EVen a WOMan should be able to change a TIRE!"

"EVen a WOMan should be able to change THAT tire!"

This is a curious and common pattern, in either variation. It's hard to set up any sentence in this pattern that *isn't* insulting, and it's so powerful that linguists use it to demonstrate how presuppositions work. When you hear a linguist-constructed example like "EVen EINstein could solve THAT equation!" you know it's ridiculous nonsense because your internal grammar tells you that it presupposes the following:

- Einstein is bad at mathematics.
- The equation being talked about is trivially easy.

Examples like "EVen a FISH can play a harMONica!" are even more compelling evidence. They make no sense; nevertheless, the fish has been insulted. And "EVen a FISH could pass THAT class!" insults both the fish and the class.

Here's the best way to respond to the "EVEN a(n)..." VAP in either of its forms:

ATTACKER: "EVen a WOMan should be able to close a SALE!"

or

"EVen a WOMan should be able to close THAT sale!"

INTENDED VICTIM: "The idea that women are somehow inferior is something you run into once in a while....I'm astonished to hear it from you."

or

> "The idea that women are somehow inferior is some-
> thing you run into once in a while....I'm sorry you feel
> that way."

Attackers aren't expecting this. They're expecting responses that
accept the victim role, take the bait and run with it, feed the hostility
loop, and guarantee a fight—like these:

INTENDED VICTIM: "Listen, women are JUST as GOOD at SELLING as
MEN are!"

or

"Hey, this is NOT an easy sale to close! YOU just don't
know what you're TALKing about!"

or

"What do you MEAN, a woman should be able to close
a sale? I'll have you know, WOMEN are EXcellent salespeople! And they know how to control their MOUTHS,
TOO, which is more than I can say for YOU!"

Here's another of the more complex VAPs:

"You could at LEAST call your MOTHer!"

"YOU could at LEAST turn in your SALES figures!"

"You could at LEAST TRY to get to work on time!"

The bait—generically speaking, "You don't even meet the <u>minimum</u>
specifications for decent human behavior"—is in there somewhere,
anchored to the real-world facts. If these utterances were being spoken
in the real world, the person they're addressed to would know exactly
what the bait is. This VAP sets up a presupposition that there is some
action that can be looked upon as the absolute bare-bones minimum
that any decent human being would do in the situation—and then
claims that the person being VAPped doesn't do even that minimum.

The appropriate response is to ignore the claim that you do or do
not do whatever it is and to agree with the presupposition that that
action is a minimum requirement. Just say, "You're absolutely right,"
putting the ball back in the attacker's court, and wait for the next
move.

You'll find that "You're absolutely right" and "I couldn't agree with
you more" are your best responses to a *number* of VAPs; it's surprising, but it's true. Look at these examples:

"YOU'RE not the ONly person around here with too much WORK to do, you know!"

"YOU'RE not the ONly lawyer in New YORK, you know!"

The chances that statements like these are false are usually zero; disagreeing with them is absurd. The bait is that *you think* you are the only whatever-it-is in question, and behave as if you were, and expect others to treat you as if you were. The response is to ignore that and address the logical presupposition: that there is more than one person, lawyer, etc., in the universe. Taking the bait—as in, "I never claimed I WAS the only one, for crying out loud!"—is a serious error. Just respond to the empty presupposition that more than one of whatever-it-is exists, by agreeing with it.

"SOME bosses would be really ANNOYED if their employees spent half the day talking on the PHONE!"

Again, this utterance has an empty presupposition—that there exist in this world some bosses of whom it could truthfully be said that they would be angry if their employees spent half the day on the phone. The bait here, tied to the real-world situation, is the claim that *you* are the employee who spends the day that way. Ignore it and respond with an immediate "I'm sure they would—you're absolutely right." And then wait for the attacker's next move.

There are still other VAPs, some of which we'll be discussing as they come up in scenarios and dialogues throughout this book. But the full set is small—probably no more than 20—and it's not necessary to discuss each one individually. When you hear one, you'll recognize it, because it's part of the grammar of verbal violence in your head. Then, to choose your response, follow the rules on page 103. When you're not sure how to proceed, you have two fallback choices:

- Use a Boring Baroque Response.
- Use a vacuous Computer mode utterance such as, "Genuinely effective solutions to problems are often elusive," or "The most interesting issues are often the most difficult to resolve."

I know only two situations in which the deliberate use of a VAP is a good strategic move:

1. When you want to test someone's verbal skills (as when someone is applying for a job with you, or when you're going into a negotiation with someone, for example)

2. When you want to give someone an opportunity to *display* his or her verbal skills for others (a junior colleague in a meeting, for example)

In both of these contexts, you can throw out a mild VAP and allow the person it's directed to to demonstrate his or her ability to respond without becoming involved in a confrontation. *But this should be a rare practice, carefully considered and chosen, and you should have a fallback plan all worked out in case things go wrong.* It goes without saying that it should never mean that *you* become involved in a confrontation! Remember, it was you who threw out the VAP in the first place, and it wasn't because you were attacking.

The Two Barriers to Using This Technique

The most difficult problem I face in teaching people to deal with the VAPs isn't a technical one. People easily understand the technique and its use, but they sometimes have trouble following through. They come back to me and report two factors that they say keep them from following the rules on page 103. Both of these barriers are based on a misunderstanding of the situation.

"Only a Wimp Would Let That One Go By!"   Over and over, I hear this kind of objection: "I understand what you're saying, and I know what you would have told me to say. But I just could not let that person get away with it!" (Because the bait in the particular attack was so cruel or so totally false or in some other way so intolerable to the victim.)

There are two basic misunderstandings here. First, you should *expect* the bait to be like that. Of *course* the bait is going to be as outrageous as the attacker can make it. Of *course,* if the attacker has personal knowledge of something that will be especially hurtful to the victim, it will be used as bait. When you go fishing, you don't bait your hook with something that will bore the fish; you choose whatever you think is most likely to get the fish's attention. "VAPpers" are doing the same thing. *They choose the bait not to hurt you, but to* hook *you; the hurt is just an unavoidable side effect.* Attackers want your attention; they want to demonstrate that they have the power to get and keep your attention; they want from you an emotional reaction that is evidence of that power. They will *always* use as bait whatever they think is most likely to be impossible for you to ignore. This should not surprise you in any way; certainly it should never surprise you into making a strategic error.

Second, it's an error to think that letting the bait go by without challenge *is* "letting them get away with it." No matter what is in the bait, it's the trivial part of the attack.

Think about it. You had a plan for how you were going to spend the next 15 minutes or so. There were things you wanted to do with that time. But the attacker has a *different* plan: that you will spend that time engaged in an undignified verbal fight in which you demonstrate how easy it is for the attacker to pull your strings and make you dance. Doing *that*—not ignoring some ridiculous insult—is letting the attacker get away with it. No matter how the fight itself ends, the loser (and wimp) is the person who provides the attacker with Victim Service, and the attacker who can *get* you to provide that service is the winner.

"But I Felt So Guilty!"   The other barrier people bring up is their feeling of guilt, especially when the verbal attacker is someone they've served as verbal victim for a long time. Suppose someone in your workplace has grown accustomed to stopping by your desk and having a VAP episode every day or two, and you suddenly stop providing that service. The attacker is likely to come at you this way:

> "You know, you used to be so much fun to be around....I always knew, no matter <u>how</u> bad my day had been, that I could come talk to you for a few minutes and go away feeling like it had all been worthwhile. But <u>now</u>, you're not any fun any more....I don't know what it is, but you've <u>changed</u>, and you know, it makes me really <u>sad</u>."

Sure it makes the attacker sad; now he or she is without a participating victim, and that's very inconvenient. But even if you feel willing to continue in the victim role for the sake of the attacker—perhaps because you view him or her with awe, or because your attacker is someone who seems too frail to fill the role—you're making a mistake. Remember, *exposure to chronic hostility is dangerous.* Chronic verbal abusers end up lonely; they end up sick and miserable. You're not being nice when you make it possible for them to indulge their habit. You're not being kind. You have absolutely no reason to feel guilty for refusing to do something that endangers both of you.

One question remains: Why can't you just state the message in Rule 3 openly and be done with it? Why can't you just *say*, right up front, Leveling all the way, "Don't bother trying that with me; I won't play that game"?

Theoretically, that's the perfect solution. In the real world, however, there are thousands of situations in which it's inappropriate or dangerous. It's an open declaration of independence; it says, "You have no power over me at all. <u>None</u>." When that is the truth, it may be the best possible response. However, you need to ask yourself two questions:

1. Are the power relationships in this situation permanent, meaning that I will never find myself subordinate to this person at some later date?

2. Are there people this person *does* have power over, people he or she is likely to punish because my response caused serious loss of face?

The Leveling response is an acceptable choice only when the answer to the first question is yes and the answer to the second question is no.

Now we can go back to Scenario Six and see how this information could be put to use there to keep the situation from degenerating into an undignified shouting match that accomplishes no useful purpose of any kind.

Another Look at Scenario Six

Here are the verbal attack patterns—and the responses they evoked—from Scenario Six. Some of the extra acoustic stresses appear underlined or in italics rather than in all capital letters, as in the original examples. This is done to indicate that the body language accompanying the VAP, including the tone and intonation of the voice, was mild or moderate rather than intense. There will be some overlap, since one person's response to a VAP is often also a VAP and brings a response from someone else.

First VAP Interaction

> WALTER: "You're not the <u>only</u> person around here who's concerned about <u>child</u> care, you know!"
>
> ANITA: "Then <u>why</u> don't you ever <u>listen</u> when we bring you a <u>plan</u>? You could at <u>least</u> give us a fair <u>hearing</u>!"
>
> RICHARD: "Anita, you're only <u>saying</u> that to cause <u>trouble</u>—you <u>know</u> it's not true!"

Walter throws out a VAP; Anita responds to it with two VAPs of her own, to which Richard responds with yet another VAP.

Suggested Rewrite

> WALTER: "You're not the <u>only</u> person around here who's concerned about <u>child</u> care, you know!"
>
> ANITA: "I know that's true. That's why I am so confident that when you've heard the facts you will agree that we can and should have an on-site child care facility."

Richard no longer has a VAP to respond to. If he *did* use the original line, however, an appropriate response is for Anita to go to Computer mode and say, "Understanding the motives of others is never a simple matter."

Second VAP Interaction

> ANITA: "If you <u>really</u> cared about the welfare of your employees, you'd stop making ex<u>cus</u>es and BORrow the capital!"
>
> WALTER: "Borrow? You are seriously suggesting that we take on <u>more</u> <u>debt</u>?"
>
> ANITA: "<u>Yes</u>! This is the biggest poultry company in the United <u>States</u>! We're not exactly short on <u>credit</u> lines—but our <u>employees</u> are! <u>They</u> can't <u>afford</u> nannies and private schools! Don't you even <u>care</u> <u>about</u> <u>the</u> <u>problems</u> <u>of</u> <u>ordinary</u> <u>people</u>?"

At this point Anita has used the "If you REALLY" pattern; Walter has responded with angry astonishment; and Anita has come back at him with a barrage of hostile language ending with a VAP we haven't yet discussed—the "Don't you even CARE" pattern. Walter's next utterance in response to all this artillery is the VAP below:

> WALTER: "EVen a WOMan should be able to discuss exPENDitures without a lot of cheap MELodrama and emotional BLACKmail!"

Suggested Rewrites

If Anita has the good judgment to use a neutral utterance instead of a VAP, she can say this:

> ANITA: "One of the clearest ways we could demonstrate that concern is by <u>borrowing</u> the capital needed."

If, on the other hand, she persists in her verbal abuse, Walter has the option of responding neutrally, as in this exchange:

> ANITA: "Then <u>why</u> don't you ever <u>listen</u> when we bring you a <u>plan</u>? You could at <u>least</u> give us a fair <u>hearing</u>!"
>
> WALTER: "All right. What is the child care problem that concerns you most right this minute? You tell us, and we will listen carefully."

Walter has done two wise things here. First, he has ignored her two insults, "You never listen and you don't even do the minimum a decent person would do." Second, he has responded directly to the presupposition that listening *never* happens, by offering to listen—making the presupposition false on the spot. This is one of the options for dealing with a

"WHY do you always/don't you ever..." attack pattern. In addition, by offering the hearing Anita is asking for, he is agreeing with her claim that such a hearing is required, just as if he had said "You're absolutely right."

In this rewrite, Walter's purpose is to counter the two VAPs and cause them to fail and at the same time to get Anita's presentation under way so that it can be heard. This is consistent with the scenario; if the managers don't want to listen to what Anita has to tell them (which would suggest a Boring Baroque Response to her two VAPs), they should not have agreed to the meeting in the first place.

In the original scenario, Anita's next move was to challenge Walter with a "Don't you even CARE" VAP; when she did so, she made him seriously angry, provoking his "EVen a WOMan" VAP with its added hostile remarks about melodrama and emotional blackmail.

The "Don't you even CARE" pattern is a vicious one; it is one of the few VAPs for which I feel that a Boring Baroque Response is very often justified. Here are some of the choices Walter has for defusing it instead of feeding the hostility loop.

ANITA: "Don't you even <u>care</u> <u>about</u> <u>the</u> <u>problems</u> <u>of</u> <u>ordinary</u> <u>people</u>?"
WALTER: "Of course I do."

Period. Without another word. The ball is now back in Anita's court, and the attack has failed.

WALTER: "Such problems are a major concern of every manager."

This is an innocuous Computer mode response; the ball is in Anita's court and the attack has failed.

WALTER: "Indeed I do. Why only the other day I saw an article on that subject in *The New York Times*...at least, I <u>think</u> it was the *Times*! No, wait—it couldn't have been. It must have been *The Wall Street Journal*, because...."

This is a Boring Baroque Response. It is well deserved but dangerous because it is happening in front of spectators and Anita will lose face. That's ill-advised unless there is a compelling *reason*, based on logic rather than emotion, why she *should* be made to lose face in public. (Notice that although many words are in italics, they don't signal hostile language; they are the punctuation English requires for writing the names of newspapers.)

Third VAP Interaction

WALTER: "EVen a WOMan should be able to discuss exPENDitures without a lot of cheap MELodrama and emotional BLACKmail!"

ANITA: "It is NOT melodrama! And it is not BLACKmail! It is the TRUTH! And my GENder has NOTHing to DO with it!"

RICHARD: "WHY do you always do this, Anita? Please try to calm down!"

ANITA: "WHY do you always tell ME to calm down? WHY don't you ever take MY side when he attacks me like that? WHY is it always ME that gets chewed out?"

WALTER: "Nobody has attacked you, Anita, and nobody has chewed you out. If you really wanted to make the case for a child care facility, you'd learn to stick to the facts instead of making emotional speeches!"

ZAP! POW! TAKE THAT! This isn't communication, this is combat. Anita's response should have been, "The idea that women are somehow incapable of rational discussion is something you run into once in a while....I'm surprised to hear that from you, Walter." Instead, she takes his bait and serves as willing and vociferous victim—and gets VAPped again by both men for her pains. By the time she gets to her final utterance she is so furious that she uses three stressed-WHY VAPs, one right after another, making Walter's comments about emotional speeches hard to refute. If he is *trying* to get her to make a spectacle of herself (something we don't have enough information to make a judgment about), she has played right into his hands.

All three of the people involved in this altercation are at fault. Anita is at fault for starting the row and maintaining it; the men are at fault for playing victim and perpetuating it. However, once each man has used a VAP and Anita has taken *its* bait, the roles are reversed. Everyone is equally guilty, except in the nebulous sense that Anita was the *first* to attack.

Because we don't know these people or their circumstances, one unsolved question remains. We don't know whether Anita behaved as she did because she likes to throw her weight around and demonstrate her ability to cause scenes and upset people, or if she did it simply because she cares passionately about her subject and is very unskilled at communication under those circumstances. Either explanation is possible, and only the people involved know which was correct. And, of course, once Anita throws out the attack that *starts* the confrontation, everyone else's motivation may well be only self-defense. Whatever the motivations may have been, the technique for dealing effectively with the VAPs remains the same.

English VAPs and Nonnative Speakers

A final note. You will have noticed that, with the exception of a single plea to Anita to speak more calmly, Mary Begay did not participate in the row in Scenario Six. This is not because she is a woman; Anita's language behavior makes it quite clear that women are as capable of this verbal fighting as men are. Nor does it mean that Navajos do not engage in verbal abuse. However, the grammar of verbal violence differs from one language to another. Nonnative speakers of English, even if very fluent, are unlikely to be comfortable using the English VAPs. This is especially true when, as with Navajo, the other grammar is from an entirely different language family and from a culture in which great value is placed on cooperation and consensus.

When interacting with nonnative speakers, it is never safe to assume that they will understand your VAPs. For one thing, you have no reason at all to assume that they will understand any attack sheltered in an English presupposition. Furthermore, if a nonnative speaker throws an English VAP at you, it's not safe to assume, on the basis of that line alone, that an attack was intended. The person may have picked up the pattern in a classroom, in conversation, or from the media, and may be completely unaware that it constitutes verbal abuse. *Always give the nonnative speaker the benefit of the doubt.* This is an important guideline. In today's multiethnic and multilingual United States, no one can any longer afford to ignore it.

WORKOUT SECTION: CHAPTER 6

1. Add to your role-playing practice sessions some in which Speaker A attacks, using one of the verbal attack patterns; Speaker B responds; and the Coach observes and critiques. *If the people involved start getting angry, stop the session; irrational hostility is just as bad for you as any other kind.*

2. For your Communication Strategy Notebook, set up a Verbal Attack Patterns file and begin keeping track of relevant information. For example:

- Record incidents in which you followed the rules for defusing the VAPs and dealing with them properly, to serve as a database for planning strategies. What did the attacker say? What was your response? What was said next? How did it turn out? What was surprising? Did anything go wrong, and if so, can you determine why? If you had it to do over again, how would you do it differently?

- Record incidents in which you were present when others became involved in a VAP session; analyze them in the usual way. (You might also record some VAP sessions from television and compare them with those you encounter in the real world to find out if and how they are different.)

- Set up a page that looks like this:

VAP Frequency Log

Month and Year: _____

Number of times I was involved in a VAP session. (Indicate by putting a check mark after the appropriate description each time.)

As the attacker

As the victim

As a bystander

Totals for this month:

As attacker (   )   As victim (   )   As bystander (   )

- On a sheet of graph paper, chart your monthly totals for each role. You should see a steady decline in frequency as you become more skilled in the Gentle Art of Verbal Self-Defense techniques.

3. Defusing and deflecting the VAPs instead of taking the bait and serving as victim can be extremely frustrating at first. Similarly, if you're accustomed to using VAPs a great deal, it can be frustrating to refrain from using them. In both cases there is a potential hazard: that you won't be able to put the encounters out of your mind so that the hostility becomes internalized, with negative effects. One of the best ways to avoid this is to go ahead and *write out* the fight you didn't have. Write down the attack you were the intended victim for; write down what you would have said had you taken the bait; and continue the dialogue for as long as you like, no holds barred. Or write down the attack you refrained from making yourself, the response you wanted from your intended victim, and as much of the hypothetical fight as you like. Seeing these confrontations before you on a page (or hearing them on a tape) lets you get them out of your system and achieve the detachment necessary to forget about them.

4. If you use the VAPs on *yourself*, you do yourself harm. It's very destructive to constantly be saying things like this to yourself:

- "If I <u>really</u> cared about making that presentation, I wouldn't keep putting it OFF the way I do!"

- "EVen a CHILD could add up THOSE figures! I can't beLIEVE I could be this STUPid!"

- "WHY can't I ever do anything RIGHT? What's the MATTER with me, ANYway?!!!"

You need to become consciously aware that you are doing this—and you need to make a conscious effort not to do it. Each time it occurs, ask yourself this question: "If someone else said that to me in this same situation, what would my response—according to the rules for managing VAPs—be?" You may find it helpful to write out the attack and response as if it were an incident between you and someone else; you may want to extend the dialogue.

5. In a story about Ford Explorers, Jerry Flint writes that, "Even the Japanese, with their obsession with quality and finish, approve" (*Jerry Flint, "Man Bites Dog," Forbes magazine, September 17, 1990, p. 64*). Is this a VAP? What does this demonstrate about deciding that you've been attacked when you have only written language to base your decision on?

6. The examples below are all VAPs. For each one: find the bait; find the attack that is sheltered in a presupposition; and construct a response according to the rules in this chapter.

a. "If you were genuinely CONCERNED about our sales figures, YOU wouldn't treat our clients like CATTle!"

b. "You could at LEAST TRY to get your slides in the right order in the tray!"

c. "You're not the ONly person in this division who deserves a RAISE, you know!"

d. "If you really underSTOOD the software, YOU wouldn't keep making stupid misTAKES!"

e. "Even a LAWyer would be able to follow THAT argument!"

f. "WHY don't you ever consider the consequences your crazy strategies have for the REST of us?"

g. "An administrator who CARED about the bottom line wouldn't waste thousands of dollars catering to the employees' every WHIM!"

h. "SOME clients would cancel the ACCOUNT if the agency was always SIX months LATE!"

i. "A REAL executive doesn't constantly pinch PENNies and cut CORners!"

j. "EVen if you DO take that file home and lose it, WE won't hold it against you."

7. Are you dubious about my claim that you have a complete mental grammar of English, access to which is limited by your lack of conscious awareness? Let's assume that I have invented a new children's game and am giving a presentation about it to your company in an effort to get you to buy the rights to my game and put it into production. Which of the following proposed *names* for my game would you find acceptable? Which would you reject, and why? Did you know you knew these rules? Where and when did you learn them?

Little the Green Spaceship Game
The Green Little Spaceship Game
The Little Green Spaceship Game
Spaceship Game The Green Little

Spaceship Grawk
Spaceship Blawk
Spaceship Grszawk
Spaceship Mgawk

Suppose you are looking out a window. In the distance you can see a utility pole rising 20 feet into the sky. You would describe the pole as "20 feet tall" or "20 feet high." Now, suddenly, a tremendous gust of wind hits the pole and knocks it flat on the ground. It's the same pole and the same size it was while it was standing. But now you would have to describe it as "20 feet long." Why? Did you know you knew that grammar rule? Can you explain it? Try to find it in a grammar book, if you enjoy wasting your time.

Quotations to Consider

a. Authors Roger Fisher and William Ury tell the story of an Englishman who—after watching an American father and son playing Frisbee in a London park—spoke to the father, saying: "Sorry to bother you. Been watching you a quarter of an hour. Who's winning?" (*Roger Fisher and William Ury*, Getting to Yes: Negotiating Agreement Without Giving In. *New York: Penguin Books, 1981*)

   Often people who are involved in VAP attacks don't really care one way or the other about the apparent subject of the attack. They only participate because of their conviction that even the most trivial disagreement must end with a clear winner and a clear loser. This idea is based on emotion rather than on reason, and is usually something they learned from adults around them while they were growing up.

b. Sun Tzu, one of the greatest and most successful strategists of all time, wrote: "To win one hundred victories in one hundred battles is not the acme of skill. To subdue the enemy without fighting is the acme of skill." (*Sun Tzu*, The Art of War, *translated by Thomas Cleary. Boston and London: Shambhala Pocket Classics, 1991*)

c. "To a limited extent it is possible to control people through fear, if only because most people will do anything to avoid a scene." (*Michael Korda*, Power: How to Get It, How to Use It; *New York: Ballantine, 1975*)

   This isn't true of chronic VAPpers. However much they may dislike scenes, their need for their victim's full attention is a stronger drive—like kids who would rather be punished than be ignored.

d. Reviewing a new grammar book, Malcolm S. Forbes, Jr., writes: "When in school, I, like many, found the subject intimidating, if not incomprehensible." (*Malcolm S. Forbes, Jr., "Fact and Comment,"* Forbes *magazine, November 12, 1990, p. 20*)

Notice that the person making this claim is the editor-in-chief of this country's leading business publication. He writes a column for every issue. The idea that he found the grammar of his own language incomprehensible is itself incomprehensible: It was that *grammar that he had to use to process the language* about *English grammar which he was reading and hearing.*

e. "The social support findings...were found to be independent of other traditional risk factors such as smoking, alcohol consumption, exercise, and obesity....The relationship persisted. The more social connectedness, the lower the death rates." (*Robert Ornstein and David Sobel,* The Healing Brain: Breakthrough Discoveries about How the Brain Keeps Us Healthy. *New York: Simon & Schuster, 1987, p. 119*)

There is no surer way to find yourself without a social support network than to be someone whose company other people do their best to avoid—and a sure way to guarantee that *situation is to engage in frequent hostile communication. The Ornstein and Sobel book is one of the best sources of detailed information about the health hazards of poor communication; I strongly urge you to read it. See also Steven Locke and Douglas Colligen,* The Healer Within: The New Medicine of Mind and Body *(New York: New American Library, 1986).*

7

"Have You Stopped Cheating on Your Taxes?"

Increasing the Power of Your Arguments

Shawna Phelps was confident about today's presentation. Because several members of the planning committee were people who routinely objected to any idea that came from another person, she didn't expect to achieve immediate agreement. But it was so *obvious*, it was so *self-evident*, that AkmeX had to go global...she couldn't imagine not prevailing in the end, even if it took several meetings to get things off the ground.

Sitting at the head of the table, Shawna spread out her notes in front of her, smiled at her five colleagues, thanked them for coming, and began.

"I'm here this morning," she said, "to talk to you about the urgent need to get started on the next stage of this corporation's development. The time has come to take AkmeX beyond the borders of the United States, beyond the borders of North America—the time has come to go global. It sounds radical, but—"

"What do you mean...radical?" asked Jeffrey Clay. "Is that a business judgment or a political one?"

Shawna frowned; for a minute she wasn't sure what he was getting at. And then she understood and said, "Business, Jeffrey, of course! I mean that it would be a major change for the company. All right?"

He nodded, and she cleared her throat and continued.

"Every company in this country that wants to be part of the economy in the future…twenty years down the road, fifty years down the road…has to take this step. It's no longer a matter of choice; it's a necessity."

"Oh, come on, Shawna," said Ellen Franklin. "That's an exaggeration. How many American companies, precisely, have gone global in the past five years?"

"Well," Shawna answered, "I can't give you the exact number, but we see the announcements in the business news every single day. Ellen, consumers in this country already have at least one of everything. Lots of us have two or three of everything. Radios, for example…who do you know that doesn't have at least two radios? Nobody!"

"I know lots of people who don't have two radios," said Jeffrey. "There are many pockets of poverty in this country where people just barely make enough money to buy food."

"Those people are not likely to be customers for our products!" Shawna objected. "Now, if you don't mind, I'd like to get back to the subject at hand!"

"That's an interesting attitude," Neil Evanson put in sharply, jabbing the air in front of him with his ballpoint pen. "Never mind the problems we have at home, just full speed ahead with the bottom line abroad! And never mind what it would cost, of course."

"It would be expensive," Shawna admitted, making a note to come back to his accusation later if she could fit it in somewhere, "but we have to start sometime. It's not going to get any cheaper."

"How do you know that?" Ellen asked.

"What?"

"I mean, how do you know it won't get cheaper? How do you know that it wouldn't be wiser to wait ten years and let some of the international messes going on right now settle down before we try moving overseas?"

"Ellen, there will always be crises going on around the world!"

"Well, then," Ellen insisted, "how do you know it wouldn't be wiser to let larger companies go ahead of us and break down some of the barriers, instead of trying to be pioneers ourselves?"

"She has a point, Shawna," put in Fred O'Brien.

"Obviously," Shawna said, trying to keep the exasperation out of her voice, "we would begin in countries where the concept of international marketing is already well established! We aren't going to start with Outer Mongolia!"

"I see," said Fred. "And what country would be first?"

"Oh, for heaven's sake!" Shawna exclaimed, her patience exhausted. "There are a thousand other things we have to decide before we make that decision!"

"Well, then," asked Neil, "why didn't you start with those things instead of bringing up this issue?"

Shawna stared at him, totally amazed. *It wasn't me who brought up the business about picking the first country to market in*, she thought. *I don't remember who it was, but it wasn't me! How am I going to get this discussion back on track?*

What's Going on Here?

Shawna's Point of View

As Shawna sees it, the need for AkmeX to go global is so obvious that no rational person could argue against it. She knows the other committee members are going to put up a ritual token resistance; they would do that if she were proposing that the napkins in the company cafeteria be yellow instead of white. But she knows they *are* rational, she is positive that they're just as familiar with the facts and the statistics as she is, and she respects their judgment both individually and collectively. Her plan was just to get through this first meeting as quickly as possible, to let them get the automatic resistance out of their systems, so that they could set up another meeting to begin tackling the *real* issues.

The Others' Point of View

The way the rest of the committee members see it, Shawna isn't even willing to permit discussion, although a switch to global marketing— even a switch to active *planning* for global marketing—would require massive changes at AkmeX. The committee has been given the task of considering the global marketing question, coming to some conclusions, and taking their final position to a meeting of the board. Shawna, in their opinion, is talking as if the decisions had already been made, as if it were a foregone conclusion that AkmeX would go global and all that was left to do was settle the minor details. She may be right about the need to start planning the shift; they know that. But they resent her attitude, and they are determined that she's not going to be able to push them around and shove her ideas down their throats.

What Went Wrong?

Shawna is guilty of a single mistake, and she makes it over and over again. She keeps making *open claims*, each of which is immediately challenged by one or more of her colleagues. She should know better. She knows that she is dealing with people who are resistant to any idea they didn't originate themselves, and who feel obligated to make objections even when they actually agree with the speaker. Unless she changes her ways, she is going to go through a whole series of wasted and infuriating meetings like the one shown in the scenario—that's guaranteed by her approach. It's as if she were trying to play tennis with people whose only strategy was to hit every ball she served out of bounds and into the trees.

There are a number of things that she can do to get past the delaying tactics her colleagues are using. We will discuss the most basic one: a way to structure her utterances so that they don't come across as open claims that trigger an immediate confrontational reflex.

Communication Technique: Using the Power of Presuppositions

Our discussions of presuppositions up to now have been primarily in the context of their use for *negative* purposes (as, for example, in the English verbal attack patterns.) The question, "Have you stopped cheating on your taxes?" is another negative example; anyone who answers "Yes" admits to having cheated in the past, while anyone who answers "No" admits to being a cheater in the present. Questions in this form are usually referred to as "trick questions," but there's no trick involved. They just use the power of presuppositions, a resource available to every native speaker of a language. In the example above, what is presupposed is the "start" that is part of the meaning of "stop."

In this section we're going to focus on the use of presuppositions for *positive* purposes, based on four areas of English grammar with which you may not be consciously familiar. The basic organizing concept for our discussion is this metaprinciple:

Anything you don't want to argue about should be presupposed.

Remember the VAP that occurs as utterances like, "If you REALLY cared about your health, YOU wouldn't SMOKE three packs of cigarettes a day!"? The attacker's expectation that the victim will respond immediately to the bait about the three packs of cigarettes—while the presupposed "you don't really care about your health" is ignored—is based on long experience with communication. People *do* tend to challenge whatever is openly claimed and let presupposed material slip by. *It is therefore always wise to provide a presuppositional shelter for items you don't want to waste time quibbling over.* To understand how this is done, we'll need to review some very basic grammar terms and facts.

Presupposing with Possessives

In English, anything that is marked by a possessive (like "my" or "yours" or "the company's") is presupposed to *exist*. If you say "We have a detergent," you have made a claim and it's open to argument; you may be asked to provide evidence for it. Suppose, however, that you say "Our detergent costs less per ounce than any existing product." Now your *claim* is that the detergent costs less than anything else available, and *that* is open to challenge. But the existence of the detergent itself has been presupposed by putting "our" in front of it.

You can go further; you can use the possessive to shelter other items you don't want to argue about. If you say, "We have a new detergent," you've made two claims: The detergent exists, and the detergent is new. But suppose you say, "Our new detergent has a pleasant fragrance." Now your only claim is the statement about the fragrance. That the detergent exists and is new is presupposed by the possessive "our." Any possessive—"The J. Wigton Company's new detergent has a pleasant fragrance," for example—will serve the same purpose.

There are languages (Navajo is one) in which a sentence like "My beautiful white horse does not exist" is unremarkable. For English, however, a thing that does not exist cannot be possessed, and the more elaborate the description attached to the possessive, the stronger the presupposition of existence. No native speaker of English would utter a sentence like this one:

"My beautiful new car with the mag wheels and the leather upholstery does not exist."

Suppose you heard someone say that sentence in ordinary conversation, rather than in a storytelling session or poetry reading, where quite different rules apply. You would assume that the speaker must have *meant* to say that the car "does not exist any longer," or some such thing; you would assume that a slip of the tongue had occurred. This feature of English allows you to put many claims into a possessive sequence and follow them either with something innocuous or with something you *do* want to discuss, as in these examples:

"Our superb new software will interest many computer owners."

"Our superb new software will be on the shelves by February 10th."

The claim that the software will interest many computer owners is hardly worth challenging; the claim about a release date may well be. But both examples *presuppose* that the software exists, is new, and is superb. Unless someone hearing this sequence is particularly opposed to those items, they will probably go unnoticed, whether they are true or not. The more detailed and plausible the possessive sequence, the stronger that probability will be. (It is of course another *negative* use of presuppositional power to use this technique to get something *false* past another person without challenge.)

One of the limiting facts about possessives, handy as they are, is that they can be constructed only with *nominals*—that is, only with sequences of language that are functioning the way *nouns* function. When the item you want to presuppose isn't a nominal, that poses a problem.

Presupposing by Nominalization

Suppose you are convinced that a colleague's secretary has destroyed one of your computer files. You could go to the colleague and say straight out: "Your secretary has destroyed one of my computer files." But that's an open claim; what if you want to shelter it with a presupposition? You can't say "her destroy" or "her careless destroy" or anything of that kind. (Notice that although I can be absolutely certain that no one ever stated that rule in your hearing, you know it; you can trust your internal grammar.) "Destroy" is a verb rather than a nominal, and verbs can't be possessed. However, English has a systematic process for solving the problem by turning verbs (and adjectives) into nominals, called *nominalization*. It allows you to say this:

"Your secretary's destruction of one of my computer files was very careless."

or

"Your secretary's careless destruction of one of my computer files is going to cause me considerable inconvenience."

That is, you can take the verb "destroy" and turn it into the nominal "destruction"; you can then treat it just like you would treat any other nominal. It can be presupposed by a possessive, and you can make the possessive sequence as elaborate as is possible in the context.

Many English verbs and adjectives have special nominalized forms of their own, as "destroy" and "careless" do. For example:

produce	production
abandon	abandonment
wicked	wickedness
futile	futility
fail	failure

The information that lets you know which nominalizing ending goes with which verb or adjective, as well as any additional changes in its form required by the sound system of English, is stored in the dictionary component (called a *lexicon*, to distinguish it from more familiar types of dictionaries) of your internal grammar. You would immediately reject the forms if someone tried to get you to use "abandonity" or "wickedtion" or "failness."

All English verbs and adjectives can be nominalized, just by adding *-ing* or a form of *be* plus *-ing*. Again, you would find it difficult to state the rules about just what form *be* takes in such constructions or precisely where the *-ing* goes—but you don't have to worry about that. Like Molière's French gentleman who was amazed to learn that he'd been speaking prose all his life, you've been nominalizing skillfully since you were a child. All those rules are stored in your internal grammar, and you know how to use them. This gives you some choices, as shown in the following examples:

"Your secretary's destruction of my file surprised me."

"Your secretary's destroying my file surprised me."

"Your constant carelessness annoys us all."

"Your being constantly careless annoys us all."

"Your having been constantly careless annoyed us all."

The choice between just adding *-ing* and using a special nominalized form, when both exist, is usually made on the basis of the context, with the addition of *-ing* being viewed as the more informal choice of the two. Both, however, will be grammatically correct.

Presupposing with Factives

There is a class of English verbs and adjectives, first described in linguistic literature by Carol and Paul Kiparsky, called "factives." Propositions that serve as objects of factives are *presupposed* to be true. This is less complicated than it sounds. Look at these examples:

1. "I knew you had been selling junk bonds."

1a. "I didn't know you had been selling junk bonds."

Both presuppose "You had been selling junk bonds."

2. "I was aware that you were the author of a prize-winning biography."

2a. "I wasn't aware that you were the author of a prize-winning biography."

Both presuppose "You are the author of a prize-winning biography."

3. "I thought you had been selling junk bonds."

3a. "I didn't think you had been selling junk bonds."

Neither one presupposes "You had been selling junk bonds."

4. "I was afraid you were going to sue us for breach of contract."

4a. "I wasn't afraid you were going to sue us for breach of contract."

Neither one presupposes "You were going to sue us for breach of contract."

These eight sentences tell us that the verb "know" and the adjective "aware" are both factives, while the verb "think" and the adjective "afraid" are nonfactives. Suppose you want to tell someone, by presupposing it, that the stock market is dangerous. You can simply state your opinion openly, like this:

"I know that the stock market is dangerous."

Your listener can still challenge you on this, of course, and may do so because you're referring to your own knowledge. You can lessen that probability by using the factive "know" and giving someone *else* credit for the knowledge, as in:

"Every successful company knows that the stock market is dangerous."

Best of all, when it can be done, is crediting the knowledge to your listener with the "As You Know" device discussed on page 22, like this:

"As you know, the stock market is dangerous."

Many variations on this pattern are available to you, depending on the context. For example:

"As I'm sure you know..."

"As we both know..."

"As you are aware..."

"As everyone in this room knows/is aware..."

"As any lawyer in a top firm like yours knows..."

"As anyone with your broad experience in the field is well aware..."

Certainly you may still be challenged. *But the challenge will be on the basis of a genuine disagreement about what is or is not a fact; it won't be because the listener doesn't like your attitude.*

This use of presuppositions allows you to state what you believe to be facts without sounding as if you consider your listeners ignorant. It is particularly valuable when you want to pass on to someone a fact that he or she badly *needs* to be aware of and you're afraid that isn't the case. Suppose your doctor certainly *should* know you're allergic to penicillin, since it's in your file in big red letters, but you're afraid she has forgotten about that....In such a case, you can save face for the doctor and avoid an inappropriate prescription by saying, "As you know, Doctor Allen, I'm allergic to penicillin." When your boss seems to have lost track of the most recent sales figures right in the middle of a meeting where they're badly needed, you can say, "As you know, our sales for this past quarter were just over two million dollars." (Or, if the boss is exceptionally touchy, "As you remember, we were all delighted that our sales for this past quarter were just over two million dollars.")

Presuppositions and Commands

As you know, adults in our culture have an automatic negative reaction to hearing direct commands from other adults. Suppose you want to tell one of your salespeople to go to Detroit without saying, "Margaret, go to Detroit." You can do that by using the presuppositions that go with a variety of English *time words*, like this:

"While you're in Detroit, Margaret, I recommend that you try the Bidalia Restaurant at least once."

or

"After you get back from Detroit, Margaret, I hope you'll have good news for us on the Cartbell account."

or

"When you're in Detroit, Margaret, you'll find that most of the construction work they were doing last year has been completed."

You can make this even more effective by combining it with what is called *an illusion of choice*. Like this:

"While you're in Detroit, Margaret, would you rather stay at the Holiday Inn or the Ramada?"

or

"After you get back from Detroit, Margaret, would you rather report on the Cartbell account in person or do you just want to write a memo?"

or

"When you're in Detroit, Margaret, would you rather take the Cartbells out to dinner or just have them meet you at the hotel?"

The people you use these sequences with will of course realize that they're being given orders. If they're strongly opposed to doing what you want and feel free to say so, they can still say, "Wait a minute—I don't want to go to Detroit." *But these challenges will be on the basis of genuine disagreement; they won't be kneejerk reactions to the speech act you're using with them.*

It should also be remembered that people who might challenge even a presupposed item when it is part of a single sentence or utterance, as in the examples in this chapter, are less likely to do so when the item is part of an ongoing language interaction, or part of a speech or presentation. In the real world, most utterances don't occur as isolated examples constructed by a linguist; *other* communicational things are happening at the same time. Politicians can say "Our bold and innovative plan for welfare reform contains the following six provisions" and go on to state those provisions, knowing that by the time they finish most people will have forgotten about challenging the presupposed "bold and innovative."

All of these presuppositional patterns can be overdone; all can be said with body language that causes them to be heard as condescending or overbearing or sarcastic. But when you use them with skill and restraint, paying attention to your nonverbal communication as well as your words, they can eliminate vast amounts of petty wrangling over things about which no one really cares. They can make it possible for you to be helpful to others in tight communication spots without anyone else knowing that's what you're doing, often a very desirable outcome. You would be well advised, especially in presentations, to make an advance list of the propositions you'd prefer not to spend time struggling over and work out ways to shield them all with presuppositions. You'll find that this quickly becomes automatic and natural.

Now let's go back and look at Scenario Seven again to see how skillful use of presuppositions, as well as several other strategic moves, could turn the meeting into a productive one.

Another Look at Scenario Seven

There are four strategies Shawna Phelps should follow in her presentation to the committee in order to accomplish her goal—which is to get the initial ritual objections over with so that the next meeting can move on to substantive issues. Three have already been discussed in detail; the fourth is discussed below.

1. She should have with her, in multiple copies, answers to every factual question she can *imagine* being asked by the other members. These "factoids" should be neatly sorted as charts and graphs for swift access; as far as possible, they should be cross-referenced. With today's computer facilities at her disposal, this is a routine task—tedious, perhaps, but routine. For the sort of audience she faces, fiercely determined nitpickers all, this is absolutely obligatory.

2. When it's appropriate, she should be prepared to do her own speaking in Computer mode—especially when there is a chance she might sound as if she were trying to set herself above the others or dictate to them.

3. Whenever possible, information she'd like to move through quickly and without discussion should be sheltered in presuppositions, rather than structured in the form of open claims.

4. She should include items specifically tailored to attract negative attention from her listeners and give them opportunities to make changes—so that their need for dominance displays can be satisfied without harming items that are important to her.

Shawna does begin with presupposed information when she says that she's there to talk about "the urgent need to get started on the next stage of this corporation's development." She has presupposed the propositions that the need exists and that it is urgent. But if she wants to begin this way, she should talk of "the urgent need to prepare for AkmeX's move to global marketing." And from this point on she makes one open claim after another, always in either Leveling or mild Blaming mode.

In the list below, you'll see each of her claims as they appear in the original scenario, followed by one of the many possible revisions that would make them less likely to trigger challenges from her listeners. English has many different linguistic devices that can be used for this purpose. Shawna needs to choose among them so that her utterances can be varied in form. Many of the revisions are in Computer mode, to reduce the listeners' perception that Shawna is trying to pull rank and demonstrate power.

- "The time has come to take AkmeX beyond the borders of the United States...the time has come to go global."

  "As all of us know, the time has come..."
- "It sounds radical, but—"

  "Some people might say that this sounds radical."
- "It would be a major change for the company."

  "After this major change has taken place, the company..."
- "Every company in this country that wants to be part of the economy in the <u>future</u>...has to take this step. It's no longer a matter of choice; it's a necessity."

  "As you all are aware, the necessity to take this step is now a challenge facing every company in this country that wants to be part of the economy in the <u>future</u>."
- "We see the announcements [*of companies going global*] in the business news every single day."

  "Announcements are made in the business news every single day."
- "Consumers in this country already have at least one of everything."

  "The fact that consumers in this country tend to already have at least one of everything is of course too well known to require discussion."
- "Those people are not likely to be customers for <u>our</u> products!"

  "The likelihood that those people will be customers for our products is, as we all know, rather small."
- "It would be expensive. But we have to start <u>some</u>time. It's not going to get any <u>cheaper</u>."

  "Because everyone is aware that the process is only going to become <u>more</u> expensive as time goes by, I'm sure you all recognize the practical benefits of making a prompt beginning."
- "Obviously we would begin in countries where the concept of international marketing is already well established...."

  "The need to begin in countries where the concept of international marketing is already well established will be obvious to everyone here."

- "There are a thousand other things we have to decide before we make that decision."

  "The many other decisions that have to be made before a first target country can be chosen will require our best efforts, and we all know that the company is counting on us to provide the background information necessary for that purpose."

It's true that the revisions above take longer to say than the direct claims and commands do, but the time they save in petty arguments and digressions avoided will more than make up for the extra time needed. At one point Shawna does something that is almost always a mistake with an audience like hers. She notes that many Americans have two or three of most consumer items, using radios as an example—and then asks, "Who do you know that doesn't have at least two radios?" She intends this to be a *rhetorical question*; she makes this doubly clear by answering it herself, with "Nobody!" But she should have been aware that this was a blatant invitation to quibblers. Rhetorical questions in contexts where argument is probable should either be of the argument-free "Do two and three make five?" variety or should be confined to questions for which no factual answer exists, like "What is truth?"

Allowing for Dominance Displays

Apes in the wild, if they feel challenged, begin pounding their chests and hooting as a way of displaying their dominance. Human beings don't pound and hoot, but they still demonstrate their kinship with other primates through dominance displays.

Shawna cannot avoid facing *some* challenges and objections and picky questions. Even if what she had to say were as completely self-evident as she personally (and mistakenly) believes, challenges and objections and questions would occur. She knows that—she's expecting it. Using some or all of the structures in the revised examples above would reduce the number of those items and help her avoid becoming hopelessly entangled in absurd wrangles to such a point that she completely loses control of her presentation. In addition, however, she should dangle before her audience some items that are *obviously* badly chosen, so that they can correct her on them and be right.

When I had to present written proposals to university committees as a college professor, I was always careful to salt them with a variety of items from my native Ozark English dialect that I knew would draw shock and dismay. I could be reasonably certain that by the time the committee members had changed all of those to Standard English—and had taken the opportunity to point out my use of the same sort of nonstandard words and phrases in my spoken comments and explanations—they would have satisfied their need for dominance displays and would leave the substance of my proposal untouched. This is always a good strategy. Propose a color scheme you know will draw objections; insert factoids that are just slightly wrong—June 8th when it should be June 10th, 32nd Street when it should be 31st Street. Anything that will provide those in your audience who feel obligated to demonstrate their authority with something to change, without posing a threat to the parts of your presentation that matter to you.

Finally, in the spirit of being prepared for every possible question, Shawna should be ready to proceed *if the committee takes a position completely opposite to what she had expected*. I once went before a curriculum committee to propose a new course, something that is always an uphill battle with endless questions over details. I thought I was ready; I thought I'd taken all the strategic steps listed at the beginning of this section. However, I had thought the committee would claim that my course was too easy for upper division students; all my information had been assembled as proof that that was false. To my complete amazement, the committee attacked me vigorously from the position that the course would be too *hard* for the students, and I was totally unprepared to deal with that.

I managed to convince the committee, but it was sheer luck, bolstered perhaps by my experience on debating teams where we were required to take one position on the assigned question in the morning and the opposite position in the afternoon. Always be prepared for the possibility, unlikely though it may be, that your audience will oppose you from a position contrary to or tangential to the one you're expecting. Especially when, as in the scenario, they are likely to be arguing with you just for the sake of argument, with no strong convictions behind what they say.

WORKOUT SECTION: CHAPTER 7

1. In the examples below, numerous claims have been sheltered in presuppositions. Make them explicit by unpacking the presuppositions and writing out the explicit claims; whenever possible, identify the method used to construct the presupposition. The first one has been done for you.

a. "Even the Japanese, with their obsession with quality and finish, approve." (*Jerry Flint, "Man Bites Dog," Forbes magazine, September 17, 1990, p. 64*)

   The claims are: "The Japanese are obsessed with quality" and "The Japanese are obsessed with finish." The method used was nominalization of the adjective "obsessed" plus insertion of a possessive "their" to strengthen it.

b. "If we continue this slavish adherence to this monumental error of our past, the MAD logicians really will have won, because any attempt to deploy a full-scale, effective SDI program is forbidden by this misbegotten treaty." (*Caspar W. Weinberger, "SDI: Weakened, But Not Killed," Forbes magazine, March 4, 1991, p. 33*)

c. "Congress should torpedo the hypocritical and confidence-destroying off-budget bailout of the thrifts..." (*Ashby Bladen, "The Countdown Has Begun," Forbes magazine, April 3, 1989, p. 182*)

d. "The bureaucratic, tax, and regulatory nightmare that businesses face is not the result of evil people." (*Walter E. Williams, "The Santa Claus Syndrome: Dumb Laws Will Not Help the Disabled," Success magazine, January/February 1991, p. 8*)

2. Now let's work in the opposite direction. Here are some open claims; use the power of presuppositions to shelter them.

a. "We are the most over-lawyered, over-insured society on earth." (*James W. Michaels, "Side Lines," Forbes magazine, September 17, 1990, p. 8*)

b. "To put it simply: whereas power in the West is masked by the illusion of principle, in Japan it is masked by the illusion of benevolence." (*Karel van Wolferen, The Enigma of Japanese Power: People and Power in a Stateless Nation, New York: Alfred A. Knopf, 1989, p. 202*)

   Note: You may find it easier to work with example 2b if you first convert the passive statements it contains into their active counterparts.

3. Like fish that are unaware of the water that makes up their physical environment, we are often unaware of phenomena that surround us in our *language* environment. Look at the examples below. What are

their presuppositions? That is, identify statements that are part of their meaning but do not appear in their surface structure—as "John is a rotten student" and "the class is trivially easy" do not appear in the surface structure of "EVen JOHN could pass THAT class."

a. "Fruit consumption has tripled in Alabama."

b. "I'm so glad you managed to win the award."

c. "No one in this department was reluctant to humor you about your title."

d. "Why don't you let us see ALL the sales figures?"

e. "It's wonderful that you've finally been promoted."

f. "His minor arthritis pain is acting up."

g. "Today our CEO didn't put his foot in his mouth even once."

h. "Oh, turn blue!"

i. "That jacket makes you look slender!"

j. "War broke out in the Bedapedap Republic today."

4. For your Communication Strategy Notebook, set up a Presupposition Power file and begin keeping track of relevant information. For example:

- Record incidents in which you followed the rules for using the power of presuppositions, to serve as a database for planning strategies. What was the situation? Who was present? In what utterances did you use presuppositions as a strategic move? What was the response? What happened? What was surprising? Did anything go wrong, and if so, can you determine why? If you had it to do over again, would you do it differently? What changes would you make?

- Use the same procedure to record and analyze incidents in which you observed others using presupposition power in language interactions.

- Set up a page on which you list words or phrases that are *Presuppositional Trojan Horses*. Like "manage to," which presupposes that the person who managed to do whatever it was had a great deal of trouble accomplishing that. Or the verb "admit," as in "Many people admitted that they had been mugged," which presupposes that they felt they were in some way in the wrong. Such items seem innocuous enough and may often slip right by the listener, leaving him or her with a vague, uneasy feeling later of having missed something important but having no idea what it might have been.

Be sure to make a special note of items that you discover have one presupposition in a particular language variety but not in another. For example, for most adult male speakers of American Mainstream English, the word "violence" presupposes that the act described could have been *avoided.* For most female speakers of AME this presupposition is not part of the definition of violence. This semantic difference lies at the heart of many cross-gender communication breakdowns.

8

"But I Said Exactly the Right Words!"

Increasing the Power of Your Body Language

"Everyone in the firm knows that you are all strongly opposed to switching to computers," said Jessica Sharp. "They know, and they understand. I certainly understand; I felt the same way myself not so long ago. It's not easy to give up equipment and processes that have become almost second nature and begin over again with something completely new and unfamiliar."

"Then why do you keep asking us to do it?" demanded Ann White, who was the most senior of the clerical staff. "It's hard enough to keep up with the work load now, when we know what we're doing!" There were murmurs of agreement from the other four; Jim Britain, the only man among them, said nothing, but the look on his face eloquently expressed his contempt for the proposed change.

Jessica's heart sank; she would have liked a response that was just a little more open-minded...not to mention a little more *polite*. She saw no reason why the group had to be so rude and so uncooperative. But they were *always* this way, and she was in no way surprised; she went on determinedly.

"Your question is well taken, Ann," she said. "And you are quite right. It will be harder for you to get the work done, and that's going to be a problem for everyone here. But it's a transition that must be made. I'm sure you realize that no one would suggest this move if it weren't absolutely necessary. And I'd like to explain to you the three reasons why we can't postpone it any longer."

Five stony faces stared back at her, silently; it was, as the cliché has it, like talking to a wall.

It got no better. Although Jessica presented all three of her arguments calmly and carefully, in words that she had spent many long hours honing until she was sure they were *exactly the right and perfect words*, she could tell that she was getting nowhere. It looked as though the firm was going to have to choose between the risk of losing the entire clerical staff and the risk of being the only law firm in the state with its clerical work still being done on typewriters.

I've failed with this bunch of turkeys again, Jessica thought miserably. *They are so stubborn, and so set in their ways, and so indifferent to the needs of this company, that I just can't get through to them.*

What's Going on Here?

This is the briefest scenario in the book, and probably the most frustrating for the reader. You're being told that Jessica, office manager for this law firm, has compelling arguments that are being expressed in the most perfect words possible. But you're not being given a chance to read those words; you're being asked to take it on faith that they are as described.

I'm not doing this to you arbitrarily; I *too* have compelling arguments. The problem is that this is a scenario for which you need an audiotape (or a multimedia format) instead of a book. Reading Jessica's words, no matter how well chosen, won't clarify the situation for you; you need to *hear* them, and that's an experience I'm unable to provide. There is therefore no point in making the text longer, nor would it be useful to return to this particular scenario later in the chapter. Our best course under the circumstances is to move on to discussion and explanation.

Jessica's Point of View

As Jessica sees things, anyone who hasn't spent the last ten years living under a rock *has* to be aware that modern companies cannot function successfully without computer capability and staffs trained to put that capability into action. The switch to electronics at her firm is years overdue; the necessity for it is obvious and beyond all question. But this isn't the only time she's had trouble with the clerical staff; she *always* has trouble with them. They are capable and competent people; she wouldn't have kept them on otherwise. But she considers them the most pigheaded group of individuals she has ever encountered in her life, and everything she wants of them is a struggle.

Because she's convinced that she would be more successful with them if she were more physically attractive, Jessica has been through several expensive "makeover" programs, but that hasn't improved matters. The five employees are the bane of her existence, and she has to fight the temptation to hope they all *will* quit, complicated as that would make her life for a while, so that she can replace them with new people who are *already* part of the twentieth century.

The Clerical Staff's Point of View

As the staffers see it, Jessica spends all her time bothering them and being a pain in the neck. It would be one thing if she'd just talk, but she doesn't. She *whines* at them. Listening to her reminds those in the group who have small children of their worst experiences with their offspring.

They not only don't feel that Jessica deserves their respect and cooperation, they cannot understand why the law firm keeps her on. She must know too much about the skeletons in somebody's closet, they feel, or she'd have been let go long since. They've tried complaining to the firm's attorneys about her, but have accomplished nothing useful, because Jessica hasn't *done* anything they can explicitly object to. The response is always the same: "You can't expect us to take negative action against Jessica Sharp—who is a loyal and competent and hardworking employee—just because you don't like her!" They are therefore determined to do everything they possibly can to make Jessica's life as office manager difficult, in the hope that she will become so frustrated and discouraged that she'll give up and go work somewhere else.

What Went Wrong?

This situation, like the "talking to a wall" line, is a cliché among workplace problems. I see it a dozen times a year; I have experienced it many times in my own life. It has two predictable characteristics:

1. One person in the group has a voice that falls far short of the mainstream ideal for American English in the United States today. The effect of the voice is so negative that it becomes a *twirk*—a characteristic of someone's language that is so distracting and/or annoying that it outweighs logic, facts, and style. And every attempt that person makes at communication with the others breaks down in one way or another as a result.

2. Everyone in the group, including the person whose voice is the source of the problem, concludes that the reason for the communication breakdown lies outside the realm of language. The breakdown is blamed on character flaws, or physical appearance, or ethnic heritage, or any one of dozens of other factors that actually have little or nothing to do with it.

In Jessica's case the problem is simply that she has a high-pitched nasal voice. She doesn't know that that's what's wrong. She thinks the problem is the character of the employees. They are, she is convinced, stubborn, uncooperative, spoiled, and indifferent to the needs of the firm. She also believes that they are prejudiced and narrow-minded— prejudiced against anyone who, like her, fails to meet their absurd standards for youth and slenderness and "beauty" in the fashionable sense of the word.

In the employees' case, the problem is their conviction that the trouble is all due to Jessica's *personality*. They don't know she believes they let her appearance interfere with their judgment, or that she makes efforts to overcome that bias. They see her as a pleasant-looking well-dressed woman in her 50s; her appearance isn't something they even think about. They could not care less about her looks. What they object to is the way she whines and nags at them. And although they assume she likes them no better than they like her, they would be astonished to hear the long list of negative characteristics she attributes to them. It is, they believe, just a "personality clash."

If people's voices were like their height, or like the size and shape of their ears—something they were essentially *stuck* with and could do nothing about—this classic situation would be rather tragic. You would observe it and think, "What a shame! If only he/she hadn't been born with that awful voice! What terribly bad luck!" But in fact, except in cases of actual physical disorder or deformity, a voice that interferes with successful communication *can* be changed. For many people, no investment of time or other resources they could make would do more to improve their lives and their careers than that of improving the quality of their voice. What *is* tragic is that most of the time they don't realize that this is what needs to be done. Instead, they assume that their problems are the result of some extralinguistic factor, and they make endless efforts to change *that*. They trek from one effectiveness seminar to another, from one health spa to another, from one image consultant to another, always trying to meet the standard they feel others are holding them to—and it never helps.

You may feel that this could not apply to you. You may be convinced that any problems you have with interpersonal relations in your workplace are fully explained by your height or weight. Or by your accent. Or by the fact that you didn't attend an Ivy League school like your colleagues did. Or by the fact that you're an Asian-American, or a Southerner, or a woman. You may be convinced that you have problems because the people you have to deal with are incompetent, or weird, or ignorant—or worse. *You could be wrong; the problem could be your voice.*

We need to stop and consider this issue in detail and with great care. Because much of what people believe about the voice and its effects is based on misconceptions or outright errors of fact. And because it's almost impossible to *over*emphasize the importance of the voice in communication strategy.

Communication Technique: Simultaneous Modeling for Voice Quality and Control

Three points must be established before we can move to the instructions for the technique of simultaneous modeling. All three frequently meet with considerable surprise in my seminars and among my clients—usually because they run counter to popular wisdom.

1. For English, nonverbal communication (informally called *body language*) is far more powerful than words. There are no words so well chosen that their meaning cannot be changed or cancelled by body language. And for English, the voice is the most powerful component of nonverbal communication.

2. What we American English speakers perceive as a desirable voice—like what we perceive as a desirable accent—is entirely a matter of *fashion.*

3. Except in the case of disorders or disabilities that require expert attention (and perhaps medical attention), anyone who wants to improve his or her voice and learn to control it effectively can do so.

The Power of Nonverbal Communication

Our culture places great emphasis on having a powerful vocabulary, and much money is spent on programs intended to provide one.

Standardized tests—which almost never test *oral* language—rely heavily on vocabulary. It's probably inevitable that we tend to get the impression that if we only knew the perfect words to say, we could easily fulfill our communication responsibilities. But the facts about spoken English in the United States prove that this cluster of ideas has little validity.

You need the exact and perfect words when the message is about such things as what time an airplane leaves, how much a stock costs, and what dosage of a medication is being prescribed how many times a day. Absolutely. In written language, where body language isn't present to affect meaning, exact and perfect words matter far more. But the evidence for spoken English is very clear. (I keep saying "for English" because it's critically important to know that this information is true *of* English, and cannot be relied upon to be true for any other language.) Here are the statistics, in their most *conservative* form:

- At least 90 percent of all *emotional* information is carried not by the words but by the body language that accompanies the words.

- At least 65 percent of all information whatsoever is carried not by the words spoken but by the body language.

In the 1980s attorney Peter D. Blanck and his associates began a series of experiments to measure the power of body language in our courtrooms. They had discovered a pattern in California criminal trials: If the judge was aware that the accused had had a prior conviction, juries were *twice* as likely to convict as when no such conviction existed—despite the fact that the judge is forbidden by law to share this information with the jury. Even when statistical weighting was done to compensate for the obvious fact that people who have a prior conviction are somewhat more *likely* to be guilty, the frequency of conviction was far too high to be chance. Somehow, the judge's feelings were being leaked to the juries.

Blanck and his colleagues assembled many videotapes of nearly identical trials. (Everything about their setting was prescribed by law, the offenses were comparable, the judges read the same printed instructions to the jurors, etc.) They analyzed the written transcripts. They analyzed the videos by freeze-frame analysis, microsecond by microsecond. They analyzed the sound tracks for the videos in similar detail, including a step that would not have been possible until recently—that of removing the *content* of the speech and listening only to the intonation. When all the analysis was completed, the results were unambiguous: *What gave away each judge's personal feelings to the jury was the intonation of her or his voice.* And *all* leakage was due to nonverbal communication rather than to words; this is to be expected, since prejudicial words are forbidden and lead to mistrials. (See Blanck et al., 1985, for complete details of this research.)

This is anything but trivial. It calls into question the fairness of our entire jury system. It proves that a judge with excellent voice quality and control can, if he or she chooses, influence the verdicts of trials in a way that is supposed to be impossible. The American Bar Association's response to Blanck's findings in this and subsequent experiments has been to create a special training program on nonverbal communication for use by lawyers and judges and to promote it vigorously, in the hope that a full *awareness* of the situation will make it better. Meanwhile, the research continues.

Naturally, most people do not want this to be true; it's the sort of thing most of us would far rather not know. We have so many things that we must take responsibility for already! The idea that we also have to take responsibility for the possible consequences of our body language is appalling. Nevertheless, these are the facts, and they will not go away. That being the case, we need to hone our body language skills, both projective and receptive, with particular emphasis on the use of the voice.

The "Ideal" Voice, for American Mainstream English

Much of what you read about the differences between male and female American Mainstream English is unreliable. But there is no question about the advantage most male speakers gain from their male voices, because the favored voice in the United States today is the deep and resonant and nonnasal voice usually associated with the adult *male*. Speakers of either gender whose voices are high-pitched are linguistically handicapped by that characteristic; when their voices are also nasal and/or breathy, the situation is even worse.

Because women's voices are more likely to be high-pitched than men's, they face a serious barrier to communication effectiveness: Their voices are all too often perceived, usually below the level of conscious awareness, as *the voices of children.* When the voice is also nasal, it is perceived as the voice of a *whiny* child. When we hear a voice from the burning bush in movies about the Bible, that voice never belongs to a woman, of *any* age, and it is never John Denver's voice. It's always the voice of Charlton Heston or James Earl Jones.

This has nothing whatever to do with logic, or even with common sense; it is a matter of *fashion*. There is no logical reason why speech that is otherwise adequate in every way should be less effective only because it is has these unfashionable characteristics. In a just world, what people say would be judged on its content; ours is not a just world. It has little to do with physiology, either. The differences between the male and the female vocal tract are far too small to account for the typical pitch difference. There are a number of countries in this world in which the favored *male* voice is higher-pitched than the typical American female voice. No physiological barrier prevents most women (or men) from pitching their voices low enough to be perceived as adults.

I want to make it very clear what I am *not* saying: I am not saying that anyone whose voice is high-pitched *should*, in some moral or aesthetic sense, deliberately pitch it low. What I *am* saying is that not to do so is inevitably a barrier to effective communication—an irrational and unfair barrier, but a barrier nonetheless. Anyone whose voice constitutes such a barrier, who knows that to be the case, and who decides as a matter of principle to make no changes, has my full support. But it's unacceptable for such people to be unaware that the barrier exists—leading them to blame their communication problems on non-linguistic factors like physical appearance, ethnic heritage, etc. And it is not acceptable for them to believe that they are stuck with an undesirable voice unless they can afford to spend years training with a professional voice coach.

Gaining Control of Your Voice

Your first step is to get a clear idea of how your voice really sounds— to *other* people. You can do this by making a tape of yourself talking. Almost any currently produced tape recorder will do. Obviously you don't want one that you picked up at a yard sale after 17 teenagers have worked their will on it, but the sort of machine you can buy for less than $50 at Radio Shack is perfectly adequate. The tape itself, however, should be of very good quality—not the three-for-a-dollar kind. Sit down and make your tape *in complete privacy*; talk about your favorite food or the teacher you disliked most or what you think of Congress. Don't read aloud; don't make a speech; just *talk*. The first five minutes or so will probably be of no use because you'll be so self-conscious, but that will wear off; keep talking until it does, and then get ten minutes of tape that sounds the way you actually do sound when you're talking in a relaxed fashion. (If you find yourself literally unable to get past the self-conscious stage, get permission from someone close to you to make tapes of the two of you in ordinary conversation, and keep taping until you *do* get ten minutes of your natural speech.) Put the tape away for at least 24 hours, and then go back and listen to it carefully.

For many people this listening process is a shock, and their immediate reaction is, "I couldn't <u>possibly</u> sound like that!" It has always been considered courteous to tell them that they're probably right and that they only hear themselves that way because sound conducted through air is different from sound conducted through bone, and so on. This may have been sensible in the past, but no more. With the kind of recording equipment available to us today, *the way you sound to yourself on that tape is almost certainly the way you sound to other people.* If you're convinced that it has to be a flaw in the equipment, try it again with a different recorder and a new tape; if you sound no different, you can rely on the result.

After you've made this baseline tape and listened to it, you may decide that you're entirely satisfied with your voice just as it is. In that case, you can skip the instructions for simultaneous modeling that are coming up below and go straight to the section on voice control that follows. Otherwise, put your baseline tape away somewhere secure, with a date on it for your reference, and read on.

Unquestionably, the *easiest* (and usually the quickest) way to improve your voice is to put yourself in the hands of an expert voice coach, just as the easiest and quickest way to improve your golf swing is to engage the services of a golf pro. But expert voice coaches with top qualifications and good references from satisfied clients are not found on every corner; they are expensive; and they of course require a regularly scheduled investment of your time. Many people can't find a coach, can't afford one, can't make time for the regular appointments, or simply prefer not to take on the commitment necessary. This does *not* mean that they cannot substantially improve their voice using the technique of simultaneous modeling.

Instructions for Simultaneous Modeling

We are accustomed in this culture to learning things by being given explicit instruction, followed by a demonstration of how much (or how little) we've learned through testing. This isn't the only way to learn, nor is it always the best way. It would be very hard to learn to walk by reading a book or listening to a lecture. When what you are learning is primarily movements of your body, much of the process is not available for your direct observation unless you are wired up to electronic monitors of some sort. Such learning then has to take place for the most part below the level of your direct conscious awareness.

The traditional methods of language teaching ignore the fact that learning the physical act of speech requires mastery of a multitude of body movements and adjustments about which you can't possibly know much. The way people sound as they speak depends on such matters as how much they tense the muscles of their vocal tract, how much they move their diaphragm and expand their rib cage, how high in the mouth they hold their tongue and how tense the tongue is, and whether they do or do not vibrate their vocal cords. If you speak in front of a mirror you can directly observe how much you round your lips and you can see some of the movements of your tongue, but by and large all of this process is as far beyond your powers of observation as the flood of neurotransmitters your brain sends throughout your body to make it possible.

However, as George Miller says, "The brain is a mismatch detector." If you just provide it with the necessary input and refrain from interfering, your brain can monitor all these physiological matters expertly for you.

This means that teaching someone language by having them listen to an utterance and then repeating what they heard—the standard method—is a very poor way to proceed. Instead, they should speak *with* the modeled utterance, simultaneously, just as *tai chi* students learn its system of movements by moving simultaneously *with* their instructor rather than by watching and then trying to repeat afterward alone. This is how foreign languages are taught in the courses of the University of California San Diego in the program developed by linguist Leonard Newmark. It works so well that students there typically achieve the same proficiency after one quarter of instruction that students learning by the traditional methods demonstrate after an entire year.

Speaking *with* a model stream of speech, live or recorded, lets your brain do what it knows how to do: *It monitors the two streams of sound, notes where they differ, and makes all the many tiny adjustments necessary to match your speech to the model.* You can't make those adjustments yourself by conscious effort, but your brain can do it superbly if you just let it happen. Here are the steps you follow:

1. Choose someone as your voice model, someone whose voice you perceive as desirable and admirable. Choose someone of your own gender and approximate age. Don't choose anyone whose voice is

considered exotic or unusual—not Michael Jackson or Jimmy Durante or any of the Gabor sisters. Unless you have *very* good reason to believe that your accent is a handicap to you, choose someone who speaks the same variety of English you speak. Otherwise, choose a model whose accent is the one you aspire to.

2. Get a 20- to 30-minute tape of your model speaker. It makes no difference whether you make the tape yourself or buy a commercial recording, as long as the tape quality is good. If you've chosen one of the anchor persons on National Public Radio (who are excellent choices), most radios you buy today are equipped to let you tape programs right off the air. Diane Sawyer is a model I often recommend for women, as is Whoopi Goldberg; Peter Jennings is a very good choice for men.

3. Listen to your tape all the way through once to become familiar with its *content*. Don't try to remember it; just get a rough idea of what it's about.

4. Choose a sentence of moderate length from the tape to work with. DON'T WRITE IT DOWN; DON'T MEMORIZE IT.

5. Listen to the sentence you've chosen once or twice, to become familiar with what it says.

6. Now, say that sentence *with the tape,* simultaneously.

7. Rewind to the beginning of the sentence and repeat step 6. Do this at least five times; ten is not too many.

8. Choose another sentence and repeat steps 5 through 7.

When you've worked with a tape so long that you know it by heart or are terribly bored with it, get another one and proceed in exactly the same way. The more time you spend at this, the more quickly you will progress; three 20-minute sessions a week is the bare minimum.

After you've completed roughly six hours of this process (and at the end of each six hours thereafter) make a *new* tape of your own natural speech like the one you did at the very beginning. Listen to it carefully; compare it with your baseline tape if that seems helpful. *When you feel that your own speech is improved to the degree that you are satisfied with it, STOP.* Your goal is not to continue the process until you match the model's voice so perfectly that the two of you could not be told apart. You're not trying to learn to do Diane Sawyer or Peter Jennings *impersonations*; your goal is to keep your *own* voice but to substantially improve its quality. If you've been working with a Diane Sawyer tape and your friends start saying, "Gosh, you sound just like Diane *Sawyer*," you've kept at it too long, and you'll need to get a different model tape to help you *un*learn Sawyer's voice.

Some people will be able to complete this change very quickly; for others, it will take a long time. It doesn't matter. You do this at your own speed, at your own convenience, and at almost no cost. There is no "correct" number of hours that it should take. Your speed will depend on your motivation, on how much time you can spend in simultaneous modeling, on how different your speech is from the model speech, on how old you are, on how many languages you speak, on whether hearing is your preferred sensory system, and other factors. As a *very* rough guide, it would not be unusual for a person 40 years of age, who speaks only English fluently and can manage only two or three sessions a week, to need six months to a year, or even longer. The point is that the change will happen and that it is under your control; it's not a contest and there is no exam to pass.

And what if you do in fact have a medical problem that interferes with your speech? In that case, it's reasonable to assume that you won't be able to achieve the results you otherwise could. However, it's also reasonable to assume that you *will* be able to make changes that are positive. Where the voice is concerned, even very small changes toward the fashionable ideal will pay back your investment of time and energy many times over.

Finally, here are two exercises (the first is a classic from voice teachers everywhere) that will increase your ability to consciously control your voice.

1. Choose a familiar simple song—"Three Blind Mice" or "Twinkle Twinkle Little Star" are about right. Instead of singing the melody to the song, speak it. That is, change your voice to produce the pitch changes in the tune, but never let yourself switch from speaking to singing.

    This is most definitely not easy to do, nor is it something you'd want to in public, but it's excellent training. As you do it, pay close attention to how it feels to speak at particular pitches; you want to gain some conscious awareness of what your vocal tract is doing. When you get good at the simple songs, choose a difficult one.

2. Working with a sequence of memorized language (or with nonsense syllables), and speaking aloud, try to perceive your stream of speech as a ribbon coming from your mouth. Make the ribbon rise and fall; make it describe lines or curves or figures. As above, pay close attention to how it feels when you do these things, so that you will learn to get feedback as you speak.

When you begin to feel comfortable with this, start doing the same sort of monitoring during real speech. Your goal is for the control to become automatic, so that you don't have to think about it while you're speaking.

As I warned you above, going back to Scenario Eight would be a waste of time. However, it will now be clear to you that if Jessica Sharp wants to communicate more effectively, she will have to take steps to improve the quality of her voice. It might help a little for the staffers to be made aware of the facts about nonverbal communication, so that when they are listening to Jessica they can try to listen with a more open mind. But that effort—having to say to themselves, "Now I have to remember to concentrate on what she's saying and not on her voice!" while they listen—will also interfere with their ability to process her language. It's no solution.

WORKOUT SECTION: CHAPTER 8

1. Your television set is a superb "exercise machine" for building your body language skills, as both sender and receiver of messages: It's always available, costs almost nothing, and is indifferent to your behavior. That's almost perfection. (The reason for the "almost" is that much televised communication is very different from real-world language.) When you're interacting with real people, you need to be so good at interpreting and remembering their body language that you can do that while carrying on your part of the communication with ease and without making others aware that you're tracking their body language. The best way to learn how to do that is to work with the television set. Here are some ways to take advantage of what it offers:

Many people—especially men—find it hard even to pay attention to body language, much less remember it after an interaction. But with more than half of all messages (and 90 percent of all emotional information) being carried by nonverbal communication, it's obvious that this is a skill you *must* have if you are to achieve understanding and commitment for your proposed strategies. It's easiest to learn it in stages.

a. Begin by watching television programs where people are talking to one another, with the sound turned completely off, so that there's nothing to distract you from the movements they're making. Observe carefully; take notes. As soon as you feel that you're getting the hang of it, turn the sound up just slightly: You want to be able to hear the intonation—the tune the words are set to—but you don't want to be able to understand the words themselves. Observe carefully; take notes. Finally, repeat the same activity with the sound at a normal setting. (You'll find this easier to do if you set up a page with columns for the various body parts you're observing and then enter the data under those headings: Chin, Hands, Feet, Knees, Eyebrows, and so on.)

b. Spend some sessions concentrating your attention on the individual body parts of the televised speakers. Watch only their chins for ten minutes; then watch only their elbows; then only their feet, and so on.

c. Watch the speakers with the sound completely off. Can you determine from their body language alone what emotion(s) they're feeling as they talk? Make a decision; then turn the sound up and check to see if you were correct.

d. When you feel comfortable with the three activities above, stop taking notes. Observe, as always, for 15 minutes. Then turn off the set and write down as much as you can remember of the body language you've been watching.

Another body language skill critical to good communication is the process called *interactional synchrony*. When people are really listening, their body language is *synchronized* with the speaker's body language. This doesn't mean that the listeners make the *same* movements the speaker makes, but that when the speaker moves the listeners move, and at the same rate of speed—as if the speaker were <u>conducting</u>. (When you're talking and this doesn't happen, you know that your audience *isn't* really listening.)

Try watching the televised language interactions WITHOUT MOVING A SINGLE MUSCLE, HOLDING ABSOLUTELY STILL. Can you do it? Can you understand what's being said while you do it? Try deliberately moving *exactly* with a televised speaker (a process called *shadowing*, or *mirroring*.) Can you do it? Can you understand what's being said while you do it?

2. When you begin to find working with the television set easy to do, switch to working with real people. *Warning:* Never try mirroring with a real person unless you have explained what you are doing and have permission. Except under those circumstances, mirroring is very dangerous. If you're caught at it—and most people will be—you can expect intense (and well-deserved) anger and resentment.

3. Edward T. Hall writes that the Japanese not only pay attention to others who are speaking, they deliberately synchronize their breathing with the speaker's breathing. Try that; try the same thing for the rate and speed at which you blink your eyes; try nodding, almost imperceptibly, in rhythm with the speaker.

This can be extremely useful, especially for dealing with someone who should not go on talking—like the individual who decides to take over your presentation from the floor and give it *for* you, or the colleague who loses his or her temper in public and is clearly going to go too far in expressing emotions. You can stop such displays by openly acknowledging that they're happening and asking (or ordering) the person to cut it out. But that causes loss of face. Before doing anything so drastic, make and hold eye contact with the person who has hijacked your presentation, or with your out-of-control colleague; synchronize your breathing and eye blink; add the synchronized nodding. You may want to also begin saying "Mmhmm" or "I understand" with each nod. Then, when the two of you are perfectly matched, slow down your *own* rate of breathing, eye blink, and nodding, gradually, until you are moving very slowly indeed. When you do this well, the other person will slow down *with* you and dwindle away into silence. At which point you break eye contact and take back the linguistic floor as if nothing had happened.

4. Speakers of American Mainstream English have rarely complained in the past about the inadequacy of English punctuation for conveying body language. Perhaps this was because with written communication there was a lot of time to work and rework the message to get it exactly right, and there was no way the person being written to could come back at you with a swift response to which you had to react quickly. But recently, with the extraordinary increase in written communication by computer, this has all changed. In computer interactions only the person who sends the opening message has time for leisurely consideration; the interaction goes very fast, once begun. People have reacted to this by creating what are called *emoticons*—a new kind of punctuation that uses existing keyboard symbols to do the work body language does in face-to-face communication. For example:

:-)	means "I'm smiling as I write this."
;-)	means "I'm winking and smiling as I write; I'm only kidding."
:+p+	"I'm sticking out my tongue at you as I write this."
:D	"I have a huge grin on my face as I write this."

What do you think? Should there be emoticons in off-line written communication? In contracts and proposals and reports of minutes from meetings? In memos? Are there some emoticons you'd really like to have?

5. Popular books on body language are often misleading; it's not safe to assume that particular postures and gestures and facial expressions reliably "mean" particular messages. Even when the information has some validity, it will be true only for a single cultural group—usually the dominant middle or upper class white adult male. However, there's one principle of nonverbal communication that you *can* count on: *Mismatch is a warning sign.* It's not true that a person who speaks to you in high pitch is probably lying. It's not true that a person whose pupils dilate as you talk is demonstrating agreement with what you're saying. It *is* true that when there is a *change* in the body language of your listener, a deviation from that person's usual nonverbal patterns, it signals you that something is going on and you should go to maximum alert. High pitch, in and of itself, doesn't signal an attempt to deceive; higher pitch than is usual for a particular individual often does, and certainly signals tension. The sudden widening of pupils doesn't signal agreement, but it does let you know that there has been an emotional reaction. Whether it's positive or negative is something you have to find out.

You can use this information to improve the chances of your presentations substantially. In the same way that you have begun recording people's preferred sensory modes and Satir Modes, set up a Body Language Record in your notebook for people you interact with and compile records of the body language that is typical of them when they are involved in casual communication. Suppose the baseline you want to establish is for your boss. Get the answers to questions like these:

How fast does he or she usually talk?
How high is the person's voice pitched?
How rapidly does he or she breathe?
How rapid is the person's eyeblink, and how often does it happen?
What is his or her usual body position when sitting down? When standing?
What are the person's typical hand movements?
How are his or her shoulders usually held?
Is there laughter or throat clearing?
How often does he or she smile?

Get the information to establish the baseline profile and be sure you're familiar with it before you go into an interaction with that person. Then watch for mismatch, the deviation from the baseline that means something is happening. (If you have to go into an interaction with someone you don't know, you can get a lot of the baseline information from a telephone conversation on some neutral subject.) This is difficult at first, but with practice, it will all become automatic; you'll do it without any conscious effort. As with all the techniques in this book, you can speed up your mastery of the skills involved by working through practice sessions in teams of three.

6. For your Communication Strategy Notebook, set up a Body Language file and begin keeping track of relevant information to serve as a database for planning strategies. For example:

- Record incidents in which you used body language as a part of your communication strategy. What was the situation? Who was present? What nonverbal communication items (or clusters of items) did you use? What happened? What was surprising? Did anything go wrong, and if so, can you determine why? If you had it to do over again, what would you do differently?
- In the same way, record incidents in which you noticed that someone *else's* body language led to a consequence worth remembering and learning from.

- If possible, have someone videotape you during a language interaction (with the permission of everyone involved, of course). Then watch the video and analyze your body language carefully in your notebook.

7. If you're not happy with your own body language, you can use the technique of simultaneous modeling to improve it. Just work with a *videotape* of someone whose nonverbal communication you admire. First, talk along with your model, as you do when working with the tape recorder to improve voice quality. Next, *move* with the model, without trying to match the spoken words. Finally, do both—speak and move simultaneously with your model speaker. As always, don't keep this up so long that you appear to be attempting an *impersonation* of the other speaker. Stop as soon as you're satisfied with your progress.

9

"And As I Was Saying... But I Digress..."

Using the Power of Metaphor for Rapid Change

Scenario Nine

"Sure, downsizing and outsourcing is the big fad right now," said Hugh Nelson, "and everybody's doing it. I know that. And just how many fads have we been through in the past ten years? Remember quality circles?"

The listening managers nodded; yes, they remembered quality circles.

"At the time," Hugh went on (and he held up the well-worn book the company had used as its guide during that phase, turning from side to side to make sure that every single member had a good view, holding each position a good ten seconds to make *doubly* sure), "there was no such thing as reading a business magazine without having to wade through yet one more article claiming that any company that didn't go for quality circles was headed for bankruptcy. I can even remember...."

"Hugh?" That was Tomas Martinez, head of marketing.

"Yes, Tomas?"

"You were going to give us the figures your committee put together—the figures this meeting was supposed to be <u>about</u>. I wonder if you could just move on to those so we could get down to cases?"

Hugh sighed, long and deep.

"I <u>told</u> you, Tomas, I'm getting to that," he said patiently. "There's a certain amount of <u>preparation</u> that's necessary if the figures are to make any <u>sense</u>."

"But, Hugh," Carolyn Anderson put in, "you've been doing 'preparation,' as you call it, for nearly ten <u>minutes</u> now!"

Hugh's eyebrows went up, and his mouth drew narrow and tight and prim. "If you have more pressing matters to attend to, Carolyn, I certainly wouldn't want to keep you <u>here</u>."

Carolyn cleared her throat. "Sorry, Hugh," she said. "Go on, please. We shouldn't have interrupted you."

They were all looking down at the presentation folders on the table in front of them now, Hugh noticed. It annoyed him. What was the point of all his effort to put this presentation together for them if they didn't even have the courtesy to listen to what he was saying?

"If I could have your attention, please," he said firmly, "I'd like to get back to our subject." And he waited. <u>He</u> knew what courtesy was; he waited with no sign of impatience.

When he was satisfied that every one of them was looking right at him, he said, "That's better. <u>Thank</u> you! Now, as I was saying, the fad for downsizing and outsourcing has been sweeping this country—and doing terrible harm to the economy in the process. It reminds me of a time when I was in the infantry, and...."

"Darn it all, Hugh!" Spencer Evans broke in. Spencer ran public relations. "<u>Don't</u> tell us about your war experiences again! Just report the figures the committee came up with, and get <u>on</u> with it!"

Hugh stared at him. That hurt. It really hurt. "Spencer," he said, "we are all well aware here of your left-wing opinions about the armed services of this great country. It's not necessary for you to make a public display of them."

"Hugh, my opinions have <u>nothing</u> to do with <u>anything</u>!" Spencer protested.

"<u>You</u> said it," Hugh pointed out, chuckling, "not <u>me</u>!"

There was a thick silence, and that was all right with Hugh. *I can give as good as I get,* he thought, well satisfied with the point he had scored over Evans, *and they'd better remember that.*

"Now," he said, "as I was saying..."

What's Going on Here?

Misery is going on here. *Boredom* and *frustration* are going on here. And we can be sure that Hugh Nelson is one of the founders of this company, or a close relative of one of the founders, or has some other hold on his position that is not connected to his skill as a speaker and persuader, or that some other special circumstance is in effect. If this were not the case, he would never have been allowed to attempt this presentation.

Hugh's Point of View

Hugh is honestly opposed to the idea that the company should begin letting permanent employees go and shifting tasks to temporary help and independent contractors. He has seen the figures comparing the costs; he knows what a saving it would be not only in salaries but in health care and other benefits. But he's convinced that in the *long* term it would be a grave mistake. He did an excellent job as devil's advocate on the preliminary committee, turning what would otherwise have been a shallow job, rushed through by a group of people with their minds already made up, into a *real* investigation of the issue. And now he is prepared to take the same dogged stance with the managers, all of whom he regards as lazy and self-indulgent. He knows the down-sizing proposal may go through anyway, but it's not going to happen because of inadequate coverage of the *facts*; Hugh will see to that. He's accustomed to being treated rudely and can tolerate a lot of that; he's determined that the managers *will* hear him out, no matter how much they would like to just slide through the material in their usual slapdash fashion.

It causes Hugh considerable distress that his hard work and loyalty and long experience inspire no respect in the managers. It seems to him to be unjust, and he resents it deeply. But he knows his duty and he intends to *do* it, even if he has to drag every manager in the room through the process kicking and screaming. And he is baffled: How come *they* are managers, and *he*, who goes out of his way to give 150 percent and has been with the company longer than any of them, is still just one of the *troops?*

The Managers' Points of View

The managers know that Hugh has every single smallest detail of the necessary information stored away in his head; he's famous for that. They know that if they are to carry out downsizing without destroying morale in the employees they *don't* let go, they will have to be able to explain and justify their actions to those people. They need to know what arguments they're likely to encounter from the staff that remains, so they can prepare adequate responses. Hugh is the best possible representative of the resistant conservatives who will be hard to win over; that was the whole point of assembling a committee to do a thorough preliminary investigation and putting Hugh in charge of it. The managers *need* the information Hugh has, and they'd very much like to get it from him.

But the way he drones on endlessly—wandering off every sentence or two into digressions about matters that have nothing to do with the subject and are tedious beyond bearing—drives them berserk. The habit he has of preparing minutely detailed charts and tables and figures and then insisting on reading all that detail *aloud* to his audience is enough to drive a saint to drink. They were all in agreement that assigning him the task would give them a taste of what was ahead, and that it would be worth it to let him demonstrate the scope of the problem. Now that it's happening, however, they're wishing they'd made some other decision. The day Hugh finally has to retire, every single one of them will go out and celebrate; in the meantime, they will do their best to endure him when he can't be avoided. And they are baffled, one and all. How can a man who is so knowledgeable and so dedicated, and who has so many years of experience, not *realize* how intolerably boring he is when he talks?

What Went Wrong?

We have all known people like poor Hugh Nelson—devoted, loyal, intelligent, hardworking, reliable, *boring,* people. We have all felt guilty because we could not control our irritation in spite of all we knew about their good points. We have felt guilty when we caught ourselves ducking into offices we weren't headed for, just because we saw those people coming down the hall toward us. We have been ashamed when we caught ourselves hoping that they would sprain an ankle or catch the flu...anything to keep them home a while and out of our hair.

This is unfortunate. There ought to be a way to make the playing field more level for such people, so that their basic goodness and good service—the qualities that make others put up with them in spite of their language behavior—can be rewarded. And of course there *is* a way. Hugh Nelson (or anyone like him) can be put into the hands of a team of top-notch communication consultants who will train him, over time, to talk in a way that is not the equivalent of two tranquilizers with a whiskey chaser. Other chapters in this book describe many things Hugh can learn to do, with help or on his own, that would improve his performance when he tries to talk to other people. In this chapter, however, we'll take the results of all those experts for granted and concentrate on just *one* strategic change that Hugh can make: that of using metaphors to cut away vast amounts of potentially boring detail.

Communication Technique:
Using Metaphors

Suppose you've been listening to me present a plan for a new project that your firm is about to begin work on. Suppose that I have so far confined myself to laying out the details that everyone *must* remember, and I'm winding down. Suppose I now look at you, add an appropriate gesture, and say only these two words: "Wagons, HO!"

If you are a native speaker of American Mainstream English, raised in this culture, that will mean many things to you. Here are just four of them:

- The project is going to be hard work, but it will be an exciting adventure that pays off in the long run.

- In order to reach our goal, we will all have to work together, filling the roles other people rely on us to fill.

- Some of the things that happen to us during the project may be not only new but also frightening, and we will need to face them with courage.

- You can count on your leaders to be out ahead of you, breaking trail, always on the alert for both hazards and benefits.

How do you know all that? How can two words, three small syllables, carry all that freight? Not to mention all the rest of the things that they bring to mind. Trail bosses, pioneers, covered wagons, salt flats, Native Americans, the bleached skulls of cattle under a burning sun...a long, long list that I can be quite sure you will have in mind just as I did. "Wagons, HO!" is a very small bouillon cube indeed to produce such a complicated soup, but it *works*. It works because it is part of one of our culture's most beloved unifying metaphors: The Old West. "Wagons, HO!" is in many ways like a piece of a hologram; all by itself, it conveys:

"This project is like a wagon train heading out across the plains to settle the Western frontier."

I don't have to fill in all the rest; I don't have to state all those messages back there openly. A metaphor, provided it is either one we all share or one we can all immediately understand, does all that work for me, saving vast amounts of time and energy. And if I happen to be a boring speaker, it won't matter—because I won't have to talk *long* enough to try your patience. Hugh Nelson's major problem is that no matter how good the content of his presentation may be, no matter how admirable his motivation for making it, and no matter how badly it may be *needed*, his speaking skills are so poor that they cancel all those things. Trying harder won't help with that, any more than trying harder would make it possible for him to speak Norwegian rather than English. But a good metaphor *would* help.

When you studied metaphors in school you probably learned that they have the form "X is Y," as in "War is hell" or "Time is money." That's accurate in the narrow sense of the term. We will be using it in a broader sense here, to mean *all the explicit and presupposed parts of such a metaphor, whatever its form, and the process of using them in communication.* "My love is like a red red rose" is a metaphor in that sense, and so is "Wagons, HO!" Nothing is more powerful in bringing about meaningful and long-lasting change than a successful metaphor; unlike change brought about by force (or such modern equivalents of force as demotions and promotions), such change is accompanied by changes in underlying *attitudes.*

I used to come to very negative conclusions about people who, when I was a guest in their homes, left the television on all the time, even when we were talking. It seemed to me that they were either rude or hypocritical; either they didn't care about being courteous to me or they were only pretending to want to carry on a conversation with me. And then came the day when I read Camille Paglia's metaphor of explanation ("Dinner Conversation: She Wants Her TV! He Wants His Book!," *Harper's,* March 1991). The television set in the modern home, she said, is the flickering fire on the hearth. SHAZAM! I understood completely. This doesn't mean that I find the set any less distracting than I did before, *but I no longer consider it to be evidence of rudeness or hypocrisy.* This is a substantial attitude change, brought about almost instantaneously, and it is probably permanent. The only thing that could turn it around would be some other, equally effective metaphor.

This matters. You can use rewards and punishments to achieve *compliance* with a strategy that you have presented, but compliance isn't enough. People who comply halfheartedly will carry out your strategy only as well as they feel they *must* to get the reward or avoid the punishment; they will not go the extra mile. And people who comply when they are actually opposed will not only do just what they must and no more, but will sabotage the strategy if they get a chance. If anyone comes along with the power to give them either a worse punishment or a more attractive reward, both groups will promptly abandon your strategy.

A successful metaphor is far more useful for moving beyond mere compliance and getting genuine *commitment* than all but the most extreme rewards and punishments. People convinced by a metaphor will go on working to implement your strategy in *spite* of severe problems and meager benefits. This is in fact what lies behind much of Hugh Nelson's behavior: he is living out a *military* metaphor. He is slogging through swamps and over mountain passes, dodging bullets and grenades, carrying out every order—whether it makes any sense to him or not—down to the last crossed *t* and dotted *i*, no matter what perils he must face to do so. It's his bad luck that he is carrying out these military maneuvers in a context where everyone *else* is operating out of the metaphor of The Football Game. If they were on a real football field in the middle of a real game and Hugh came marching along under a heavy pack and tried to carry the ball for them, or defend them while they carried it, the fact that his intentions were good would not help matters—he would be a *terrible* burden to the team. In the situation shown in Scenario Nine, where a business team is trying to accomplish a task and all its other members are filtering their perceptions through the metaphor of football, he is equally a burden.

The Significance of the Football Metaphor

One of the major sources of communication breakdowns in the United States today is the metaphor "X is a football game." For most adult *male* speakers of American Mainstream English, X is anything that involves negotiation in public; for some, it extends into private life as well. Business is therefore a football game, and every project in the workplace is a football game. For most adult *female* speakers of American Mainstream English, however, the dominant metaphor that serves as perceptual filter in public life is not football but The Traditional Schoolroom. The semantic differences this leads to are devastating to cross-gender communication, because common and important words—like "lying," "cheating," "fair," "violence," and "betrayal"—have radically different meanings in these two settings.

In a football game, pretending that you have the ball when you don't, or that you'll be throwing the ball to one person when you intend to throw it somewhere else, does not constitute *lying*. On the contrary; it's how you play the game. Working together is not considered *cheating*; pushing another player down and falling on top of him is not considered *violence*; sacrificing one player for the sake of the team is not *betrayal*. Nor is it anything *personal* when you knock someone down or shove him out of your way or deceive him about your intentions; your action is taken because that person is in a particular role relative to the game being played.

Now consider what goes on in a traditional schoolroom. Any false statement or act is considered a lie, working together instead of independently is called cheating, pushing or shoving another student is violence and is forbidden, sacrificing one student for the good of the whole class is never acceptable—and *all* these actions, if carried out, are taken personally. The distance between these two semantic environments is wide and deep and dangerous.

Most of the time, when you find a man and a woman involved in an argument where she keeps saying "You lied!" and he keeps saying "I did not!," they both agree that lies are wrong and they agree on what he said—their disagreement is on how a "lie" is *defined*. And most of the time, it's because he operates from the football metaphor and she operates from the schoolroom metaphor, and neither one of them is aware that that's where their communication breakdown originates.

Precisely the same thing happens when most of the men in a group use The Football Game as perceptual filter, but there's one man present who—like Hugh Nelson—is using a different one. If the man's metaphor is close to football, if it's baseball or basketball or some other team sport, it may not matter a great deal. But the further apart the metaphors are, the greater the communication problems will be. Fortunately, however, this is one of the rare cases in which *awareness of a problem's existence* is enough to bring about dramatic improvement. If both metaphors involved are familiar to members of the culture, knowing that another person has a particular one as perceptual filter will immediately clear up many misunderstandings and make it possible to prevent many future ones.

Hunting and Finding Metaphors

The question is, of course, how do you *find* an appropriate and powerful metaphor? How do you choose among the possibilities? How do you make sure that your choice doesn't clash with the one being used by others around you, the way Hugh's Good-and-Noble-Soldier metaphor clashes with the managers' football metaphor? Metaphors can have negative effects as well as good ones; you don't want to make a bad choice.

A few years ago I was amazed to read an article in a medical journal in which a professor of obstetrics took up the problem of patients' reactions to the fees for delivering babies, and advised doctors to compare that cost to the cost of embalming the dead. This is a powerful metaphor, for sure, but its effects are disastrous! Metaphors say "Let's think of X and Y as an analogous pair, based on the characteristics they have in common," and they rely on the human brain to match up those characteristics point by point. Hearing "Delivering babies is like embalming corpses," the brain starts matching up the delivery table with the embalming table, the amniotic fluid with the embalming fluid, the delivery room with the morgue, the ambulance with the hearse, the doctor with the mortician. Point by point, the brain fastens it down, and it's *awful*. The choice must be carefully made.

Semantic Features and Reality Statements

There are two devices that can be used productively for stalking metaphors. Suppose you were asked to explain why a bat is not a bird. Both are living creatures, both are winged, and both are small; it's easy to understand why a child, seeing a bat in flight for the first time, might call it a bird. Using the linguistic device called the *semantic feature*, we would have to say that birds and bats have in common the semantic features [+ANIMATE], [+WINGED], and [+SMALL]. We need a feature to separate the two. The usual solution is to use [+FEATHERED] because it sets birds apart not only from bats but from all other creatures. A bird is the *only* one that has feathers. A bat would be marked as [− FEATHERED].

This is a clear either/or decision; things are either plus or minus feathered, and that's the end of it. When the features you use can be specified that unequivocally, it simplifies matters. When they can't, you can add a measure of the degree of some characteristic by using multiple pluses and minuses. Thus, if you wanted to describe Hugh Nelson in terms of the feature [BORING], you might want to write it as [+++BORING] rather than using only one plus sign.

You could also explain the bird/bat distinction by expanding the semantic features into reality statements—brief statements that are part of the definition people have of the reality we live in. For both bats and birds, we have the reality statements "It is animate" and "It is small" and "It has wings"; but only for birds do people agree that "It has feathers." Semantic features are quicker to use, but sometimes they're not readily available; reality statements are particularly helpful when no single word or brief phrase exists that you can use as a feature. And using both will often help you find out where there are gaps that need filling and where there are pitfalls of the "A newborn baby is like a corpse" variety.

Suppose I had gone looking for a metaphor to change my attitude about television sets left playing softly while people talk, instead of just coming across one by accident. I would first have set up the metaphor pattern: "A television set turned down low is a(n) X" Then I would have made a list of features and/or reality statements that, for me, define that TV set. The list might have looked something like this:

Television Set Turned Down Low

[−ANIMATE]

[+CONSTRUCTED]

[+SMALL]

- It gives off a soft light.
- It makes a soft hissing or crackling noise.
- It is kept in a house.
- You can see pictures on screen.

There might have been a few more items on the list; I would not have included "It is used for entertainment" because it's not entertaining to watch a television set when you can't hear the sound well enough to know what's going on. When I was satisfied that I had at least a preliminary list, I would have asked myself the question: "What else is there in my reality that shares some of the characteristics listed?" It probably would not have taken me long to think of a hearth fire as the answer to my question, and my task—solving for the empty X in the pattern—would then have been complete.

Obviously, there will be characteristics that the two parts of this (or any other) metaphor *don't* share. A fire is not a constructed object; it does not have knobs or buttons; you can't buy one on the installment plan. A television set can't be used to cook your lunch; you can't make one by rubbing two sticks together; you can't turn it off by blowing it out. And obviously, once the metaphor was complete, my brain would have supplied features I had overlooked at first. I would have realized that the TV picture is framed by the screen as the fire is framed by the fireplace, and that people gather around a TV set just as they gather round a fire.

This is how it's done. To choose a metaphor for a proposal you want to make, proceed as follows:

Step 1: Write down the defining characteristics of your project, goal, etc., using semantic features and/or reality statements.

Step 2: Look for something else that shares *enough* of those features to make the metaphor plausible and effective.

Step 3: Check to make sure it doesn't carry *other* features that would make its effects negative.

As a shortcut, you can always run through the list of unifying metaphors for our American Mainstream English culture to see if one of those will serve your purpose. For example, is what you are proposing and trying to persuade people to commit themselves to like

The Football Game?

The Old West?

The Old South?

The Proud Ship Sailing?

The Glorious Battle?

One Big Happy Family?

The Rose-Covered Cottage?

The Traditional Schoolroom?

Climbing the Highest Peak?

Catching the Big One?

Driving a car?

Sailing a boat?

Flying a plane?

Running away to join the circus?

If so, you may need to say little more than "Charge!" or "We're heading for a touchdown!" to get your point across.

Finally, you can often find metaphors in *stories*. When you say, "We've got to stop chasing Tinkerbell and go after Captain Hook!" or "We're not Robin Hood and his merry men, you know; we're the crew of the Starship Enterprise!", most people in our society will know exactly what you mean. One of Ronald Reagan's favorite stories was the one about the boy who, faced with the task of shoveling out a shed full of manure, cries, "There's got to be a pony in there *some*where!"; you can tell that one for a laugh, and urge people to be ponyfinders rather than the alternative.

It's not important for metaphors (outside of "literature") to be new and striking. When what you are proposing is new and striking itself—perhaps even new and frightening—one of the good old familiar metaphors may be exactly what you need. When persuading people to commit themselves to a plan, you want to tie the worrisome new to the comforting old. It makes your listeners feel that they'll still know where they are after the change takes place.

Now, let's go back to Scenario Nine and see what a metaphor might do to help Hugh Nelson argue against downsizing and outsourcing at his company.

Scenario Nine, Revised

"Good morning, everyone," said Hugh Nelson, smiling at the group of managers sitting around the table, "and thank you for coming."

He leaned forward, his hand on the presentation folder before him. "As you know," he said, "the committee charged with investigating the potential for downsizing and outsourcing at BixTech has spent almost three months studying the issue and assembling the necessary facts and figures." He tapped the folder gently. "I'm not going to waste your time going <u>over</u> those numbers; they're all in your folder, written out for your careful examination. As I'm sure you expected, they show beyond all question that BixTech would save money—a <u>lot</u> of money—if we followed the current fashion and went that route. That's not at issue. And when you go over the figures at your leisure, you'll find your expectations borne out. You may even find that you've <u>under</u>estimated the potential savings!"

He paused; they were all looking at him and listening carefully. "However," he said, "I want to talk to you very briefly about something that doesn't have a dollar figure attached to it. Let's just suppose for a moment that this company is a baseball team. All right? Let's suppose it is a <u>winning</u> baseball team, headed right for the top of the league. Imagine yourself on that team. You know every other team member. You know how well Tomas Martinez can hit…you know how well Carolyn Anderson can pitch. You not only know <u>those</u> things, things that can be written down and turned into charts and graphs, you know the most <u>important</u> thing: *you know what each of the members of the team can be counted on to do, in a routine game and in a crisis.* You know who will respond to a crisis by hitting the ball out of the park; you know who it's a bad idea to bring up to bat when the bases are loaded. You're a <u>team</u>.

"And then one day the owner stops in to tell you that it's not going to be like that any more. Because he and his accountant have discovered that they can save a fortune by keeping just a pitcher and a catcher and maybe one batter and hiring <u>temps</u> to play all the other positions. You wouldn't know those temporary people—those independent contractors. You wouldn't know when you could rely on them, or what kinds of things might distract them when you needed their full attention on the ball, or what they might do when things got rough."

Hugh paused again, and then he spoke as seriously as he knew how: "Think about it—think about what that would be like. Would you like that?"

The Baseball Team metaphor lets Hugh get his message across to the managers without having to set out each of his arguments separately and specifically. The others *can* imagine what it would be like to have a constantly shifting team and have to function on the field without ever knowing who is a rock and who is a lily pad. The metaphor is familiar; people can fill in the details for themselves easily. Hugh is being careful not to clutter it up with specialized baseball jargon that might not be understood by everyone present; he's being careful not to go on too long. He may say, "Play ball!" or "Batter up!" at least once before the meeting ends, but he's not going to start talking about his war experiences or the company's previous fling with quality circles. The presentation by metaphor may not be enough to convince his audience that he's right, but it will give him a *chance* to convince them. They won't disagree with him only because he has bored them stiff and made them angry. This is a significant improvement.

WORKOUT SECTION: CHAPTER 9

1. For your Communication Strategy Notebook, set up a Metaphor file and begin keeping track of relevant information to serve as a database for planning strategies. For example:

- Record incidents in which you used metaphor(s) as a part of your communication strategy. What was the situation? Who was present? What did you say to activate the metaphor? What was said in response? What happened? What was surprising? Did anything go wrong, and if so, can you determine why? If you had it to do over again, would you choose a different metaphor?

- In the same place where you record the preferred sensory and Satir Modes, body language baseline profiles, and so on for other people with whom you interact, begin recording their dominant metaphors. Do they filter their perceptions in the workplace through The Football Game metaphor? The Traditional Schoolroom metaphor? The Old West metaphor? Something else? Often, in the process of finding *out* someone's dominant metaphor, you discover things to say that make the process go more quickly and smoothly. *Be sure you write these down, so you can use them the next time you're investigating metaphors.*

- In your ordinary contact with other people and the media, you will frequently encounter interesting metaphors. Set up a page on which you can record them, so that when you're seeking a metaphor for your own use they'll be there to get you started. A good metaphor is a treasure; take care of it.

- Pay attention to the metaphors you use in your daily life and make a list of them. When you have a dozen or so, look for patterns. If what you see is a lot of negative thinking—as in, "This job is killing me" or, "Every time I see that rep, my blood boils" or, "Every salesperson I have is a royal pain in the neck"—that's toxic language, and it's polluting your language environment. Your brain bases its acts on the messages you send it. If they're constantly negative, it will take negative action, resulting in such unpleasant items as migraines, ulcers, allergies, depression, heart disease, and many other tribulations. Stop giving yourself negative messages; they're equivalent to beating yourself over the head with a hammer.

- Find out what metaphor serves *you* as a perceptual filter in business and public life. The easiest way to do this is to write out in detail the definitions that you use in *business contexts* for "cheating," "lying," "betrayal," "cooperation," and "violence." Make a list of three or four examples that illustrate your definitions. What would one of your colleagues/employees/superiors have to do before you'd say, "He lied to me" or, "She betrayed me" or, "What they did was way out of line—it hurt me badly"? When you have this information completed, ask yourself: In what *other* situation do the rules I'm using apply? Football? Schoolroom? Battlefield? Wagon train going west? Chess? *Almost nothing that you could find out about yourself is more valuable to you than this single piece of information.*

2. In *The Enigma of Japanese Power*, Karel van Wolferen writes that, "Japanese are treated by their...superiors in the way a landscape gardener treats a hedge; protruding bits of the personality are regularly snipped off" (New York: Knopf, 1989). Consider that last verb carefully. Why "snipped off"? Why not "hacked off" or "chopped off" or "amputated"? In your Communication Strategies Notebook, set up a page with four columns, one for each of these choices. Then use semantic features and reality statements to investigate them and give them definitions that will make it clear why one would be used rather than another. Such choices, done properly, are not "just a matter of style"; different choices carry different messages, and the choice will be "stylistic" only when more important semantic reason holds.

In a *Forbes* magazine story on the history of swizzle sticks ("Stirring Story," November 12, 1990), Joshua Levine explains that they were developed during the Great Depression to replace silver demitasse spoons. The progression was from silver spoon to wooden spoon to wooden stirrer to plastic stirrer, and—for McDonald's—to *cocaine* spoon, causing the company to redesign the stirrers so that they would be too flat to serve that forbidden purpose. Use semantic features and reality statements to define the members of this set.

Using semantic features and reality statements, find out why so many newscasters during the Gulf War used the following sequence of language: "Our boys and...[Pause] Our men and women in the Gulf..." We've always referred to our military as "our boys"; what's the problem with "Our boys and girls in the Gulf?" Does this give you any insight into the objections many women have to being referred to as "the girls"?

3. In item 1 above I told you that negative metaphors are dangerous and should be taken out like any other trash. Just getting rid of them is good for you. Even better, however, is replacing them with positive *substitutes*. For example, here is Mike Way, quoted in "Don't Get Mad—Get Ahead," by Scott DeGarmo (*Success* magazine, January/February 1991): "Each rejection is a stepping stone to the guy

who is going to say yes." That is: not "A no from a client is a knife in my back" but "A no from a client is a stepping stone to a client who will say yes." Not "I'm a drowning person—my company is failing" but "I'm a free person—I can start a different and better business now that my company is failing." Take a good and thorough look at your own negative metaphors and work out positive replacements for them.

4. Many reasons have been proposed to explain why Japan has made so much more extensive use of robots in manufacturing than the United States has. One reason that you may not have heard about is discussed in "Inside the Robot Kingdom," by Michael Colpitts (*BCS Tech* newsletter, November 1991). Colpitts explains that when the Japanese think of robots they think of the robotlike wooden dolls called *karakuri* used as tea-serving devices in Japan in the twelfth century. When Americans think of robots, what is the association? How would the semantic features for the two associations differ? For more details, see *Inside the Robot Kingdom* by Frederik L. Schodt (New York: Kodansha International, 1991).

5. For an example of an extended metaphor used throughout an entire article, read "Prospecting in the Wild East," by Paul Klebnikov (*Forbes* magazine, November 12, 1990). The final sentence reads: "Dodge City, Russia, is too good an opportunity to ignore, but it's still too early to bring along the covered wagons and the families."

6. Here's a metaphor that badly needs fixing; determine what's wrong with it and make the necessary repairs: "The most basic precept of portfolio management is to let your winners run. The takeover craze nips that rose in the bud." (*Kenneth L. Fisher, "I Call Them 'Take-Aways'"* Forbes *magazine, April 3, 1989, p. 180*)

7. Often you can use an existing metaphor as a pattern to create new ones. For example, in "Zombie bonds," Matthew Schifrin opens with this sentence: "Where there's a carcass, there's a vulture" (*Forbes* magazine, April 3, 1989). What is the older metaphor that was used as pattern for this? What additional variations could you devise?

8. In his excellent and useful book *Getting Past No* William Ury says that breakthrough negotiation is "the art of letting the other person have *your* way" (New York: Bantam, 1991). What makes this metaphor work? Why is it so intriguing? Take a look at the definition of the verb "let" and its presuppositions. Another example of the same kind comes from Alan Watts's book, *Cloud-Hidden, Whereabouts Unknown:* "Fire is water falling upwards" (New York: Vintage Books,

1974). The key to the metaphor is in the definition and presuppositions of the verb "fall."

9. In 1970, Lewis Thomas gave a talk that was a compelling extended metaphor, with significant real-world results. It was called "Adaptive Aspects of Inflammation" and began with a detailed description of the things that actually go on inside a human body in response to infection. Thomas told his audience that we lose track of what's really going on because we perceive it as a "catastrophe." He said that it's as if we had to use our first view of a multiple collision on the highway, with the road littered with smashed cars and glass and debris, as "our only source of information for a general theory about the normal operation of the modern four-wheel brake, or the traffic light, or the seat belt." (You can find the text of this brief talk in the February 1994 issue of *MD* magazine.)

10. Sometimes an entire strategy is based on a metaphor that not only doesn't achieve the intended goal but actively works against it. For example, there's an educational television station I'm familiar with that sets up its semiannual fundraising efforts as a "festival." The metaphor is supported by an elaborately decorated set in the studio, by half a dozen or more people on the set dressed in evening gowns and tuxedos, by elaborate graphics, and so on. But the dominant messages are (1) the logistics of making your pledge and getting your premium in return and (2) the constant reiteration of the dismal fact that only one in twelve of the station's viewers contributes—phrased as, "We know you're out there, but only one in twelve of you is paying your fair share." The total failure of this metaphor is well demonstrated by the following statistics. Five years ago, one in ten viewers contributed; now that ratio has fallen to one in twelve. What's wrong with this metaphor as strategy? What could be done to fix it?

10

"Hey! Not So Fast!"

Moving from Metaphors That Fail to Metaphors That Succeed

Scenario Ten

Leonard Bauer was a *very* happy man. It had been a rough year—a year of long days, of tension and suspense, of having to be Mr. Total Confidence even when he was far from sure he could do the things he was claiming he would do. Having it all work out perfectly at last, the investors satisfied and enthusiastic, the new capital in the bank and ready to be poured into the business, gave him more pleasure than he could express. He couldn't wait to get started on the transformation of his company, couldn't wait to share the good news with all his people. He looked around the conference room, glad he'd spent the money to bring them all here to the lake hotel instead of just calling a meeting back at the office, glad to see them relaxed and interested and eager to hear his speech.

"People," he said, "I know you're all wondering what I'm going to say, and I'm not going to keep you in suspense one minute longer. This is the day...this is the day when I finally get to share the <u>future</u> with you! And I'm here to tell you that the future is <u>bright</u>. This company—<u>our</u> company—is getting ready to go through a transformation that will move us out of the parking space and into <u>cyber</u>space. We are moving out onto The Information Highway, my friends, and we are going to <u>thrive</u> out there!" He drew a long breath of satisfaction, rubbing his hands together briskly, and leaned toward them. "Let me tell you what we're going to do," he said, and began the list.

- ArborNews was no longer going to be a company that prepared and sold a product called "horticulture newsletters." Now it was going to be a company that sold <u>information</u> about every aspect of the horticulture and gardening business.

- ArborNews was no longer going to cut-and-paste the newsletters and send them out to be typeset and printed. Now they were going to do the whole production task in-house, with their own desktop publishing equipment and software.

- ArborNews was no longer going to just answer letters by mail and phone. Now there would be an on-line bulletin board where every customer and client with a modem could get an instant answer to questions, interact with <u>other</u> customers and clients, call up the latest figures and news bulletins, access a library of horticultural information, and download anything of interest—plus attend teleconferences and on-line seminars and discussion groups.

- ArborNews was no longer going to be tied to just two or three uniform publications, all alike. Now it would have the technology to custom-tailor them, add special regional inserts and bulletins, offer special issues on demand, and vary the newsletters to fit the narrowest of niches.

- ArborNews staffers would no longer have to spend their time doing the same old boring tasks one after another. Now they were going to be intrapreneurs!

"We want your ideas," he said, bringing the speech to a close, knowing he had only barely touched on the wonderful opportunities that were ahead but that it was time he stopped monopolizing the floor and let <u>them</u> talk. "We want a flood of new ideas from you—you are never again going to have to hesitate with a proposal for a new product or service because it might be 'too far out'! Hey…we're not just going to be out there on the Information Highway! We'll be moving so fast, and so far, we may just find ourselves <u>flying over</u> it!"

The End, he thought. *That's a wrap!* He stepped out from behind the podium to the edge of the riser and told them he was ready now to take their questions and listen to their comments, and he waited for the enthusiasm he knew was coming.

But it *didn't* come. There was a long, uneasy silence. And then there were a few questions, obviously posed only because the silence was so embarrassing. *How soon would all this be starting? How much time would they be given for training with the new equipment and software?* Things like that. Logistics! And one of his most valuable people actually wanted to know if *every*body would have to make these changes or if maybe there'd be some exceptions!

Leonard was stunned and hurt—and baffled. Sure, this would mean a lot of big changes, but they were all changes for the better, all terrific opportunities. They should have been popping the champagne corks, but they looked as if he'd told them the company was going into bankruptcy! He couldn't believe it; he just couldn't *believe* it. What was the *matter* with them, *anyway?*

What's Going on Here?

Leonard's Point of View

As Leonard sees it, he's just handed his employees everything they could possibly want in their working lives. No more stodgy old product-driven company; no more days stuck in slots where every move is rigidly prescribed; no more *tedium.* He's always been good to them; he's sure they know he can be counted on to provide plenty of training in the new procedures and to give them ample transition time. He was expecting them to rejoice with him and to be, like him, chafing at the bit to get back to work and start implementing the transformation. To have them listen to his presentation and then sit there frowning and fretting at him was totally unexpected, and it was awful. He doesn't know what to *do* now to turn that reaction around and get the kind of enthusiasm he thought would be forthcoming. His employees have definitely ruined *his* day.

The Employees' Points of View

As the employees see it, Leonard Bauer has lost his mind and wants them to join him in his insanity. They've been with the company for many years. They know what they're expected to do, and they know how to do it *well.* They're familiar with every smallest detail of the business, and they're proud of the way they carry out their duties. And there he stands, telling them they have to start over from square one, and thinking they're going to be *pleased* about it.

If Bauer thinks they are going to go along with this wild scheme *willingly,* he can just think *again!* They will do what they are called on to do—it's that kind of company, and they are that kind of loyal and dedicated employees. But they are going to fight it every step of the way, as strongly as they dare. *He* may think they're going to be flying along above the information highway, but *first* he's going to have to get them to break camp and head for the on-ramp.

What Went Wrong?

The outcome of Leonard Bauer's big announcement speech should not surprise him. He has managed to inflict on his workforce a severe case of what Leon Festinger called *cognitive dissonance:* a kind of mental misery that descends on people when they have to face ideas that appear to be inescapable and that are in drastic conflict with their model of reality. The cognitive dissonance in this case comes from the following conflict:

- The workers believe that they are valuable employees because there's *nothing* the company does that they can't do blindfolded, nothing that they could not do even under the worst of crisis conditions—*because they know it all so well.*

- Bauer's speech confronts them with the idea that valuable employees are those who can start from scratch with equipment they've never seen before, who not only *do* new things but think of even *more* new things to do, all by themselves.

The employees are overwhelmed; the cognitive dissonance is excruciating.

People afflicted with cognitive dissonance have limited choices. They can either give up what they have always believed is true and accept the new reality model as the "real" truth, or they can cling to their current reality and reject the new ideas as wildest fantasy. Finding any kind of compromise instead of that either/or—perhaps by making changes in one or both models—is extremely difficult. If the two alternatives weren't seriously incompatible, the cognitive dissonance wouldn't occur in the first place. Leonard has wisely tried to bring the change about by using a metaphor, instead of just lecturing at his people or burying them in facts and figures, but he has made a serious mistake. *When you say that* X *is* Y, *with* X *as the status quo and* Y *as your goal, you need to be sure that the distance between* X *and* Y *is small enough to be bridged.* From "parking space" to "cyberspace" is a vast and terrifying gulf, and the reaction Leonard gets is predictable.

There's a better way, using the semantic features and reality statements already introduced in Chapter 9. It's called *semantic modulation.*

Communication Technique: Semantic Modulation

Suppose a traditional composer wants to move from one key to another in a composition—using the process called *modulation*—and the target key is very distant in musical space. Unless the goal of that move is to shock and startle listeners, the composer will not simply leap from the original key to the target key. Instead, he or she will modulate first to a key or keys closer to the original one and go step by step through those bridging keys to the target. We can build on that process in music and incorporate it into semantics for use in moving an individual or group from one metaphor to another through one or more bridge metaphors.

Here are the six steps in semantic modulation:

Step 1: Identify the metaphor that is the status quo—the metaphor from within which the individual or group is operating.

Step 2: Identify the metaphor that is the target—the one from within which you *want* the individual or group to operate.

Step 3: Build a description of the status quo and target metaphors, using semantic features and reality statements. *Because human beings are integral to the metaphor, the description must always include the* roles *they play in it.*

Step 4: Compare the two descriptions. If they share a number of important characteristics (four is a desirable minimum), move directly from status quo to target. Otherwise, go to Step 5.

Step 5: Find a bridge metaphor by identifying some *other* metaphor that shares four or more features with both the status quo and target metaphors. (If necessary, locate several of these at various points along the path from status quo to target in semantic space.)

Step 6: Move from status quo to bridge(s) to target.

Often you will recognize the status quo metaphor without difficulty. If not, you will have to talk to the people involved, asking them questions and discussing their culture, until you do know what it is.

In the case of Leonard Bauer's company, the status quo metaphor is an old familiar one: One Big Happy Family. A description in terms of semantic features and reality statements would look something like this:

Semantic Features

[+ LOYAL]

[+ NUMEROUS]

[+ HAPPY]

[+ CONTENTED]

[+ AFFECTIONATE]

[+ CLOSE-KNIT]

[+ COOPERATIVE]

[+ TRADITIONAL]

Reality Statements

- Everyone puts the welfare of the family ahead of his or her own welfare.
- Everyone does his or her share, dutifully and cooperatively.
- The roles include parent, offspring, and close relatives.
- The parent(s) are clearly in charge and have the final say, but the leadership is caring rather than tyrannical.

Notice that any of the semantic features could be expanded into a reality statement. But there is often no word or brief phrase of English that will convert a particular reality statement into a semantic feature. (This situation—an idea for which no word or brief phrase exists to provide it a convenient surface shape—is called *a lexical gap*.)

We know what Leonard's target metaphor is because he identified it explicitly in his speech. The Information Highway. "Highway" isn't a term that can be applied to a group of people the way "family" can, but that's not a problem. As we would have to do with the metaphors of The Old West or The Old South, we specify that we are describing the *people* of the metaphor. A group of "Information Highwaypersons," as Leonard perceives them, might be described like this:

Semantic Features

[+ LOYAL]

[+ NUMEROUS]

[+ INNOVATIVE]

[+ AMBITIOUS]

[+ FEARLESS]

[+ HARDWORKING]

[+ TECHNOLOGICALLY SOPHISTICATED]

Reality Statements

- Everyone puts the welfare of the group ahead of his or her own individual welfare.

- Everyone does his or her share, eagerly and enthusiastically.
- No one is afraid to propose or try something new.
- Everyone is constantly seeking new and different ways to move the group ahead.
- Everyone strives to do his or her tasks by the most up-to-date methods possible.

When you compare these two descriptions, you can tell immediately that the metaphors are very distant indeed. They share only two semantic features relevant to the discussion (as opposed to accurate, but irrelevant features, such as [+ANIMATE]) and they share only one reality statement. That's bad—but it's not the worst of it. The worst of it is that the most important reality statement of all—*the list of roles that people play in the metaphor*—is completely missing.

When we think of the familiar metaphors of our culture, as with One Big Happy Family, we know the roles right away. For example:

The Old West: Wagonmaster, Cowboy, Indian, Dancehall Girl, Good Old Doc.

The Old South: the Southern Lady, the Southern Gentleman, the Handsome Scoundrel, the Selfless and Devoted Servant, the Trashy Poor Sharecropper.

The Football Game: Quarterback, Tight End, Fullback, Coach, Halfback, Referee, Cheerleader.

But The Information Highway? It's too new. No one knows as yet what the roles are, though the cyberpunk youth culture and the science fiction authors who write about it are working on the problem. Maybe, just as *Star Trek* is *Wagon Train* in Space, The Information Highway is *Wagon Train* in Cyberspace—but that seems unlikely when you look at the description.

This tells us that Leonard didn't just choose a metaphor that was too distant from the status quo, he chose the wrong metaphor entirely. He needs one that is at least well enough understood to make it possible to specify the roles with confidence. Asking his workforce to go from Happy Family to Information Highwaypersons (whatever they may be) is asking them to make a leap of faith into a *void*. If these people were a religious group burning with passionate devotion to some sacred goal, that might be a reasonable request, but they're not. They're a *business* group. If Leonard were the sort of charismatic superstar speaker who inspires *instant* passion and devotion, he might be able to get them to *agree* to leap—but they'd change their minds once they were out of range of his rhetoric. Leonard wants his people to commit themselves to his vision for ArborNews, willingly and enthusiastically; he wants a complete shift in their attitudes and a major shift in their actions. To achieve that goal, he needs to choose a more conservative metaphor to carry his message. Now let's go back to Scenario Ten and see how that could be done.

Another Look at Scenario Ten

Let's assume for purposes of discussion that Leonard Bauer is fully informed about metaphor as a process and understands how he can use it to evoke in his employees the necessary enthusiasm for and commitment to the transformation of the company. This is a *major* transformation, remember, and has the potential to cause severe cognitive dissonance. He needs to follow the steps on page 179 carefully.

First, he will identify the metaphor his employees are using now— the status quo metaphor. Chances are, he already *knows* that it's One Big Happy Family; he has probably heard employees say "We're just like one big happy family around here!" and he may have said it himself. We know that he shares that metaphor—that's why he was expecting everyone to be enthusiastic about his new project and was *hurt* when they disappointed him. He expected them to support him as family members are supposed to support one another, even when they may not fully approve. If he *isn't* consciously aware that that's the metaphor now operating, he can fix that by sitting down and talking to his employees, asking them to discuss how they feel about the company and about their jobs and about one another. This particular metaphor is obvious enough and common enough that it's not likely to be mistaken for something else.

Next he will identify the target metaphor, and since he is the one making that choice he can choose anything he likes. Suppose he chooses The Information Highway, and wants his employees to join him in being Information Highwaypersons. We know what will happen if he does that. When he goes on to Step 3 and tries to prepare his definitions for the two metaphors, he'll find himself facing the situation outlined on page 181: His metaphors have almost nothing in common, making the distance between them too great—and worst of all, he doesn't even know what the *roles* in his target metaphor would be. At this point he needs to ask himself this question: *What other metaphor exists that has some of the characteristics of my first choice for target but has more in common with the status quo? What metaphor exists that meets those criteria and for which I would be able to specify the roles people will play?*

Given what we know about Leonard, it's safe to hypothesize that his new choice could be The Proud Ship Sailing in *Space*. Not just an oceangoing ship to get his employees and his company off the land, but a *space*going ship; and not just a vehicle tied to an orbit, but the spaceship of science fiction that freely roams the galaxies. With that as his target, he can set up the following descriptions:

One Big Happy Family

[+ LOYAL; + NUMEROUS; + HAPPY; + CONTENTED; + AFFECTIONATE; + CLOSE-KNIT; + COOPERATIVE; + TRADITIONAL]

- Everyone puts the welfare of the family ahead of his or her own welfare.
- Everyone does his or her share, dutifully and cooperatively.
- The roles include parent, offspring, and close relatives.
- The parent(s) are clearly in charge and have the final say, but the leadership is caring rather than tyrannical.

The Crew of the Proud Ship Sailing in Space

[+ LOYAL; + NUMEROUS; + HAPPY; + CLOSE-KNIT; + COOPERATIVE; + COURA-GEOUS; + HARD-WORKING; + INNOVATIVE]

- Everyone puts the welfare of the group and the ship ahead of his or her own welfare.
- Everyone does his or her share, dutifully and cooperatively and enthusiastically.
- Everyone is interested in doing new things, going new places, gathering new information.
- The roles include captain, other officers, and crew.
- The captain is clearly in charge and has the final say, but the leadership is benign rather than tyrannical.

This is *much* better. There are differences, certainly; but the two metaphors have many elements in common. Not everything Leonard wanted is there—for example, the independence and creativity of the intrapreneur is missing. But the spaceship metaphor comes pretty *close*.

Leonard's only question now is whether his employees can easily handle the distance between status quo and target. If he thinks they can, he can structure his presentation in terms of the spaceship metaphor. If not, he can look for something that will serve as a *bridge* metaphor—something that still meets his criteria but falls somewhere between One Big Happy Family and the spaceship crew. The obvious choice then would be to use as bridge the metaphor of The Proud Ship Sailing but to keep that ship on *Earth*. Almost everything would be the same; and after a while, when people were comfortable with it, he could present to them the advantages of moving their voyage out into space.

Let's rewrite the opening of his speech to reflect the second choice, in which he assumes that he'll need to do this in stages.

"People," Leonard said, "I know you're all wondering what I'm going to say, and I'm not going to keep you in suspense one minute longer. This is the day...this is the day when I finally get to share with you the adventure that lies ahead of us. And I'm here to tell you that this is an adventure that we'll be going into with a solid keel beneath our feet and a steady wind at our backs. This company—<u>our</u> company—is getting ready to go through a transformation that will let us move beyond the four walls holding us in right now. We are going to move out into the open seas of commerce, where we will have the freedom to set our own course, to do things we were only able to <u>dream</u> of doing before, to move as quickly as we <u>want</u> to move. And, my friends, we are going to <u>love</u> it out there!" He drew a long breath of satisfaction, rubbing his hands together briskly, and leaned toward them.

"Let me tell you what we're going to do," he said. "I'll just mention some of the opportunities we now have, opportunities we never could have had as landlubbers. I won't go into the details—we have <u>plenty</u> of time for that, later, when we're back at the office. I'm just going to mention a few of the possibilities...a few of the ports of call and the tropical islands...so you'll be able to see what a wonderful voyage we have ahead of us." And he began the list.

You see, *that's how it's done.* This is much less terrifying to his listeners. They know themselves as family members; they will be able to imagine themselves as crew members. And if Leonard is careful in listing the new tasks ahead, touching lightly on their technological wizardry and offering abundant reassurance about training and transition time, he won't find himself listening to that terrible silence that means nobody else is ready to come aboard.

WORKOUT SECTION: CHAPTER 10

1. What is your company's dominant, unifying metaphor—the one that serves the company as perceptual filter? (If there is more than one, identify each of them and decide how the fact that you don't all operate from within the *same* metaphor affects performance.) Is the dominant metaphor the one you'd *like* it to be? If not, what would your target metaphor be? How far is it from the one that constitutes the status quo?

2. In *In Search of Excellence*, T. Peters and R. Waterman, Jr., quote James March as saying that "organizations are to be sailed rather than driven" (New York: Warner, 1984). Think about your own company. Is it driven? pushed? sailed? flown? something else?

3. Complete the following sentences by "solving for X." Turn each into a metaphor and then consider the consequences.

a. "A law enforcement officer is a(n) ....X......."

b. "A doctor is a(n) ....X..................."

c. "A lawyer is a(n) ....X..............."

d. "A member of Congress is a(n)..........X.........."

I once did a seminar for a group of law enforcement officers who, when I asked them to identify their metaphor, immediately and unanimously told me that "Cops are garbage collectors." I was stunned. The usual metaphor for law enforcement is "a soldier on a battlefield" or "a knight on a white horse." Sometimes, when "It's a jungle out there!" is a dominant metaphor, the officer is seen as a lion or a hunter. "Garbage collector" was a shock, not only to me but to the commanding officer present. We worked with that metaphor a while; the only roles it contains are "garbage collector" (who, they told me, cleans up trash other people don't want to deal with), the garbage itself, and the people whose garbage is being collected. A very serious morale problem existed in that group.

4. In "Steal This Strategy," Joshua Hyatt says of Jack Kahl, "What's more, Kahl doesn't copy ideas; he replants them" *Inc.* magazine, February 1991). Do a semantic modulation from "copy ideas" to "replant ideas." Can you do it without using a bridge metaphor?

5. "You can't try to alter people's habits. That's why Pampers were white and looked just like cloth diapers in the beginning. Once you get people hooked, you can move them to colors." (*Scott Cook, quoted by Julia Pitta in "The Crisco Factor," Forbes magazine, July 20, 1992, p. 307.*)

This is a perfect example of semantic modulation. What kind of cognitive dissonance did the company avoid by beginning with a white disposable diaper that looked exactly like the product it was intended to replace? Notice that Scott Cook, if quoted accurately, thinks "habits" are the source of the problem; that is, people would resist going from cloth diapers to disposable ones because they were "in the habit" of using cloth diapers. Do you agree?

For a very long time, Americans strongly resisted the idea that acupuncture was useful for dealing with pain. They had a reality statement that went, "Only chemicals can control pain," and acupuncture was obviously not a chemical. When it proved to control pain in horses (and in an American official who had an emergency appendectomy in China), much cognitive dissonance was created. Only when endorphins—painkilling chemicals manufactured by the body itself—were discovered did we accept acupuncture, because now it fit our model of reality: It was something that triggered the body's production of chemicals. Which, as we know, are the only things that can control pain...

6. For your Communication Strategy Notebook, set up a Cognitive Dissonance file and begin keeping track of relevant information, to serve as a database for planning strategies. Record incidents (from your own life or incidents you've read or heard about) in which cognitive dissonance clearly was the source of problems. What was the situation? Who was present? What was said that activated the cognitive dissonance? How did people react? What were their alternatives? What did they say? What happened? What was surprising? What could have been done to prevent the cognitive dissonance from occurring, or to resolve it after it occurred?

For example, suppose that a woman strongly believes that the *looks* of a presentation—the slides, the printed materials, the physical setting, the presenter's appearance, etc.—are critically important. She believes that anyone who doesn't "realize" this is deficient in some way. Then she encounters a man who is very powerful, a leader in their field and who considers looks to be trivial. The result is cognitive dissonance. Her immediately obvious alternatives include "I was wrong; looks aren't important after all" and "He is wrong; he must not be a powerful person after all...He must be a phony." Her behavior toward the man—and, as a result, his behavior toward her—will be significantly affected by the choice she makes. Are there any other alternatives?

7. In *The Mind of the Strategist*, Kenichi Ohmae tells us that "In business as on the battlefield, the object of strategy is to bring about the conditions most favorable to one's own side, judging precisely the right moment to attack or withdraw." (New York: McGraw-Hill, 1982).

And, "The central notion of Japanese business strategy is to change the battleground." Apparently the dominant metaphor for both Japanese and American business in the early 1980s (when the book was written) was "Business is war." But is it safe to assume that "Business is war" means the same thing in both cultures? (Remember the Japanese metaphor, "A robot is a helpful big doll.") For the Japanese, what are the *roles* available for people to play in the "Business is war" metaphor? For the Americans?

8. Ferdinand F. Fournies published a book in 1978 called *Coaching for Improved Performance* (Bridgewater, N.J.: F. Fournies & Associates). It's a very good book on face-to-face communication in business, although, as is typical of books on communication, its dialogues provide no information whatsoever about intonation. Nonetheless, I recommend it. The metaphor Fournies uses throughout the book is "The manager is the coach." By contrast, in "Crafting Strategy," Henry Mintzberg writes, "In my metaphor, managers are craftsmen and strategy is their clay" (in *The State of Strategy*, Harvard Business School, 1991).

Set up a page in your notebook with four columns—"Manager Is King/Queen," "Manager Is Parent," "Manager Is Coach," "Manager Is Craftsperson"—and do a semantic analysis with features and reality statements. Could you move easily from any one of these to any one of the other three? Could some of them serve as bridges for the others? What are the consequences of each metaphor, in business terms? Which of these metaphors holds for your company, or do none of them hold? (And for your company, in that case, what *is* a manager?)

11

"Next, I'll Go Over the Nine Subsections of Section Ten for You..."

Talking to People from Other Cultures

Scenario Eleven

Chet Filmer and Leslie O'Connor were well aware that making a presentation to a group of seven Japanese executives would be a bit different. They'd been thoroughly briefed, and their boss had seen to it that they each got a copy of a long list of tips on doing business with the Japanese. They knew they had to be extremely polite and must be careful not to come across as back-slapping klutzes. They knew that the executives' business cards should be given long and detailed examination and then put respectfully away as if they were art objects. Leslie knew she should not be aggressive; Chet knew he should not try to tell jokes. There was an ample supply of champagne and tea and fruit and elegant pastries. They were ready for this cross-cultural experience.

"Good morning, gentlemen," Chet began. "Ms. O'Connor and I are very grateful to you for letting us join you this morning and giving

us this opportunity to explain to you why your corporations should
sponsor the Elwood J. Duner Art Exhibition." And he asked for the first
slide.

He and Leslie had designed the script that went with the slides as if it
were being entered in a literary competition. Each took six slides,
alternately. For each slide, carefully and courteously, they did three
things: explained the theme of the painting, said a few words about the
artist, and explained why the work was a perfect expression of one or
more principles dear to the three Japanese firms represented. It took
a while, but they were willing to give it all the time and care necessary.
And then Chet took the last few slides—the ones that set out the
necessary information about expenses, tax benefits, and other financial
details—and wound up the session.

"There you have it, gentlemen!" he said in conclusion. "And now my
associate and I would be happy to answer any questions that you
might have."

He waited through a long silence, not wanting to rush them, realizing
that all the things he'd heard about "inscrutable" Japanese were true. The
body language he was observing in his audience gave him no clues
to their reactions; he couldn't interpret it at all. "No questions?" he asked
uneasily.

"No questions," came the answer. "Yes. No questions."

"Well, then!" Chet rubbed his hands briskly together. "Then may I
suggest that we move now to the atrium, where we can be more
comfortable?" *Don't push them,* he reminded himself. *Don't try to get them
to commit themselves to anything yet. Be patient.*

The boss had warned Leslie and Chet that it might be like this. "You
may have a hard time telling how they feel about it afterwards,"
she'd said. "That's predictable. Don't let it get to you. Just stay calm, take
them to the atrium, socialize…give them plenty of time."

Even so, Chet was sure something was wrong. The first time he was
able to get close enough to Leslie to check with her, he whispered, "What
do you think?"

"I'm not sure," she said softly, the smile on her face never wavering,
"but I don't have the feeling we were a smash hit."

Chet nodded slowly; he was very much afraid that she was right.

What's Going on Here?

We can sum up the points of view here in two sentences. As Chet and
Leslie see it, they have bent over backwards to be courteous, to avoid all
of the hard-driving aggressive tactics they would have used with a
group of American executives in the same situation, and all they have to
show for it is a funny feeling in the pit of their stomachs. As for the
Japanese executives, they are too polite to say so openly, but they are
deeply offended; they will look for some other cultural event to sponsor.

What Went Wrong?

This problem has been discussed at great length by anthropologist Edward T. Hall, who identifies cultures as either *high-context* or *low-context*, with Japan being a high-context example. In *The Dance of Life*, Hall tells us that cultures differ in how much information they believe should be made explicit. He says that "one of the great communication strategies, whether addressing a single person or an entire group, is to ascertain the correct level of contexting of one's communication." In the same book he states:

> Americans lacking extensive experience with the Japanese...have difficulty knowing what the Japanese "are getting at."...The Japanese think intelligent human beings should be able to discover the point of a discourse from the context, which they are careful to provide. (*Edward T. Hall*, The Dance of Life: The Other Dimension of Time. *New York: Doubleday/Anchor, 1983, p. 63.*)

Chet and Leslie were right to try hard to be courteous. Japanese sentences contain multiple grammatical markers that indicate an awareness at all times of the relative *ranking* of speaker and listener. A Japanese person speaking English feels awkward without those markers and tends to use politeness markers from English as substitutes. But the Americans' attempt at courtesy failed for an equally basic reason: it was interpreted as talking down to their listeners. The Japanese executives in the scenario did not perceive the careful and explicit detail in Chet and Leslie's presentation as courtesy but as evidence that the two Americans found them lacking in both intelligence and sophistication. The Japanese, like all high-context cultures, expect adults to rely heavily on presupposed information when communicating with other adults. Only in speaking to children would you fill in the details and make them part of the surface structure of the language.

We have a phenomenon in English that will serve as a metaphor. Think of a couple who have had a vicious argument that both of them regret afterward. The husband comes home the next evening ready to pretend that the fight never happened and tries to be exceptionally affectionate and considerate, but the wife's response is unrelentingly chilly. When he asks for an explanation, she tells him grimly that he should have suggested going *out* to dinner; but when he agrees and proposes that they leave immediately for their favorite restaurant, she refuses. *Why?* "Because I shouldn't have had to <u>tell</u> you," she says bitterly. "You should have <u>known</u>!" This attitude strikes the husband as totally irrational, and the end result is another argument. It comes from the wife's mistaken assumption that the two of them agree on what information can be presupposed and what information should be made explicit.

Although the problem is the other way around in Scenario Eleven—the Japanese are offended because the Americans have made information explicit that, in their opinion, should have been left unstated and presupposed—the source of the breakdown is the same: *A mistaken assumption that speaker and listener* agree *on how heavily to rely on context in communication.* If the scenario had been written to illustrate the same communication failure for two Japanese speaking to an audience of seven Americans, the Americans would have been annoyed because they perceived the Japanese as vague and noncommital and unwilling to provide the information needed for making decisions.

The remedy for cross-cultural misunderstandings of this kind won't be found in the sort of vague suggestions that turn up in travel brochures. The breakdown is in the communication—in the language—and that is where you have to go for the solution.

Communication Technique: Cross-Cultural Translation

If you've ever taken a foreign language course, you probably remember your first attempt at translating an English sentence into that language. Most people tackling that task for the first time get a dictionary of the foreign language and follow a two-step procedure. First, they substitute a foreign word for each English word, using the dictionary to make their choice. Second, they try to "foreignize" the result according to their understanding of the grammar of the other language, by such tactics as changes in word order. Sometimes this does produce an accurate translation, but that's an accident; more often, the result is hilariously bad. Unfortunately for communication across cultures, this continues to be the accepted idea of what translation *is* for most people.

An accurate way to define translation is as follows: To translate a sequence of Language A into Language B, find the sequence that a native speaker of Language B would say or write *in the same context and situation.* The resulting sequence may or may not turn out to contain the same words in the two languages.

The Navajo translation of "What is your name?" doesn't contain the Navajo word for "name." Because it's extremely rude to ask for someone's name in the Navajo culture, the Navajo question is, "Where do you come from?" That is, in the context of one adult encountering another adult for the first time and needing to establish basic information about identity—where an English speaker would ask about names—a Navajo speaker would begin by asking about origins.

Similarly, translations into Laotian of English "if" sentences—like "If you want to work for this company, you'll have to go back to school and get a degree"—will begin with the Laotian word for "suppose." The sequence will mean, "Suppose you want to work for this company. You'll have to go back to school and get a degree." The reason for this isn't that the English word "if" is translated by the Laotian word for "suppose." It's because in a context where an English speaker would use an "if" sequence, a Laotian speaker would use a "suppose" sequence.

Suppose an American English speaker addressing another American English speaker uses a sequence like this one:

"Okay, let's get right down to business. The first thing we have to decide is the price of the product. What's your proposal?"

In exactly the same situation, the opening sequence for speakers of Arabic would be a comment about the weather and/or the landscape. It would "mean" the same thing—"Well, here we both are and now we can get started on the task of working out the contract for this product"—but the shared words would be few and far between.

Finally, in a context where the American would say, "Now, this painting is a view of the Bay of Fundy in springtime seen from the top of a nearby cliff, contrasting the awe the painter feels for the power of the waves with the feeling of serene pleasure evoked by the flowering trees in the foreground—and of course the eagle in the upper lefthand corner is a symbol of courage," a Japanese speaker would use a sequence meaning something like "I sincerely believe that you will enjoy this painting." The Japanese speaker assumes that the listener is capable of understanding what the painting portrays, what it is "about," what symbolism it contains, and so on, and that all that information can be considered as presupposed. Furthermore, the Japanese speaker believes *it would be insulting to the listener to assume otherwise.*

When your task is to present a strategy to a speaker or speakers of a language other than English, or a dialect of English other than your own, you need to do cross-cultural translation. Many factors in this communication situation will be entirely familiar. Your goals will remain the same as always: You want to make sure that as long as *you* understand what you're saying, your audience will understand it too; and you want everything you say to achieve its maximum potential for persuading your audience to share your commitment to the strategy. And the steps you take will also be familiar. *The process you follow is exactly the same as the one you use in sensory mode matching or in matching metaphors.*

If you are sight dominant and want to respond to something said by a touch dominant speaker, you ask yourself: "What would a touch dominant person say in this situation?" If the metaphor you use as perceptual filter is The Traditional Schoolroom and you want to make a proposal to someone for whom it is The Football Game, you ask yourself: "What would a football-metaphor person say in this situation?" That, on a very small scale, is cross-cultural translation. The difference, of course, is that in translating between sensory modes and between metaphors from your own culture you are working from a shared linguistic database. Although you prefer one sensory mode above the rest, you speak *all* of them; although some of the details of a metaphor from your culture may be unfamiliar to you, you know a great deal about it from your personal experience.

Translating between dialects is harder. A large proportion of the data will be common to both dialects. But the more linguistically distant the dialect is from yours, the more likely you are to be without some of the information you need to answer the question, "What would a speaker of the_____dialect of English say in this situation?" Translating between whole languages—especially when, as with English and Japanese, they come from completely different language families—is the hardest of all. How do you get the information you need, in either of these situations?

The best solution is always the simplest one: Ask a native speaker. If you want to convince a group of speakers of Language X to give your company a large order for tractors, the ideal solution is to find a native speaker of Language X who is also a speaker of English and ask for help. Here are the steps you follow:

Step 1: Describe the context. Explain your goal. Ask, "What would you say, *in your own language,* to open that meeting and start your presentation?"

Step 2: Listen to the utterance.

Step 3: When the utterance is over, ask the speaker to give you its *literal* English translation, to the extent that that's possible.

Step 4: If Step 3 leaves you baffled, ask the speaker to explain. Ask *why* that particular utterance is used; explore the subject until you feel that you understand adequately.

The word-for-word translation probably won't be what any English speaker would have said in that context, but it will give you valuable clues and help you ask the necessary questions. And it may surprise you. The literal translation of the sentence a Navajo speaker would say when an English speaker would say "I was riding a horse" is "A horse was animaling about with me." Sentences about tractors might be equally illuminating; the best way to find out such things is by asking a native speaker and listening carefully.

When consulting a native speaker—or even a nonnative but *fluent* speaker—is impossible, you have to fall back on the information in books and magazines, on tapes, and in other media. As you saw in Scenario Eleven, such sources aren't always reliable. Often what you read about "doing business with speakers of Language X" gives you information sufficient to make a list of tips (like the one about not treating Japanese business cards casually), but it tells you nothing about what lies *behind* the tips.

All the guides to doing business with the Japanese tell you to use very polite English and avoid informality, but they leave it to you to decide *why* that's called for. Common—and incorrect—conclusions among Americans are that the Japanese tendency to fill every English sentence with markers of politeness signals toadying, or hypocrisy, or elitism, or insincerity, or an attempt to "put on airs." The guides *don't* tell you what I've already told you: that equivalent Japanese sentences carry markers for rank and status without which the Japanese speaker feels uncomfortable and rude, and that English politeness markers are substituted for these missing items. That information is essential to keep you from basing your behavior on misunderstandings and incorrect conclusions. Similarly, a guide that tells you to be polite—but doesn't explain that a crucial element of courtesy for the Japanese is to rely heavily on context and assume that the adult listener will be able to work out the details—leaves you badly prepared for any presentation to a Japanese audience.

You are always safer reading about the other culture and language in the work of anthropologists and linguists. Supplement their writing with material by experts in business, but never rely on the business literature alone. Business experts aren't trained in cultural analysis—no reason why they should be—and what they "know" will often be based on their understanding of their personal experiences. When the understanding is actually *mis*understanding, much confusion will be created. You need both kinds of literature, so that you can check one against the other, and you need to be sure that what you're reading is relatively current. Even a superb discussion of the language and culture of Russia in 1904 is likely to be little use in presenting a strategy to the Russians of 1994. The books of Edward T. Hall—which are easy to find in libraries, regularly published in updated editions, and not impenetrably technical—are a good place to start. His bibliographies will lead you to other sources.

Another Look at Scenario Eleven

It will be obvious to you how Chet and Leslie should have handled their presentation; there's no need for me to insult *your* intelligence by providing a detailed revision. They should have introduced their slides of the paintings by saying, "We want to show you some examples of the paintings that will be in the exhibition," and confined their remarks about each slide to statements like "This is 'April Twilight,' painted by John J. Smith." They should have allowed the Japanese executives to make their own connections between their corporate cultures and the paintings in question, instead of presuming to tell them what those connections were. When they came to the point of providing the financial facts, Chet and Leslie should have asked themselves "If I explain this, will I sound as if I am talking down to my listeners?" If the answer was yes, those items should have been made discreetly available in writing or diagrams, without additional explanation. Then, when Chet closed the presentation by asking if there were any questions, there would have been ample opportunity to fill in any blanks—*at the option of the people he was trying to convince.*

Certainly handling it this way would have involved some risks. Some important information might have been overlooked; some important message might not have been transmitted. But the risks of handling it the other way—treating the Japanese listeners, as they perceived it, like *children*—were far greater.

WORKOUT SECTION: CHAPTER 11

1. In "C. Northcote Parkinson: An Appreciation," John Train mentions Parkinson's admonition not to take oneself too seriously. It is, he writes, "almost an echo of Talleyrand's famous advice to a young diplomat, 'Surtout point de zèle'; very roughly, 'Don't get carried away.'" (*The American Spectator*, June 1993). Train's words demonstrate the popular wisdom about what a translation is; his translation is not rough, but perfect. In the same situation where a French person would say, "Surtout point de zèle," an American English speaker would say "Don't get carried away." The literal translation—"Above all, absolutely no zeal whatsoever"—would not be nearly as accurate.

2. For your Communication Strategy Notebook, set up a Cross-Cultural Translation file and begin keeping track of relevant information to serve as a database for planning strategies. Record incidents in which you used (or observed someone else use) cross-cultural translation as part of a communication strategy. What was the situation? Who was present? What were the circumstances in the two cultures that caused translation to be necessary? What was said? What happened? What was surprising? Did anything go wrong, and if so, can you determine why? How could it have been done better?

Note: I strongly disagree with the popular idea that there are two distinct cultures for American Mainstream English speakers, one male and one female. However, I could certainly be wrong. You could investigate this important issue by looking for incidents in which you observe cross-cultural translation being done between the two genders. *Be careful not to confuse a clash in metaphors—as when one person filters perceptions through The Football Game metaphor and the other through The Traditional Schoolroom metaphor—with the more complex situation in which two different cultures exist. A man operating from the Traditional Schoolroom metaphor in a group where everyone else is using the Football Game metaphor—or a woman using the Football metaphor in a Schoolroom group—faces equally severe problems. This is independent of gender.*

3. In public life, and in any negotiation, Arabic speakers follow a rule we can summarize as, "Any serious language interaction must begin with a reference to history; the more serious the situation, the more elaborate the reference must be." Knowing that, how would you begin a presentation in which your final goal was to persuade a group of Arabic-speaking businessmen to contract for your company's services?

4. Within your own culture you have a heuristic process, based on empathy, that often works very well: "If I said [X], I would be feeling [Y]. Therefore, the speaker who has just said [X] must be feeling [Y]." Can you use that heuristic with individuals from a different culture?

5. In *Beyond Culture,* Edward T. Hall explains that to the American observer the Chinese seem to put up with a great deal, behave as if no problem exists, and permit endless hassles without objection (New York: Doubleday/Anchor, 1977). Hall points out that this behavior could lead Americans to conclude that the Chinese are weak and timid, which would be an error. Their tolerance is based on the fact that in the Chinese culture, once you have openly acknowledged that something you object to has happened, you are obligated to *do* something about it, and that can have grave consequences. (We have seen this graphically demonstrated in recent years, in the case of the young demonstrators in Tiananmen Square.) How should this affect your communication strategy in interactions with potential Chinese investors or business partners? Is there any counterpart to this Chinese cultural concept in your own culture?

6. In *The Enigma of Japanese Power,* K. van Wolferen tells us that "being openly contradicted in Japan entails a loss of face" (New York: Knopf, 1989). One of the consequences of this fact is that Japanese speakers will do everything they can to phrase questions in such a way that a "yes" answer will be appropriate. This is not only to avoid being contradicted themselves, but also to avoid putting the other person in a bind where contradiction seems to be the only option. Knowing this, what can you predict about the reaction of Japanese speakers to English negative questions like "You're not ready to leave yet, are you?" or "You're not concerned about the price, are you?" What sort of communication problems do you predict if such questions are used? How can such questions be avoided? And how can you structure your own communication so that *you* don't force a Japanese speaker into an open contradiction?

7. In "Do Not Pass Go," Damon Darlin recommends that Americans who are interacting in business with Asian nations make a serious effort to become competent players of the board game called *Go* (*Forbes* magazine, June 21, 1993). He lists the following as three important concepts of that game:

1. "Don't exploit the obvious move."

2. "The entire game is important, not the next move."

3. "A move that works toward one goal is a wasted move."

Darlin claims that Go reflects Asian business strategy "much the same way poker reflects American strategy." How would you relate the three Go concepts to communication strategy? And do you agree with Darlin that poker is the best example of American business strategy?

12

"Four Score and Six or Seven Years Ago, I Think..."

Increasing the Power of Your Words

Scenario Twelve

His name was Justin Draybar, he was the bearer of bad news, and he looked the part. He stood on the small stage at the front of the company auditorium, hanging on to the podium and looking grim. The audience looked grim right back at him; they knew he was there to try to convince them to accept a pay cut. It was enough to make anybody nervous. Justin cleared his throat a couple of times, took a deep breath, and began.

"People," he said, "I know how you feel. This is scary; I know it is. I expect most of you know what I'm going to say...you've heard the rumors going around...and I know you're upset. I understand what it's like for you, I really do. But I know what you're thinking out there. You're wondering how I can possibly have the brass gall, making three times as much as you do...and I'm pretty well fixed, I've got a nice house and a big car...you're wondering how I can stand up here and tell you that I understand what you're up against.

"I don't blame you for feeling that way, but I want to explain this situation to you. I won't keep you very long; I know it's no fun listening to me talk. Maybe it'll help a little if I tell you that the talking is as hard for me as the listening is for you? No? Well, it was worth a try!

"Anyway, you want to remember that I worked on the line once, too, just like you. Things were hard for me. Lots of times I wondered where I was going to get the money for the rent. I'd ask myself how my family

and I were going to make it. You don't forget that, you know. It
stays with you all your life and you always remember how it was.
So even though I'm part of management now, that doesn't mean I don't
understand how hard this is for all of you.

"I know what else you're thinking. You're thinking that all of us up on
the third floor are crazy if we believe for one minute that you're going
to say yes to a cut in your pay when you're only just barely getting by as
it is; you've just been waiting for your chance to tell us no. Let me tell
you, I wish this <u>was</u> some crazy person's wild imaginings! It would be a
lot easier on everybody. But it's not like that. No, I am here to tell you
the cold hard truth, and here it comes: This company is in <u>big</u> trouble. We
are about to go down the tubes, and that's the truth. We've got just
two choices: We can lay off a bunch of people, or you can agree to a pay
cut for everybody. And I do mean everybody, all the way to the top!
We can't hit the CEO and top execs as hard as we hit you—I'm not going
to lie to you, okay?—because if we do, they'll quit, and we can't make it
without them. But they <u>will</u> take a cut, I promise you.

"Okay. Let's remember that this is temporary. All we have to do is ride
it out. Things will get better, and we'll all be looking back at this and
laughing. But right now we're stuck with conditions as they are, and we
have to live with it.

"It's hard to choose between your jobs and your paychecks. You know
that the pay cut will hit everybody; that's fair. Because every single one
of you deserves to keep your job, there's no way we can promise you
layoffs would be fair. We'd try, sure, but we can't promise. Both of those
choices are bad ones; I only wish there were at least one <u>good</u> one. The
decision is up to you; because this is America, it doesn't get made
by some imperial decree, you get to <u>vote</u> on it, and the majority wins.

"Okay, I guess I've talked long enough. Too long, right? I know how
you feel. I'm going to stop now and give you a chance to talk it over and
decide what you want to do. And when you vote tomorrow morning, I
know you'll do the right thing.

"God bless you, and God bless this great country where everybody has
just as good a chance to make it to the top as everybody else.

"Thank you; that's all I have to say. Except that everybody in
management is really sorry about this, and I <u>personally</u> am sick about it,
and I want to be sure you know that. Thank you."

He stood there a minute looking at them, seeing them looking back at
him, their faces hard and cold as stone. And then he shrugged his
shoulders and told them one more time that he was sorry, and he walked
off the stage and down the hall, moving fast to get away from the
uproar he heard breaking out in the auditorium behind him.

What's Going on Here?

This is a typical example of an attempt by management to accomplish
three things: to tell the company's employees some bad news; to apol-

ogize for the bad news; and to persuade the workers to do what management wants them to do in *response* to the bad news. Those in charge hope all this can be done without completely destroying the relationship between workers and management. To make it clear that management takes the situation seriously, the method chosen is a brief speech in the company auditorium rather than something more informal. The man selected to make that speech has tried hard—and failed.

Justin's Point of View

Justin knows he's not a *great* public speaker, but he feels that he's a competent one. He's careful not to talk too long; he knows how to stick to his subject; he talks loudly enough and clearly enough so that people can understand what he says; he doesn't use a lot of stuffy, inappropriate big words or tell rambling personal anecdotes. He gets called on for speeches pretty often. This time, because he knew it wasn't something to just toss off casually, he spent a couple of evenings planning what he was going to say and practicing his delivery.

As Justin saw it, there were four points he had to make. First: That he remembered what it was like to be in the ranks and have a hard time getting by, so that he understood how hard this was going to be for the employees and felt bad about it. Second: That things were so bad, even if the squeeze was a temporary one, that the only choices open to the company were layoffs or paycuts. Third: That the decision between those two bad choices would be made by majority vote of the employees themselves, not by some decree from above. And fourth: That everything would be done to make the action taken as fair as it possibly could be.

He gave a lot of thought to how he could get all that into a short speech, he made *sure* it was all in there, and he feels that he did a decent job. He just wishes that he'd been able to get through to his audience at some point and bring them around to the idea that although it would be hard, this was their chance to work together so that eventually things would be better for *every*body. He knows that didn't happen. He knows he left the employees resentful, with their only solidarity based on their conviction that, "It's us versus them." He regrets that, but he has no idea what he could have done to achieve a better outcome.

The Employees' Point of View

It seems to the employees that they have been thoroughly shafted and that expecting them to be nice about it is irrational. They understood Justin's four points, but not as he intended them. As they heard it, he said, "We've made such a mess at the top that we have to cut your pay or lay you off. We're going to make you choose your own poison, and we expect you to be grateful for the chance. If you don't like it, tough; we're trying to be fair." They heard him say that he's sorry, and that management is sorry, and they believe it. Why *wouldn't* they be sorry, when the company they're supposed to be running is in so much trouble that it threatens *their* paychecks? But being sorry doesn't pay the rent or put food on the table. They are furious about what's happening, and not one word Justin said gave them a reason to feel anything but rage and resentment.

What Went Wrong?

When you have good news for people, it really doesn't matter much how you say it. Nobody who hears you say, "Everybody's going to get a raise, starting next week!" is going to complain that you should have said that more elegantly. But when the news is *bad*, when you have only terrible choices to offer, that's a different matter; then the way you phrase your messages becomes critically important, and you have to make choices based on style rather than on content.

When you are the bearer of bad news, as Justin Draybar was, the only thing you have to fall back on is *emotions.* You need to be able to inspire a feeling of rallying around the flag on the sinking ship, a feeling of "We're all in this together, and what matters is working together and helping each other face this challenge, because then it will all turn out right in the end for every one of us!"

You can't do that with facts alone. You can't do it by just "being yourself," unless, unlike most of us, you have irresistible charisma. You have to use the full power of language, which offers you a wide array of tools for getting *past* the facts and convincing people to let their feelings take over in *spite* of the facts.

Let's take a look at some of those tools.

Communication Technique: Using the Power of Rhetoric

You may have taken a course called "English Rhetoric." You have almost certainly taken an English course in which your instructor discussed "rhetorical devices." Rhetoric is one of the most ancient of disciplines—if you had been a pupil of Aristotle, you would have studied rhetoric. Many and varied definitions of rhetoric exist, depending on the person doing the defining and the field from which the definition is taken. For our purposes, we can define it here very simply: *Rhetoric is the science of persuasion based on language.* (It's traditional to speak of the "art" of rhetoric, but it's more accurate today to call it a science.)

The "devices" of rhetoric (simile, metonymy, oxymoron, synecdoche, and the like) fill up entire shelves in our libraries, where you are free to examine them at your leisure if they interest you. In this chapter we will be concentrating on two *rhetorical processes* under which most of the devices can be filed: metaphor and parallelism. Because metaphor has already been discussed at length in Chapters 9 and 10, our major focus here will be on parallelism.

Parallelism

Parallelism means shaping the chunks of your language in a connected discourse so that they are as much alike as is possible while maintaining their separate meanings. It's used in written language, but has to be handled with great care in that medium because it so easily becomes overobvious and excessive. In spoken language, however—in speeches and talks and oral presentations of every kind—it can be used much more freely. People listening to language don't have the text before them, and they find the repetitiousness of parallel items helpful for processing what they're hearing.

The most famous example of parallelism is probably Caesar's, "I came; I saw; I conquered." Each of the clauses in that sequence has two constituents: a subject nominal ("I"), and a single verb. (A *constituent* is either a single word or a chunk that could, by itself, answer a question about the content of a sentence, like "Who did it?" or "Where did it happen"?) The clauses are absolutely parallel, as was the Latin, "Veni; vidi; vici," from which they were translated. They don't *have* to be that way, however. You could convey the same three messages with any of an infinite number of alternatives, including the following:

- I came; I saw; and then I whipped the enemy.
- I came; I saw; the enemy was conquered by me.
- In the end I won, but I first I had to get to the scene and see what was happening.
- After I arrived and looked things over, I went on to conquer the enemy.
- First, you know, I got there. And I saw the whole scene...like what was going on, you know? And then finally I, like, turned out to be the winner.

These examples differ in style and focus. The final example comes from someone whose speech contains twirks—the speaker's use of "like" and "you know"—that would distract from the message and capture far too much of the listener's attention. However, although they all say roughly what the original said and convey the same three messages, none of them uses parallelism as the original did, and none of them has the original's power.

The steps you follow in using parallelism go like this:

1. Write down your basic message—the set of sentences that express the thoughts you want to get across to your listeners—without worrying about style.

2. Divide your sentences into their major constituent parts in terms of the *function* the parts serve.

3. Do everything possible to see that constituents which have the same function also have the same structure.

4. When you have only one constituent in a particular role, add another one—better yet, add two—and make it parallel.

5. Read the result into a tape recorder and listen to it.

6. Tidy up; where there is too *much* repetition, make substitutions and condense.

This is much more complicated to read about than it is to do. The best way to clarify it is to go through the process for a very simple brief text.

Suppose a speaker wants to tell a group of employees that management has decided to go along with some demands they've been making for a while. Without parallelism, the speaker might say this:

"I know you people have wanted a new parking lot for at least ten years. We have decided to go ahead with it. And while we're putting in the parking lot, I think we'll put in some picnic tables, too; they're something else you've been wanting. We hope you'll be pleased."

A first run through the six steps would give you this rough revision:

"We know you have wanted a parking lot for ten years; we know you have wanted picnic tables for a long time. We have decided to put in the parking lot; we have decided to put in some picnic tables. We hope you'll be pleased; we hope you'll be satisfied."

People have a strong fondness for things that come in threes. We like Three Little Pigs, and three meals a day, and three wishes, and Three Bears; we like a beginning, a middle, and an end. The speaker above has only two parallel constituents in each set; let's add one more for our next rewrite:

"We know you have wanted a parking lot for ten years; we know you have wanted picnic tables for a long time; we know you have wanted a coffee machine since the old one broke down. We have decided to put in the parking lot; we have decided to put in the picnic tables; we have decided to put in the new coffee machine. We hope you'll be pleased; we hope you'll be satisfied; we hope you'll be delighted."

Now we have perfect parallelism; all constituents filling the same role in a sentence have the same structure. But if you listen to a tape recording of this version you'll notice immediately that the repetition is too heavy and too obvious for such an informal topic. Let's get rid of some of it by making a few judicious changes, like this:

"We know you have wanted a parking lot for ten years; we know you've wanted picnic tables for a long time; we're aware that you've been wishing for a new coffee machine since the old one broke down. We've decided to put in the parking lot; we've decided to set out the picnic tables; we've made up our minds to get the new coffee machine. We hope you'll be pleased, satisfied, and delighted."

Those who teach "language arts" in this country are constantly telling us that we must strive for variety and avoid repeating ourselves. They have a point, particularly for written language. However, you would be amazed at how *much* parallelism an audience will accept, and even enjoy, in a speech. Listening with full attention when you don't have a written text to look at is difficult, and in our society we get little practice doing it. You have to really run the process of parallelism into the ground to overdo it, and when you listen to your recorded words, your own ear for language will tell you if you've gone too far. Even the "pleased, satisfied, and delighted" line above, which would get an emphatic red-penciling from most English teachers, is unlikely to produce a negative reaction in those you're talking to. One more adjective—as in, "We hope you'll be pleased, satisfied, delighted, and thrilled"—would be too much; people would think you were being sarcastic. But you can get by with three in an enthusiastic closing line.

Parallelism and Rhythm

Using parallelism gives perceptible *rhythm* to your language—patterns of rhythm that can be recognized and enjoyed by your listeners. When "Veni; vidi; vici" was translated, it would have actually been more perfectly parallel to make it "I came; I saw; I won." Then you would have had three instances of "I," followed by three verbs that were only one syllable long. Perhaps the rhythm established by "I came; I saw; I conquered" was more pleasing to the ear of the English translator. This choice is a matter of taste, and was no doubt helped along by the fact that "to conquer" is understood as a *bigger* victory than "to win." But either choice establishes a rhythmic pattern for the ear of the listener. This is one of the predictable effects of parallelism, and the natural love that human beings have for rhythmic patterns causes them to take pleasure in listening to such sequences.

This is one of the reasons for having three or more instances of a parallel constituent. If I use two parallel items in a row, the second time could have been a coincidence or an accident, and may be perceived that way. If I use *three* in a row, however, the listener knows it's almost certainly deliberate. If I say "Will you please pick the peas?" the rhyme and rhythm is probably accidental and you may not notice any pattern. If I say "Will you please pick the peas under the trees?" the pattern is unlikely to have been unintentional and it would be hard for a listener to miss. The human brain is always scanning for pattern, and when it perceives three like things in a row it assumes that a pattern has been found.

You don't have to add rhyme to your speech to take advantage of this love for pattern. The act of setting up parallel structures will *automatically* create a rhythmic pattern a great deal of the time. The only additional factor you might need to consider is the number of syllables in your words. When you can choose between a set of three words that are all appropriate to your message—one set in which all three words have two syllables and one in which all three have a different syllable count—the two-syllable set is usually your best choice.

Another Look at
Scenario Twelve

Now, let's go back to Justin Draybar's failed speech from Scenario Twelve to find out how he could use parallelism and metaphor to make his speech more effective and more compelling and give himself a better chance to create a more positive attitude in his audience.

Scenario Twelve, Revised

"I know how you feel," Justin began, his voice as solemn as if he were speaking at a funeral. "I know what you fear; I know what you need. And I know what you're thinking when you hear me say that! Oh, you're polite; you keep a civil expression on your faces, the way your mothers taught you to do. But you're thinking, how can I stand here in front of you, earning three times what you earn, me with my big house and my big car, and make those claims? How can I have the brass gall to claim that you and I have anything more in common than our basic humanity?

"Well, I don't blame you—but let me explain. Let me explain that like you, I was once a worker on the line; like you, I once lived from paycheck to paycheck. Like you, I often wondered how my family and I were going to make it till payday. I do remember what that was like. Let me tell you: You don't ever forget it! Sometimes in the darkest part of the night I still wake up in a cold sweat, I still sit bolt upright in the blackness and think, "Oh Lord, where am I going to get the money for the rent?" I don't need to do that any more—thanks to hard work, both yours and mine, and my great good fortune in being born in a country where opportunities are out there on the trees for anybody's picking—but it still happens. You never...never...forget.

"And now here I come, here I am, coming to you to ask you to do something that sounds crazy. You know what I'm going to ask. You've been hearing the rumors; you've been thinking that the people in management have gone clear out of their minds; you've been practicing up to say NO. I understand that, and I don't blame you. You can barely make it as it is, and now I'm here asking you please to take a pay cut, to somehow make it on even less!

"I don't blame you for wondering how I can do that and still be allowed to walk the streets, free and unattended like a rational man. You're thinking, 'Take him away in a net...put him somewhere and look after him...if he thinks there's a prayer of getting us to go along with cutting our own salaries, he is stark raving mad.'

"Frankly, I almost wish you were right. I wish this whole thing were only the delusions of a broken mind. Unfortunately, I stand here as sane and sober as any one of you; I can't take refuge in mad fantasies, or comfort in wild dreams.

"You are my friends; I would not lie to you. I am here to tell you the cold and bitter truth. We are in serious trouble; we face grave dangers; we are out on a cliff in a high wind, and it will take very little to push us over the edge. Let me tell it to you fast and clear and simple: *We have just two choices, and they're both bad.*

"If this company is to survive, either we cut jobs or we cut paychecks—that is the truth. We know this is temporary trouble. If we can hang on, if we can ride out this storm, we will turn this ship around, and when we do, the skies will be bright again, I promise you that! But unless we do one of two things—cut everybody's paycheck...and that means management, too, not just you people on the line—or cut two jobs or more in every ten, the only place <u>we're</u> going is right straight down to the bottom of this economy's harshest sea! That's just the way it is. This is the <u>real</u> world! We can't go surfing the channels looking for a different set of circumstances; we're stuck with the ones we face right this minute.

"Now it's up to you. We in management feel that the pay cut is the better choice, the choice that offers an opportunity for every one of you to stay on and help us set things right—the choice that offers an opportunity for every one of you to <u>share</u> in the success that we know lies ahead. But <u>you</u> have to choose. This is the United States of America, and that means you have the privilege of making this choice, by casting your own vote, voting your own conscience, standing up for your own principles. <u>You</u>, not management, get to decide which it will be.

"If you vote to cut paychecks, at least you know it's going to be fair— the pain will come to every one of us. I won't lie to you; I won't claim that those at the very top are going to be hurt as badly as you are. If we hurt them that badly, they won't stay, and we can't survive if they leave. But they <u>will</u> take a cut, along with you; I give you my word. If you vote to cut jobs, on the other hand, there's no way to know who will get thrown over the side. It could be you; it could be me; it could be your neighbor. There's no way to make that fair, because every last one of you has worked your hardest and done your best and given us one hundred and ten percent every time, and every last one of you deserves to <u>stay on</u>. It's just cruel hard fate that everybody <u>can't</u> stay on…not at the salaries we're paying now, not if we're going to be able to go on paying <u>anybody's</u> salary for very long. It's not fair—but if you decide against the pay cut, some of you will have to go.

"It's a hard choice and you're the only ones equipped to make it. I've said enough. I'm going to leave you now to think this over and discuss it among yourselves and come to a decision. And I know that when you vote tomorrow morning we can count on you. I <u>know</u> that. I know it because I once stood where you stand and faced the same hard choices you face. I know that you will do the right thing.

"God bless you all, and thank you for hearing me out."

He stood one more long minute looking at them, gripping the podium in both hands, and then he gave them a solemn but confident smile and a thumbs-up sign and walked off the stage and down the hall. He couldn't be absolutely sure that he'd won them over—you never know until the votes are in and counted—but at least what he heard behind him didn't sound like an angry riot. It sounded like the excited discussion of people who wanted to talk and were feeling a little bit more positive than they had when he started to speak to them. Maybe, just maybe, this was going to work out after all.

I'm sure you will agree with me that this rewrite is a great deal better than the speech at the beginning of the chapter. It carries the same basic messages; it makes the same four points; but it does it very differently. It's a little longer, but that's all right—the few extra minutes spent in persuasion will pay off many times over if they achieve their purpose.

We don't need to go over this revision word by word. You will see what's been done without that. But a brief analysis that just hits the high points might be helpful. Let's begin with a list of the parallel structures that were set up, and then we'll close by considering a few additional tactics Draybar could have used to give the speech its maximum potential for success.

List of Parallel Structures

1. "I know how you feel; I know what you fear; I know what you need." (Plus, "And I know what you're <u>think</u>ing...," which is almost parallel.)

2. "You're polite; you keep a civil expression on your face...; (but) you're <u>think</u>ing...."

3. "How can I stand here...; How can I have the brass <u>gall</u> to claim..."

4. "My big house; my big car"

5. "Let me explain; let me explain"

6. "Like you, I was once a worker on the line; like you, I once lived from paycheck to paycheck; like you, I often wondered..."

7. "I still wake up in a cold sweat; I still sit bolt upright in the blackness and think..."

8. "Here I come; here I am"

9. "You've been hearing the rumors; you've been thinking...; you've been practicing..."

10. "Refuge in mad fantasies; (or) comfort in wild dreams"

11. "We are in serious trouble; we face grave dangers; we are out on a cliff in a high wind..."

12. "(Either) we cut jobs (or) we cut paychecks"

13. "If we can hang on; if we can ride out this storm..."

14. "The choice that offers an opportunity for every one of you to stay on...; "the choice that offers an opportunity for every one of you to share..."

15. "Making this choice; (by) casting your own vote; voting your own conscience; standing up for your own principles."

16. "If you vote to cut paychecks...; If you vote to cut jobs..."
17. "It could be you; it could be me; it could be your neighbor."
18. "Worked your hardest; done your best; given us one hundred and ten percent..."
19. "Every last one of you has worked...; every last one of you deserves..."
20. "I know...; I know...; I know...; I know..."
21. "Stood where you stand; (and) faced the same hard choices you face."

Twenty-one sets of parallel constituents, many with smaller ones inside them. That's a lot, but it's not too many.

Additional Rhetorical Choices

What else did Justin do to use the power rhetoric gives us? He used metaphor, more than once. When he said, "We are out on a cliff in a high wind, and it will take very little to push us over the edge," he was using the metaphor "Being in our current business situation is like standing on a cliff in a high wind." And then, in the next paragraph, he made extensive us of this metaphor: "Our company in its current business situation is a ship at sea in a storm." The people he was speaking to all can imagine vividly what it's like to be at the edge of a cliff in high wind, in danger of falling over the edge; they may never have gone to sea in a ship, but they know that experience well from books and movies. Justin doesn't have to fill in all the details. Instead he relies on the context, with all its presupposed parts, and on the way human language processing works; he lets his *listeners* fill in all the blanks for themselves. Long before "interactive" became a buzz word in the electronic media, this was one of the most efficient ways to make a *talk* interactive.

In both versions of the speech we also see an allusion to "the United States of America," along with "God and country" (and, in the revision, "mother") to back it up. These items are used to remind the audience of the ties that bind them together, of their shared culture and heritage, of our long tradition of "united we stand, divided we fall," and of the good old-fashioned virtues of loyalty and duty. The speaker's hope is that this will ring the sort of note in people's minds that causes *them* to think of the metaphor that goes, "This company is like the United States of America, like a *nation*, with citizens who have shared duties and shared privileges." Both versions make three references to this overarching metaphor. To my mind, it's a little heavy-handed in the first version, and I prefer the second—but that judgment would depend on the company culture.

In several places where a single descriptive word could have been used, the revised speech uses two or more. Justin says, "great good fortune" and "free and unattended" and "cold and bitter" and "right straight down to the bottom." This is a kind of very *condensed* parallelism—"cold and bitter truth" condenses "cold truth and bitter truth," for example—and it introduces variety while at the same time attending to the human fondness for pattern.

Finally, Justin uses the device of the *rhetorical question*, which you'll remember from Chapter 7. We hear these constantly from politicians, as in "Why do I say that? I say that because..." and "Do I think that's a good idea? Yes, I do, because..." Rhetorical questions let speakers "ask" a question that they think the audience would like to (or ought to) ask, or a question that speakers want made explicit; speakers can then provide the answer themselves if that suits their purposes. This is a useful device that gives the ear an occasional rest from the otherwise unbroken sequence of statement after statement after statement after statement.

Your decision about how many rhetorical processes and devices to use, and how often, should be based primarily on two factors: the seriousness of the issue to be raised, and the formality of the setting. In the original version of the speech, Justin tried to joke with his audience a time or two, in keeping with his claim to be one of them. Given the seriousness of a forced choice between a pay cut and a layoff, plus the formality of an obligatory assembly in an auditorium, this was a mistake. It also weakened his attempt to bring in duty to God and country and, by analogy, to the company. On the other hand, although the revised speech is less casual, it has not been given the highly formal and technical vocabulary and structure of a keynote speech or an inaugural address or a plea before a federal court. Tailor your rhetoric to the occasion, the setting, and the audience.

WORKOUT SECTION: CHAPTER 12

1. The quotations that follow contain examples of deliberate use of rhetorical devices and processes. Identify them; where it's possible, improve on them. (It's not necessary to give them their technical names; just state what's been done, in ordinary language.)

a. "Parker I would never underestimate. They have the distribution, the awareness and the muscle." (*Shaun Lattin, quoted by John Marcom, Jr., in "Penmanship with a Flourish,"* Forbes *magazine, April 3, 1989, p. 154*)

b. "More troubling still are long periods of joblessness for many of these workers." (*Susan Dentzer, "Secretaries Down the Chute,"* U.S. News & World Report, *March 28, 1994, p. 65*)

c. "TQM asks not how a business can spend less or make more, but challenges it to improve workers' relationships with one another and with management." (*Kristie Perry, "What Worked for Japan Could Work for You,"* Medical Economics, *October 25, 1993, p. 87*)

d. "What is natural is beautiful. What is beautiful is powerful. What is natural and beautiful and powerful is worth holding on to." (*Jerry Flint, "How Do You Build a Luxury Image?"* Forbes *magazine, April 3, 1989, p. 60*). The sequence comes from marketing language for the Infiniti automobile.

e. "Medicine is becoming less an art than a formula, less a privilege than a right, less a profession than a trade." (*Arthur Kavanaugh, "Medicine Is Becoming Just Another Job,"* Medical Economics, *April 26, 1993, p. 33*)

f. "See what your revenues really are; accept that as reality; spend less than that." (*W. M. "Trip" Hawkins, "Winning a Dangerous Game,"* Success *magazine, March 1991, p. 10*)

g. "Bill Clinton...has suffered from the smears of resentful state police officers in Arkansas, the continuing backwash from the Whitewater affair and the bizarre withdrawal of his defense secretary-designate." (*Mortimer B. Zuckerman, "Bill Clinton, One Year Later,"* U.S. News & World Report, *January 31, 1994, p. 68*) (It would be worth your while to unpack the presuppositions in this last example and list the claims Zuckerman has sheltered.)

2. Find the claims that have been sheltered in presuppositions in the revised version of Justin Draybar's speech and make them overt.

3. "It's like you say on Wall Street: Bears make money, bulls make money, but hogs get eaten." (*Terry Erich, quoted by Jerry Flint in*

"Publisher's Heaven," Forbes *magazine, November 12, 1990, p. 78*) The author of this remark had an opportunity here to use parallelism, but he didn't. He switched the third potentially parallel chunk from active to passive; in addition, he used the "get" passive rather than the "be" passive. Can you explain why? If the three items had been kept perfectly parallel, what would the third one say? (*Note:* For many varieties of American English, the "get" passive implies some degree of responsibility, while the "be" passive implies none. That is, the person who says "I got fired" is assumed to be admitting responsibility, if only for being in the wrong place at the wrong time, while the person who says "I was fired" is assumed to be claiming total innocence of responsibility.)

4. For your Communication Strategy Notebook, set up a Rhetoric file and begin keeping track of relevant information, to serve as a database for planning strategies. For example:

- Record incidents (from your own life, or incidents you've read or heard about) in which rhetoric was used to make some sequence of language more clear or more compelling. What was the situation? Who was present? What was said? How did people react? What happened? What was surprising? Did anything go wrong, and if so can you identify it? What could have been said to make a better outcome more likely?

- Keep a record of good examples of rhetoric you come across in reading or in observing the media. You never know when you might be able to adapt one for your own use.

- One of the most common communication phenomena is what the French call "l'esprit d'escalier"—literally, "the wit of the staircase." It describes that moment after a presentation, a conversation, or a confrontation, when you're on your way to somewhere else and you suddenly think of all the things you *could* have said. (This demonstrates the difference between linguistic competence—represented by the flawless grammar stored in your long-term memory—and performance.) Begin taking advantage of this human frailty and putting it to good use. After a presentation, sit down with your notebook and do a revision while it's all still fresh in your mind. Record all the things you *could* have said that might have been improvements on what you actually did say.

5. For classic examples of good rhetoric superbly presented, read (or better yet, listen to recordings of) some of the brief speeches of John F. Kennedy and of Martin Luther King, Jr. These two men had different

native dialects of English. Do you notice any rhetorical differences that reflect this fact?

6. "If I know somebody very well, in ten minutes, if I set my mind to it, I could perhaps say to them things so cruel, so destructive, that they would never forget them for the rest of their life. But could I in ten minutes say things so beautiful, so creative, that they would never forget them?" *(Bishop Kallistos Ware, in an interview titled "Image and Likeness," Parabola, Spring 1985, pp. 66–67)*

This is a striking, and troubling, question. Why should it be so much easier to think of unforgettably cruel utterances than unforgettably beautiful ones? Is it a comment on human character, or some limitation in language itself, or could it just be a matter of lack of practice?

13

"It Just Popped into My Head from Out of Nowhere!"

Using the Fresh Perceptions of Your Right Brain

Scenario Thirteen

"This isn't going to <u>work</u>, Nate," Cecily James predicted softly, as she and Nathan Anderly met outside the conference room door.

"You just watch!" he answered. "You're going to be surprised."

"Right!" Cecily snapped. "If <u>anything</u> happens, I'm going to be surprised! Let's go on in there and get this <u>over</u> with."

Nate grinned at her. "Your Head Nanny is really giving you a hard time, isn't she?"

"What? What does <u>that</u> mean?"

"Everybody's got a Head Nanny, Cecily, standing guard by their right brain with her arms folded over her chest and her jaw set, wearing a badge that says 'Keep Out! <u>No</u>body Gets Past <u>Me</u>!'"

Cecily didn't dignify that with a response. She just glared at him and jerked her head at the door to get him moving, and they went into the room where the 12 department supervisors were waiting for them. The supervisors were seated in groups of three, staring grimly at the giant sheet of white paper that covered each of the four tables.

"Okay, everybody," Nate said, "we're all set. You're going to use the sheet of paper on your table to create a semantic map. You've all got your colored markers with you, and we—"

"Wait a minute!" said Gail Clearing. "What are we supposed to be <u>doing</u> here?"

"Preparing a semantic map, Gail, so that we can agree on a name and a logo for the new communications training program."

Nate didn't wait for her to continue. He knew what she would say if he did: "Why can't we just discuss it and make our choices the way we <u>a</u>lways do?" That had already been tried, and the group had picked "The Communication Training Program" for a name and a parrot on a perch for a logo. Instead, he went right ahead and explained the semantic mapping process to them, illustrating what he said on the board at the front of the room as he went along.

"The seven words you see in the boxes are the keywords," he told them. "They're the seven characteristics that we all agreed describe the kind of training program we want. Around each keyword you're going to write down <u>other</u> words...or brief phrases, two or three words long...that the keyword makes you think of. You want to work fast, now! Don't struggle, don't mull it over, just write down the first thing that pops into your head. If you get stuck, just skip that word and come back to it later. That gives you Level One on your map. Draw a circle around each Level One word—like this...."

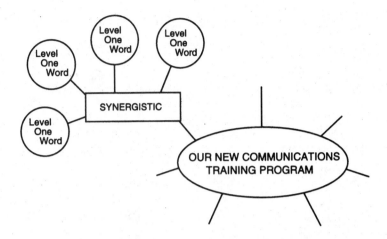

and connect it to the keyword it goes with. When you've got three, four, maybe half a dozen words in circles around each keyword, you repeat the process for each of the circled words, to get to Level Two. Like this...

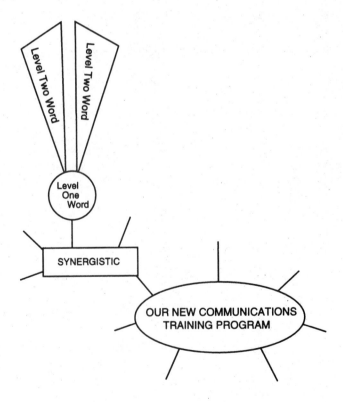

"For Level Two you want to use a different colored marker so you can keep the levels straight. You may decide you want to go on to more levels, in which case you'll use a different color for each one. Okay so far?

"Now, when you've got at least two levels you stop and look for connections—words from different parts of the map that you realize you can hook up together. You connect those with a line of a different color...like this...

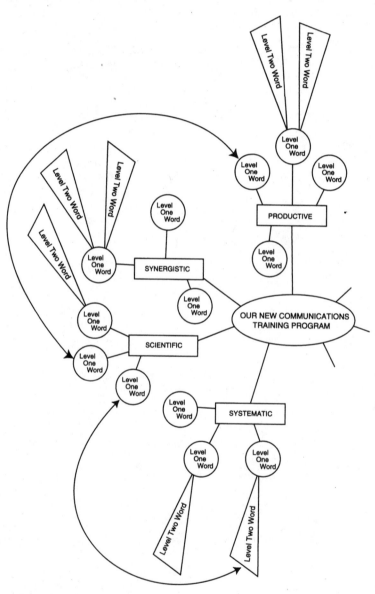

"All right! Cecily and I will be moving around the room from table to table to help you out, to answer questions, stuff like that. Let's get started!" And he stepped back to be sure they could all see the board.

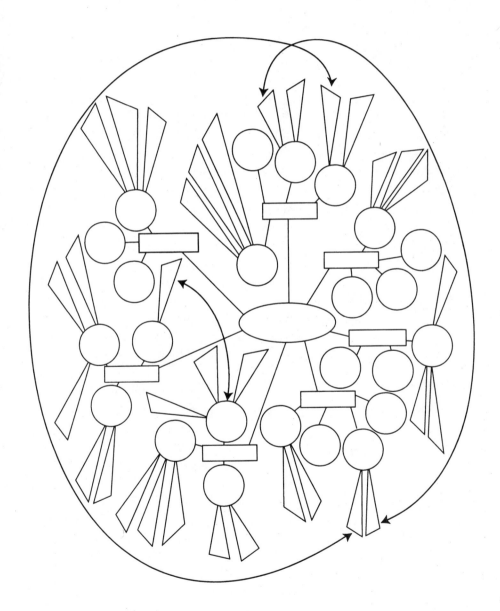

The objections he was hearing from the supervisors were predictable. He'd heard them all before; they were standard Head Nanny talk. "Why do we have to go through all this nonsense just to pick out a name and a logo?" "Whose idea was this, anyway?" "This is a silly waste of time, you know that? We've got work to do!" "What difference does it make what we call the stupid training program? Who cares what we call it?"

"Who <u>cares</u> what we call it?"

That was the one that made the semantic mapping process necessary. It was these 12 people that the company was counting on to convince all the other employees that the training program was something to be enthusiastic about; the supervisors were supposed to do the motivating. You can't inspire enthusiasm for a project in other people when your own level of interest is so low that you don't even care what the project is called. Nate just stood and smiled at them, saying, "I hear you," once in a while, until it became clear to everyone that the quickest way to get out of the meeting and back to their desks would be to get on with the task.

It went slowly at first. Cecily kept nodding her head; just as she had predicted, it wasn't working. But then there was a flurry of talk at one of the tables, and then at the others, and suddenly the room was humming with the sound of work being done—and being enjoyed.

"Hey, I don't see what 'cybernetic' has got to do with 'innovative'! I…No, wait a minute, I get it! Okay, put down 'cybernetic'!"

"The only thing 'explosives' makes <u>me</u> think of is a suitcase. You know, like at an airport terminal? Can I put that down?"

"Just <u>skip</u> that one, remember? He said to work fast and if you get stuck go on and then come back? I'm gonna put down 'investigation' here for 'systematic,' okay?"

"What was that Fuller guy's first name? Buckley? Buck something?"

"Will you look at this? Is there going to be enough room on this sheet of paper?"

Cecily stared at them, amazed, and Nate smiled at her. "I <u>told</u> you," he said. "Sometimes it's takes a while to get people started…but it works. It <u>always</u> works."

"And they'll come up with a name? And a logo?"

"You can count on it. They'll come up with several, and then they can vote on which one they're going to use."

"Will the names be any <u>good</u>?"

"Maybe. Probably. It really doesn't matter."

Cecily stopped and frowned. "I don't understand," she said.

"Whether the names—or whatever the map is for—are any good isn't important," he explained softly, "although they often turn out to be surprisingly good. What matters is that by the time these people finish their maps the communications training program will have become their baby, and they will care what it's called! What matters isn't how good the name or logo is, but that it comes from them, and has meaning for them, and is their choice. *The important thing about semantic mapping is that it gives people a perception that they personally have some degree of control—without that, they won't invest in the project.* Now, I'll take that table over there and you pick one of the others and let's see if we can keep things moving."

At the end of the session the group had five proposed names to choose from: Synergy Factory; Metacommunication 101; Mechanics of Synergy; Cybertactics; and Bees (for Building Efficient Effective Speech). And they had three candidates to replace the parrot logo.

What's Going on Here: What Went Right?

This scenario is a little different from the other 12 we've examined in this book. It shows the typical responses most business people have when it's suggested that they should solve a problem using one of the procedures that are called *right-brain techniques.* (We'll come back to what that actually means in a moment.) There is ordinarily strong resistance at first, especially if no one present has had any encounter with that sort of thing before, but it's forgotten once the procedure is under way. The initial attitude responsible for the resistance—that right-brain techniques are silly and childish and a waste of time—changes drastically when the technique pays off. Right-brain techniques are particularly useful in two types of situations:

- When everyone trying to deal with a problem is well and truly "stuck," so that no new ideas are forthcoming and the general consensus is that they never will be.

- When people trying to solve a problem have only a very vague and murky grasp of it, so that they are simply spinning their wheels—and the vagueness cannot be fixed by providing them with a list of "facts."

Communication Technique:
Semantic Mapping

Your Left Brain's Connected to
Your Right Brain

The first thing we have to do is clarify this "left-brain/right-brain" concept. Much of what you read and hear from the media on this subject is distorted and misleading. The brain does have a left hemisphere and a right hemisphere, and they differ in the tasks they handle best. However, the two hemispheres are connected, allowing information to move back and forth between them; they don't function in isolation from one another. Furthermore, most of what is stored in the brain is *redundantly* stored—that is, it's stored in more than one place, or can be managed by more than one neurological area if necessary. There are many competing models of the brain and memory, and the evidence is by no means all in. (For a nontechnical review, see Charles Hampden-Turner, *Maps of the Mind*, New York: Macmillan, 1981.) The safest course and the one least likely to lead to confusion is to treat all but the most literal information about brains/minds as a metaphor.

The common idea that the left brain is "specialized for language and math" and the right brain is "specialized for art and music" is a distortion. Remembering that we are speaking metaphorically, it's accurate to say that the left brain is best at processing information arranged as one discrete unit after another—like written English and Morse code and columns of figures, while the right brain is best at processing non-linear information, such as pictures and metaphors and music. (But remember that when people are trained in music theory and learn to "read" music, they switch to processing it in the left hemisphere.)

The left brain tries hard to impose logical order on the nonlinear thoughts of the right brain. And the left brain is, as would be expected, very fond of *lists*. Once someone's left brain has created a list and named it "all the possible solutions to this problem," it's almost impossible for that person to think of any new ideas on the subject. Some sort of pump-priming is needed, and the right brain is the best source for that.

The left brain is also determined to make everything neat and tidy the way a row of numbers is neat and tidy, and it will work hard to exclude metaphors and puns and jokes and wordplay of every kind. This is why I refer to the censorship function of your left brain as your "Head Nanny." It behaves exactly like a rigid disciplinarian determined to keep you from ever having an untidy thought—for your own *good*, of course. The reason dreams often seem so bizarre is that the left brain, appalled by the lack of order, takes the *language* of dreams... which is nonlinear and metaphorical and pictorial and filled with wordplay...and forces it into the form of a narrative.

When you look for a solution by using a right-brain technique, you are trying to get *past* the censoring left brain so that your right brain will have a chance to play around with the problem. Your left brain, if you encourage it at all, will do everything possible to dissuade you from doing that; it doesn't approve of playing around. It will supply you with an immediate conviction that you're wasting time, that the activity is silly and childish, and so on—the ideas expressed by the managers in Scenario Thirteen. You should be prepared for that reaction and you should rigorously ignore it.

What Is Semantic Mapping?

Semantic mapping is a *free association* method for accessing the right brain. Free association comes from psychoanalysis, in those therapeutic models where the analysis of dreams is considered important. Outside psychiatry, free association is the basis of the *clustering* technique developed by Gabriele Lusser Rico and the *mind maps* of Tony Buzan; it is the foundation of the *dream-mapping* technique used in the Gentle Art system. Often it provides just the sharp jog you need to let you solve a problem in some new and different way—instead of, as Edward De Bono puts it, only digging the same old hole deeper and deeper.

The left brain organizes different items logically, on the basis of well-defined criteria. If given the task of writing down a list defined as "English words that are spelled differently but pronounced the same," it might well think of both "piece" and "peace"; but if it were told that an attempt was being made to associate "nonviolent" and "peace" and "piece"—as in the semantic map for Scenario Thirteen—it would exclude "piece" from the set and call the attempt illogical. The right brain, however, moves serenely from "nonviolent" to "peace" to "piece" and will move right on from there to "pie" and "cherries" and "George Washington" and "minuet" if not stopped. That's why this way of doing things is called *free* association. You can usually demonstrate that each pair of items is linked, but they form a chain only—in left-brain terms—by coincidence.

Semantic mapping is never going to be an algorithmic process. The steps involved in deciding "what the word makes me think of" cannot be specified and their order is probably irrelevant. It's difficult even to describe what's happening while it's going on. You can, however, make the effort somewhat less random by using a heuristic process. Assume that the keyword you're considering is "leaf." Ask yourself the following questions, and others like them that occur to you, in any order:

- Where do you find a leaf?
- What is a leaf made of?
- What does a leaf do?
- What is a leaf for?
- Who or what values a leaf?
- What does a leaf look like? Sound like? Feel like? Smell like? Taste like?
- Where can you put a leaf?
- How long does a leaf last?
- What words rhyme with leaf?
- What is the same thing as a leaf?
- What is the opposite of a leaf?
- What can you make with a leaf?
- What familiar story has a leaf in it?
- What familiar song has a leaf in it?
- What other thing resembles a leaf?
- If a leaf were an animal, which animal would it be?

When your keywords are abstract items like those in Scenario Thirteen—items like "cost-effective" and "synergistic," or "freedom" and "justice"—such questions are almost impossible to answer. You may have to work through several levels of mapping before you arrive, by free association, at words for which the questions are useful. That's all right. Just use a big enough piece of paper and enough different colors. The effect is exactly like the priming of a pump.

Although it's impossible to describe this process in any tidy left-brain way, we all are familiar with the end result, in which solutions seem to "just pop into our head out of nowhere." They don't come out of nowhere, actually, but out of the right brain. Semantic mapping is a reliable way to get them to emerge.

Why Does Semantic Mapping Work?

One reason semantic mapping leads to new ideas and involvement is precisely because it is different from the usual aways of solving problems. It's a nice change from business as usual, and anything novel that isn't perceived as a threat tends to interest and involve people, at least temporarily.

However, there's another reason that is less obvious. Many research studies exist which compare the performance of two groups of people on some task in a situation where the performance is interfered with by some kind of annoying phenomenon—a blinking light, an unpleasant noise, inaccurate feedback, unpredictable interruptions, etc. In every case, the group that feels it has some control over what's happening performs better. In a typical experiment with noise as interference, one group has access to an on/off switch for the noise and the other doesn't. Always, the group with access to the switch does better than the other group. And what is most interesting, and most significant, is that this is true even when—as usually happens—*the switch is never used.* It's not the *exercise* of control that leads to improved performance, but the perception that it exists.

People whose perception is that a project has simply been dumped on them and that they have no control over it feel no involvement, and performance suffers. Expecting them to motivate others to feel involved in the project is absurd. Working through a right-brain technique like semantic mapping is a good way to provide the necessary perception of control.

Another Look at Scenario Thirteen

Here is part of the final semantic map from one of the four groups of supervisors, for your examination...

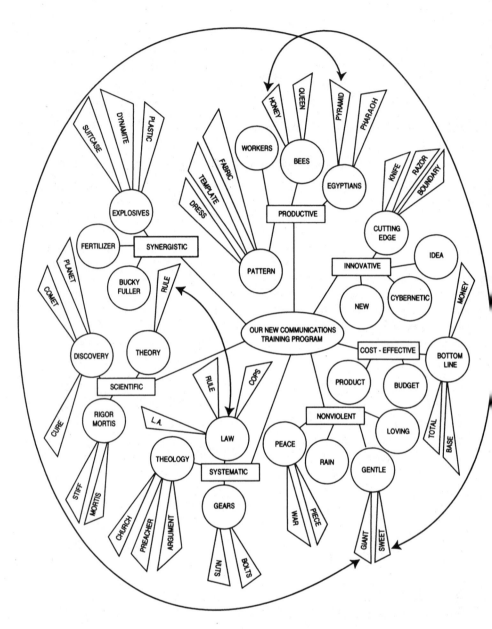

The method of persuasion used by Nate and Cecily in this scenario was coercion: It was made clear to the participants that they weren't going to be allowed to leave without first creating semantic maps. It worked, and presumably the payoff will be satisfying enough to the 12

supervisors that they won't resent having been leaned on in this way. Sometimes this is the only choice available. It would be better, however, to use some or all of the techniques presented in the earlier chapters of this book to construct a presentation about the theory and purpose of semantic mapping that would cause people to participate willingly.

WORKOUT SECTION: CHAPTER 13

1. Using all the resources you've learned about in this book, write a brief presentation that could have been used in Scenario Thirteen to persuade the group of managers to join in the semantic mapping session willingly and enthusiastically.

2. For your Communication Strategy Notebook, set up a Right Brain file and begin keeping track of relevant information to serve as a database for planning strategies. Record incidents (from your own life, or incidents you've read or heard about) in which right-brain techniques and strategies were used rather than left-brain ones. What was the situation? Who was present? How was the right-brain activity presented? How was it carried out? How did people react? What did they say? What happened? What was surprising? If things went badly, what could have been done to avoid that outcome?

3. In *Maps of the Mind* (New York: Macmillan, 1981), Charles Hampden-Turner presents and discusses a model of "the synergistic mind." He writes that Buckminster Fuller defined synergy as "the behaviour of whole systems unpredicted by the behavior of their parts" and provides an illustration on page 149 that shows a box containing the statement, "1 + 1 = 4." What is your left-brain reaction to the statement? Right-brain reaction? Why is the *definition* so bad? How could you fix it?

4. In my opinion there is no better source for a thorough and accurate presentation of the research about the human mind—in a form sufficiently nontechnical to make sense to the general reader—than Morton Hunt's book, *The Universe Within* (New York: Simon & Schuster, 1982). I strongly recommend that you read it.

5. For an equally good discussion of the controversy about "right-brain/left-brain" research, read "Of Brains and Rhetoric," by Jeffrey Walker. (*College English*, March 1990)

6. A right-brain technique that is currently fashionable is the holding of a session in which a group of people from a company work together to create an "icon" for the company—a picture that in some way represents the company's culture, principles, etc. This ordinarily produces a much more elaborate illustration than finding a *logo*. For one thing, there's no need to consider such matters as how easily the result could be added to your company letterhead. Try this for your company; don't be surprised if you face an immediate barrage of complaints from your left brain, up to and including "This is imPOSSible!" You might read a brief article on reli-

gious icons in an encyclopedia or other reference work, as a way of preparing yourself.

7. One of the best right-brain techniques is called "creative imagery" or "visualization" or, in the Gentle Art system, "percepting." It works because, provided the perception is vivid and detailed, the human brain cannot distinguish between perceptions based on external "real" stimuli and those based on "imaginary" ones. To test this, imagine that you're holding a fresh raw lemon in your hand; imagine bringing it up to your mouth; take a deep breath to smell its sharp sour fragrance; imagine that you're biting into it, *hard*; feel your teeth crunching through the lemon peel; taste the lemon juice on your tongue; swallow. Notice the effect on the muscles of your face and throat: *It's a phantom lemon, but your brain sends exactly the same messages it would send for a "real" one.*

Most accounts of the technique place an overwhelming emphasis on vision (as the word "visualization" would lead you to expect); however, no scientific reason for that emphasis exists. The more senses you involve in constructing the perception, the more vivid it will be and the greater your chances of success with it.

Athletes have long used the technique to rehearse ski slopes, golf courses, figure skating routines, and the like. Evidence shows that such mental rehearsals produce as much improvement as physical ones. *You* can use it to rehearse a language interaction you're headed into—a presentation, a negotiation, an interview, any session where you must perform and/or persuade. See yourself in the room where you'll be talking; see the people you expect to be there with you. Hear the sounds in the room; smell the smells; feel the textures and sensations you will encounter. Observe yourself going through the entire session, in the most vivid detail you can summon up with your mind's senses. *Imagine yourself doing this with total success—never rehearse forgetting what you intended to say, or similar misadventures!* Do this properly, and by the time you're actually there talking you will have the serene confidence of the seasoned expert. (For a scientific neurological account of this process—with the usual focus on the sense of sight—read "Aspects of a Cognitive Neuroscience of Mental Imagery" by Stephen M. Kosslyn, *Science*, June 17, 1988.)

8. Suppose a storm has struck your neighborhood and knocked out the utilities. You have no electric lights, no heat (or air conditioning, if it is a summer storm), no water—your bathroom doesn't function. You can't use your stove, or your shower, or your television set. The metaphor that we typically construct in such a situation is, "This is a disaster." And "I am a victim—call out the National Guard to rescue me!" However, the very people who react in this way will also spend their own hard-earned

money to do something called "going camping." The metaphor then is, "This is a pleasure, a fun thing to do." Compare the two experiences. What is the crucial difference that determines how they are perceived? What does this tell you about our tendency to let our perceptions rather than "the facts" determine our attitudes and our behavior?

9. As examples of the power of perceptions, consider these quotations:

a. "If people think they have even modest personal control over their destinies, they will persist at tasks. They will do better at them. They will become more committed to them." (*Thomas J. Peters and Robert H. Waterman, Jr.,* In Search of Excellence, *Warner Books, 1982, p. 80*)

b. "And…a study of elderly men and women in convalescent homes showed that, among other things, changes increasing their control over their lives—allowing them to decide what to have for meals, or letting them turn their telephones off or on—lowered their mortality rate over a period of 18 months by 50 percent, compared to residents in the same homes for whom things did not change." (*Daniel Goleman, "The Mind Over the Body,"* New York Times Magazine, *September 27, 1987, p. 60*)

14
Conclusion

The Four R's of
Excellent Communication

You are now equipped with a set of techniques for implementing your communication strategies, which is the critical first step without which your *business* strategies cannot be successfully carried out. These techniques are based solidly on contemporary science and are thoroughly tested. For every person involved in a language interaction, they work together synergistically to create and maintain the Four R's of excellent communication:

1. Reduce tension
2. Reduce hostility
3. Reduce the burden on short-term memory
4. Reduce loss of face

The scenarios in this book have shown you how the set of techniques would be used in a variety of common and typical business situations. Common as they are, however, it may be that you will never encounter any one of them yourself. That's all right. The reason a system is better than a list is because a system can handle something new.

Consider what happens when you play golf. Every golf course is different in some way from every other course. Even the course you play on Monday morning, if a severe storm hits on Tuesday, will be a slightly different course on Wednesday. But the *techniques* you have learned for the sport—choosing the proper club, standing correctly, swinging correctly, connecting with the ball in *exactly* the right way and with *exactly* the right angle and amount of force—are always the same, no matter what course you're playing on. They are *synergistic*; they work together to produce an effect that is more than the sum of all its separate parts. And when you *understand* them, you can adapt them to any course whatsoever.

The Gentle Art of Verbal Self-Defense techniques you have learned as you read this book are like that. No matter what communication situation you find yourself in, you will know how to tailor those techniques to your needs and use them expertly. The more you practice them, the more valuable they will be to you.

Yes, you *are* an expert in your language.

Yes, you *do* understand.

Yes, you *can* use language effectively and successfully.

References and Bibliography

Articles

A. F. G. "Notes: Judges' Nonverbal Behavior in Jury Trials: A Threat to Judicial Impartiality." *Virginia Law Review* 61 (1975): 1266–1298.

Addington, D. W. "The Relationship of Selected Vocal Characteristics to Personality Perception." *Speech Monographs* 35 (1968): 492–503.

Albert, M. "Universal Grammar." *Z* (December 1988): 99–104.

"Art of Negotiation, The." *The Royal Bank Letter* (July/August 1986): 1–4.

Beattie, G. W. "The Regulation of Speaker-Turns in Face-to-Face Conversation: Some Implications for Conversation in Sound-Only Communication Channels." *Semiotica* 34 (1981): 55–70.

———. "Interruption in Conversational Interaction and Its Relation to the Sex and Status of the Interactants." *Linguistics* 19 (1981): 15–35.

Bell, C. "Family Violence." *JAMA* (September 19, 1986): 1501–1502.

Bladen, A. "The Countdown Has Begun." *Forbes* (April 3, 1989): 182.

Blakeslee, S. "Cynicism and Mistrust Tied to Early Death." *New York Times* (January 17, 1989).

Blanck, P. D. "Off the Record: Nonverbal Communication in the Courtroom." *Stanford Lawyer* (Spring 1987): 18–23, 39.

———. "What Empirical Research Tells Us: Studying Judges' and Juries' Behavior." *The American University Law Review* 40 (1991): 775–804.

———. "The Appearance of Justice: Judges' Verbal and Nonverbal Behavior in Criminal Jury Trials." *Stanford Law Review* (November 1985): 89–163.

Bolinger, D. "Contrastive Accent and Contrastive Stress." *Language* 37 (1961): 83–96.

Brimelow, P., and L. Spencer. "Ralph Nader, Inc." *Forbes* (September 17, 1990): 117–129.

Brokaw, L. "Play by Play." *Inc.* (September 1989): 64–73.

Cassileth, B. R., et al. "Psychosocial Correlates of Survival in Advanced Malignant Disease." *New England Journal of Medicine* (June 13, 1985): 1551–1555.

Check, W. E. "Homicide, Suicide, Other Violence Gain Increasing Medical Attention." *JAMA* (August 9, 1985): 721–730.

Cohn, C. "Slick'ems, Glick'ems, Christmas Trees, and Cookie Cutters: Nuclear Language and How We Learned to Pat the Bomb." *Bulletin of the Atomic Scientists* (June 1987): 17–24.

Colpitts, M. "Inside the Robot Kingdom." *BC Tech* (November 1991): 1–3.

Cosmides, L. "Invariance in the Acoustic Expression of Emotion During Speech." *Journal of Experimental Psychology* (December 1983): 864–881.

Darlin, S. "Do Not Pass Go." *Forbes* (June 21, 1983): 112.

DeGarmo, S. "Don't Get Mad—Get Ahead." *Success* (January/February 1991): 4.

Dentzer, S. "Secretaries Down the Chute." *U.S. News & World Report* (March 28, 1994): 65.

Dimsdale, J. E. "A Perspective on Type A Behavior and Coronary Disease." *New England Journal of Medicine* (January 14, 1988): 110–112.

Douglis, C. "The Beat Goes On." *Psychology Today* (November 1987): 38–42.

Ervin-Tripp, S., et al. "Language and Power in the Family." In C. Kramarae et al., eds., *Language and Power* (Beverly Hills: Sage Publications, 1984): 116–135.

Fellman, B. "Talk: The Not-So-Silent Killer." *Science 85* (December 1985): 70–71.

——. "A Conversation with Ira Progoff." *Medical Self-Care* (July/August 1978): 11–12.

Fincher, J. "Inside an Intensive Journal Workshop." *Medical Self-Care* (July/August 1978): 6–10.

Finkbeiner, A. "The Puzzle of Child Abuse." *Science Illustrated* (June/July 1987): 14–19.

Fisher, K. L. "I Call Them 'Takeaways.'" *Forbes* (April 3, 1989): 180.

Flint, J. "How Do You Build a Luxury Image?" *Forbes* (April 3, 1989): 60–63.

——. "Man Bites Dog." *Forbes* (September 17, 1990): 64.

——. "Publisher's Heaven." *Forbes* (November 12, 1990): 76–78.

Forbes, M. S. "Fact and Comment." *Forbes* (July 24, 1989): 19–21.

——. "Fact and Comment." *Forbes* (October 2, 1989): 19–21.

Forbes M. S., Jr. "Fact and Comment." *Forbes* (November 12, 1990): 19–20.

Fox, B. H. "Depression Symptoms and Cancer." *JAMA* (September 1, 1989): 1231.

Friedman, M. "Type A Behavior and Mortality from Coronary Heart Disease." *New England Journal of Medicine* (July 14, 1988): 114. (See also other letters under same title through page 117.)

Gary, F., et al. "Little Brother Is Changing You." *Psychology Today* (March 1974): 42–46.

Gold, P. W., et al. "Clinical and Biochemical Manifestations of Depression: Relation to Neurobiology of Stress." Part One, *New England Journal of Medicine* (August 11, 1988): 348–351; Part Two, *New England Journal of Medicine* (August 18, 1988): 413–420.

Goldberg, J. "Anatomy of a Scientific Discovery." *Science Illustrated* (January/February 1989): 5–12.

Goleman, D. "Studies Point to Power of Nonverbal Signals." *New York Times* (April 8, 1986).

———. "Research Affirms Power of Positive Thinking." *New York Times* (February 3, 1987).

———. "The Mind Over the Body." *New York Times Magazine* (September 27, 1987): 36–39 and 59–60.

———. "Researchers Find That Optimism Helps the Body's Defense System." *New York Times* (April 20, 1989).

———. "Researchers Trace Empathy's Roots to Infancy." *New York Times* (April 28, 1989).

———. "Sensing Silent Cues Emerges as Key Skill." *New York Times* (October 10, 1989).

Haden, R. "A Comparative Exploration of the Expression of Anger in Fourteen Languages, and Some Implications." *Arktesol Post* (Summer/Fall 1987): 7–10.

Hall, E. "Giving Away Psychology in the 80's: George Miller Interviewed by Elizabeth Hall." *Psychology Today* (January 1980): 38–50, 97–98.

Hall, S. S. "A Molecular Code Links Emotions, Mind and Health." *Smithsonian Magazine* (June 1989): 62–71.

Harris, T. G. "Heart and Soul." *Psychology Today* (January/February 1989): 50–52.

Harvey, J. B. "The Abilene Paradox: The Management of Agreement." *Organizational Dynamics* (Summer 1974): 1–18.

Heins, J. "Why Ingersoll Picked St. Louis." *Forbes* (July 24, 1989): 52–55.

Henley, N. M., and C. Kramarae. "Gender, Power and Miscommunication." In N. Coupland et al., eds., *"Miscommunication" and Problematic Talk* (Newbury Park, Calif.: Sage Publications, 1991): 18–43.

Higgins, L. C. "Hostility Theory Rekindles Debate over Type A Behavior." *Medical World News* (February 27, 1989): 21.

Hollien, M. "Vocal Indicators of Psychological Stress." *Annals of The New York Academy of Science* 347 (1980): 47–72.

House, J. S., et al. "Social Relationships and Health." *Science* (July 29, 1988): 540–544.

"Image and Likeness" (interview with Bishop Kallistos Ware). *Parabola* (Spring 1985): 62–71.

Jones, E. E. "Interpreting Interpersonal Behavior: The Effects of Expectancies." *Science* (October 3, 1986): 41–46.

Kamiya, G. "The Cancer Personality." *Hippocrates* (November/December 1989): 92–93.

Kartunnen, L. "Implicative Verbs." *Language* 47 (1971): 350–358.

Katz, J. J., and D. T. Langendoen. "Pragmatics and Presupposition." *Language* 52 (1976): 1–17.

Kavanaugh, A. "Medicine Is Becoming Just Another Job." *Medical Economics* (April 26, 1993): 30–33.

Kempton, W. "The Rhythmic Basis of Interactional Synchrony." In M. R. Key, ed., *The Relationship of Verbal and Nonverbal Communication* (New York: Mouton, 1980), 67–75.

Kiparsky, C., and P. Kiparsky. "Fact." In M. Bierwisch and K. E. Heidolph, eds., *Progress in Linguistics* (The Hague: Mouton 1970): 142–173.

Kipnis, D., and S. Schmidt. "The Language of Persuasion." *Psychology Today* (April 1985): 46.

Klebnikov, P. "Prospecting in the Wild East." *Forbes* (November 12, 1990): 138–144.

Kobasa, S. O. "Test for Hardiness: How Much Stress Can You Survive?" *American Health* (September 1984): 64.

Kohn, A. "Beyond Selfishness." *Psychology Today* (October 1988): 34–38.

Kosslyn, S. M. "Aspects of a Cognitive Neuroscience of Mental Imagery." *Science* (June 17, 1988): 1621–1626.

Krier, B. A. "Conversation Interruptus: Critical Social Skill or Just Plain Rudeness?" *Los Angeles Times* (December 14, 1986).

Levine, J. "Stirring Story." *Forbes* (November 12, 1990): 308–310.

Long, D. J. "Emoticons," *CHIPS Newsletter* (July 1993): 13, 26.

Lynch, J. J. "Listen and Live." *American Health* (April 1985): 39–43.

———. "Interpersonal Aspects of Blood Pressure Control." *Journal of Nervous and Mental Diseases* 170 (1982): 143–153.

Mack, R. A. "What's the Real Reason Women Outlive Men?" *Medical Economics* (August 3, 1992): 172–184.

Marcom, J., Jr. "Penmanship with a Flourish." *Forbes* (April 3, 1989): 95–120.

Michael, J. W. "Side Lines." *Forbes* (September 17, 1990): 8.

Miller, S. M. "Why Having Control Reduces Stress: If I Can Stop the Roller Coaster, I Don't Have to Get Off." In J. Garber and M. E. P. Seligman, eds., *Human Helplessness: Theory and Applications* (New York: Academic Press, 1980.)

Milstead, J. "Verbal Battering." *BBW* (August 1985): 34–35, 61, 68.

Miron, M. S., and T. A. Pasquale. "Psycholinguistic Analysis of Coercive Communication." *Journal of Psycholinguistic Research* 7 (1985): 95–120.

Morais, R. C. "Tale of Two Tombs." *Forbes* (November 12, 1990): 174–176.

Newbergh, C. "State of Emergency: Hospital Emergency Rooms Turning into Combat Zones; Angry Patients Attacking Personnel." *Oakland Tribune* (September 27, 1992).

Olsen, E., et al. "Beyond Positive Thinking." *Success* (December 1988): 31–38.

Oppenheim, G. "How to Defuse a Hostile Patient." *Medical Economics* (September 5, 1988): 125–134.

Parlee, M. B. "Conversational Politics," *Psychology Today* (May 1979): 45–86.

Pennimay, N. "Why Ingersoll Picked St. Louis." *Forbes* (July 24, 1989): 52–55.

Perry, K. "What Worked for Japan Could Work for You." *Medical Economics* (October 25, 1993): 84–93.

Phillips, P. "Domestic Violence on the Increase." *Cortlandt Forum* (November 1992): 48DD–48EE.

Pines, M. "Psychological Hardiness: The Role of Challenge in Health." *Psychology Today* (December 1980): 34–45.

Pitta, J. "The Crisco Factor." *Forbes* (July 20, 1992): 306–307.

"Renegades '91." *Success* (January/February 1991): 23–30.

Rozanski, A., et al. "Mental Stress and the Induction of Silent Myocardial Ischemia in Patients with Coronary Artery Disease. *New England Journal of Medicine* (April 21, 1986): 1005–1012.

Ruby, M. "The Children's Crusade." *U.S. News & World Report:* 112.

Sacks, H., et al. "A Simplest Systematics for the Organization of Turn-Taking for Conversation." *Language* 50 (1974): 696–735.

Schaffer, R. H. "The Breakthrough Strategy." *Success* (September 1989) 48–49.

Scherwitz, L., et al. "Self-Involvement and the Risk Factors for Coronary Heart Disease." *Advances* (Winter 1985): 6–18.

Schifrin, M. "Zombie Bonds." *Forbes* (April 3, 1989): 70.

Seligman, J., et al. "The Wounds of Words: When Verbal Abuse Is as Scary as Physical Abuse." *Newsweek* (October 12, 1992): 90–92.

Shea, M. J. "Mental Stress and the Heart." *CVR&R* (April 1988): 51–58.

Smith, M. E. "Sexual Harassment: Now You See It, Now You Don't." *Sojourner* (December 1991).

"Swiftness of Spouse's Death Affects Mate's Mortality Risk." *Medical World News* (September 11, 1989): 27.

Thomas, L. "Adaptive Aspects of Inflammation." *MD* (February 1994): 15–16.

Train, J. "C. Northcote Parkinson: An Appreciation." *The American Spectator* (June 1993): 56–57.

Weinberger, C. W. "SDI: Weakened, but Not Killed." *Forbes* (March 4, 1991): 33.

Weiner, E. J. "A Knowledge Representation Approach to Understanding Metaphors." *Computational Linguistics* 10 (1984): 1–14.

West, C., and A. Garcia. "Conversational Shift Work: A Study of Topical Transitions Between Women and Men." *Social Problems* 35 (1988): 551–575.

Whaley, B. "Toward a General Theory of Deception." *Journal of Strategic Studies* (March 1982): 179–192.

Wilber, J. F. "Neuropeptides, Appetite Regulation, and Human Obesity." *JAMA* (July 10, 1991): 257–259.

Williams, R. "Curing Type A: The Trusting Heart." *Psychology Today* (January/February 1989): 36–42.

Williams, W. E. "The Santa Claus Syndrome." *Success* (January/February 1991): 8.

Willoughby, J. "Teasing the Teasers." *Forbes* (April 3, 1989): 68.

"Winning a Dangerous Game." *Success* (March 1991): 10.

Zimmerman, J. "Does Emotional State Affect Disease?" *MD* (April 1986): 30, 41–43.

Zonderman, A. B., et al. "Depression as a Risk for Cancer Morbidity and Mortality in a Nationally Representative Sample." *JAMA* (September 1, 1989): 1191–1195.

Zuckerman, M. B. "Bill Clinton, One Year Later." *U.S. News & World Report* (January 31, 1994): 68.

Books

Ader, R., ed. *Psychoneuroimmunology*. New York: Academic Press, 1981.

Argyle, M. *Bodily Communication*. London: Methuen, 1975.

Antonovsky, A. *Health, Stress, and Coping*. San Francisco: Jossey-Bass, 1979.

Barsy, A. J. *Worried Sick: Our Troubled Quest for Wellness*. Boston: Little, Brown, 1988.

Beattie, G. *Talk: An Analysis of Speech and Non-Verbal Behaviour in Conversation*. Milton Keynes, England: Open University Press, 1983.

Benson, H. *The Mind/Body Effect.* New York: Simon & Schuster, 1979.

——— and W. Proctor. *Beyond the Relaxation Response.* New York: Times Books, 1984.

Bierwisch, M., and K. E. Heidolph, eds. *Progress in Linguistics.* The Hague: Mouton, 1970.

Birdwhistell, R. L. *Kinesics and Context: Essays on Body Motion Communication.* Philadelphia: University of Pennsylvania Press, 1970.

Blumenthal, M. D., et al. *Justifying Violence: Methodological Studies of Attitudes and Behavior.* Ann Arbor: University of Michigan, 1975.

———. *More about Justifying Violence: Methodological Studies of Attitudes and Behavior.* Ann Arbor: University of Michigan, 1975.

Bolinger, D. *Intonation.* Harmondsworth, England: Penguin Books, 1972.

Bolton, R. *People Skills: How to Assert Yourself, Listen to Others and Resolve Conflicts.* Englewood Cliffs, N.J.: Prentice-Hall, 1979.

Borysenko, J., with L. Rothstein. *Minding the Body, Mending the Mind.* Reading, Mass.: Addison-Wesley, 1987.

Buzan, T. *Using Both Sides of Your Brain.* New York: Dutton, 1983.

Capaccione, L. *The Well-Being Journal: Drawing on Your Inner Power to Heal Yourself.* North Hollywood, Calif.: Newcastle Publishing, 1989.

Charlesworth, E. A., and R. G. Nathan. *Stress Management: A Comprehensive Guide to Wellness.* New York: Ballantine, 1982.

Chesney, M., and R. H. Rosenman, eds. *Anger and Hostility in Cardiovascular and Behavioral Disorders.* Washington, D.C.: Hemisphere Corporation, 1985.

Clark, V. P., et al., eds. *Language: Introductory Readings, 3rd Edition.* New York: St. Martin's Press, 1981.

Cole, P., and J. L. Morgan, eds. *Syntax and Semantics, Volume 3: Speech Acts.* New York: Academic Press, 1975.

Craig, R. T., and K. Tracy. *Conversational Coherence: Form, Structure, and Strategy.* Beverly Hills: Sage, 1983.

Edwards, B. *Drawing on the Right Side of the Brain.* Los Angeles: Tarcher, 1979.

Ekman, P. *Telling Lies.* New York: Norton, 1985.

Elgin, S. H. *What Is Linguistics? 2nd Edition.* Englewood Cliffs, N.J.: Prentice Hall, 1979.

———. *The Gentle Art of Verbal Self-Defense.* New York: Barnes & Noble, 1985. (Originally published by Prentice Hall, 1980.)

———. *More on the Gentle Art of Verbal Self-Defense.* New York: Prentice Hall, 1983.

———. *Manual for Gentle Art Syntonics Trainers: Level One.* Huntsville, Ark.: OCLS Press, 1991.

———. *Language in Emergency Medicine: A Verbal Self-Defense/Syntonics Handbook.* Huntsville, Ark.: OCLS Press, 1987a.

————. *The Last Word on the Gentle Art of Verbal Self-Defense*. New York: Prentice Hall, 1987b.

————. *Success with the Gentle Art of Verbal Self-Defense*. Englewood Cliffs, N.J.: Prentice Hall, 1989.

————. *Mastering the Gentle Art of Verbal Self-Defense*. Englewood Cliffs, N.J.: Prentice Hall, 1989. (Audio program.)

————. *Staying Well with the Gentle Art of Verbal Self-Defense*. Englewood Cliffs, N.J.: Prentice Hall, 1991.

————. *The Written Art of Verbal Self-Defense*. Englewood Cliffs, N.J.: Prentice Hall, 1993a.

————. *Genderspeak: Men, Women, and the Gentle Art of Verbal Self-Defense*. New York: John Wiley, 1993b.

Elgin, S. H., and R. Haden. *Raising Civilized Kids in a Savage World*. Huntsville, Ark.: OCLS Press, 1989.

Festinger, L. *A Theory of Cognitive Dissonance*. Evanston, Ill.: Row, Peterson, 1957.

Fisher, R., and W. Ury. *Getting to YES: Negotiating Agreement without Giving In*. New York: Penguin Books, 1983.

Frank, J. *Persuasion and Healing*. Baltimore: Johns Hopkins, 1973.

Friedman, M., and R. H. Rosenman. *Type A Behavior and Your Heart*. New York: Knopf, 1974.

————, and D. Ulmer. *Treating Type A Behavior and Your Heart*. New York: Knopf, 1984.

Goleman, D. *Vital Lies, Simple Truths: The Psychology of Self-Deception*. New York: Simon & Schuster, 1985.

Gordon, T. *Leader Effectiveness Training: L.E.T.* New York: Wyden, 1972.

Hall, E. T. *Beyond Culture*. New York: Doubleday / Anchor, 1977.

————. *The Silent Language*. New York: Doubleday / Anchor, 1959.

————. *The Dance of Life: The Other Dimension of Time*. New York: Doubleday / Anchor, 1983.

Haley, J. *Uncommon Therapy: The Psychiatric Techniques of Milton H. Erickson, M.D.* New York: Anchor Books, 1977.

Harvard College. *The State of Strategy*. Boston: Harvard Business School Publishing Division, 1991.

Hindle, T. *Field Guide to Strategy: A Glossary of Essential Tools and Concepts for Today's Manager*. Boston: Harvard Business School Press, 1994.

Hunt, M. *The Universe Within: A New Science Explores the Human Mind*. New York: Simon and Schuster, 1982.

Justice, B. *Who Gets Sick?: Thinking and Health*. Houston: Peak Press, 1987.

Key, M. R., ed. *The Relationship of Verbal and Nonverbal Communication*. The Hague: Mouton, 1980.

Kramarae, C., ed. *The Voices and Words of Women and Men*. Oxford: Pergamon Press, 1980.

——, et al., eds. *Language and Power*. Beverly Hills: Sage, 1984.

Lakoff, G., and M. Johnson. *Metaphors We Live By*. Chicago: University of Chicago Press, 1980.

Lakoff, R. *Talking Power: The Politics of Language in Our Lives*. New York: Basic Books, 1990.

Lazarus, R. S., and S. Folkman. *Stress, Appraisal, and Coping*. New York: Syringer, 1984.

Leech, G. *Principles of Pragmatics*. London: Longman, 1983.

Levy, S. M. *Behavior and Cancer*. San Francisco: Jossey-Bass, 1985.

Lewis, D. *The Secret Language of Success: Using Body Language to Get What You Want*. New York: Carroll & Graf, 1989.

Locke, S., et al., eds. *Foundations of Psychoneuroimmunology*. New York: Aldine, 1985.

Locke, S., and D. Colligan. *The Healer Within: The New Medicine of Mind and Body*. New York: New American Library / Mentor, 1987.

Lynch, J. J. *The Broken Heart: The Medical Consequences of Loneliness*. New York: Basic Books, 1977.

——. *The Language of the Heart: The Body's Response to Human Dialogue*. New York: Basic Books, 1985.

Montagu, M. F. A. *Touching: The Human Significance of the Skin, Third Edition*. New York: Harper and Row, 1986.

O'Barr, W. M. *Linguistic Evidence: Language, Power, and Strategy in the Courtroom*. New York: Academic Press, 1982.

Ohmae, Kenichi. *The Mind of the Strategist: The Art of Japanese Business*. New York: McGraw-Hill, 1982.

Ornstein, R., and D. Sobel. *The Healing Brain: Breakthrough Discoveries about How the Brain Keeps Us Healthy*. New York: Simon & Schuster, 1987.

——, and C. Swencious. *The Healing Brain: A Scientific Reader*. New York: Guilford Press, 1990.

Pascale, R. T., and A. G. Athos. *The Art of Japanese Management: Applications for American Executives*. New York: Warner Books, 1981.

Peale, N. V. *The Power of Positive Thinking*. Englewood Cliffs, N.J.: Prentice Hall, 1961.

Peters T., and R. Waterman, Jr. *In Search of Excellence*. New York: Warner, 1984.

Rainer, T. *The New Diary*. Los Angeles: Tarcher, 1978.

Rico, G. L. *Writing the Natural Way.* Los Angeles: Tarcher, 1983.

Renkema, J. *Discourse Studies: An Introductory Textbook.* Philadelphia: Benjamins, 1993.

Robert, M. *Strategy Pure and Simple: How Winning CEOs Outthink Their Competition.* New York: McGraw-Hill, 1993.

Rothwell, J. D. *Telling It Like It Isn't.* Englewood Cliffs, N.J.: Prentice Hall, 1982.

Samovar, L. A., and R. E. Porter. *Intercultural Communication: A Reader, 4th Edition.* Belmont, Calif.: Wadsworth, 1985.

Satir, V. *Conjoint Family Therapy.* Palo Alto: Science & Behavior Books, 1964.

————. *Peoplemaking.* Palo Alto: Science & Behavior Books, 1972.

Scott, G. G. *Mind Power: Picture Your Way to Success in Business.* Englewood Cliffs, N.J.: Prentice Hall, 1987.

Sattel, J. W. *Men, Inexpressiveness, and Power.* Rowley, Mass.: Newbury House, 1983.

Sheikh, A. A. *Imagery: Current Theory, Research and Application.* New York: Wiley, 1983.

Tannen, D. *That's Not What I Meant! How Conversational Style Makes or Breaks Relationships.* New York: Morrow, 1986.

————. *You Just Don't Understand: Women and Men in Conversation.* New York: Morrow, 1990.

Thorne, B., et al., eds. *Language, Gender and Society.* Rowley, Mass.: Newbury House, 1983.

Van Dijk, T. A., ed. *Handbook of Discourse Analysis.* London: Academic Press, 1985.

Van Wolferen, K. *The Enigma of Japanese Power: People and Politics in a Stateless Nation.* New York: Knopf, 1989.

Watzlawick, P., et al. *Pragmatics of Human Communication: A Study of Interactional Patterns, Pathologies, and Paradoxes.* New York: Norton, 1967.

Index

About the Author

Suzette Haden Elgin, Ph.D., is the author of *The Gentle Art of Verbal Self-Defense* series which has sold more than 1 million copies. Always in demand as a seminar and workshop leader, she is an expert in applied psycholinguistics, the founder of the Ozark Center for Language Studies, and the author of 23 books.